Women/Writing/Teaching

Women/Writing/Teaching

Jan Zlotnik Schmidt

STATE UNIVERSITY OF NEW YORK PRESS

Published by
State University of New York Press, Albany

©1998 State University of New York

All rights reserved

For information, address State University of New York Press,
State University Plaza, Albany, N.Y., 12246

Production by Diane Ganeles
Marketing by Nancy Farrell

Library of Congress Cataloging-in-Publication Data

Women/writing/teaching / [edited by] Jan Zlotnik Schmidt.
          p.   cm.
     Includes bibliographical references.
     ISBN 0-7914-3591-1 (acid-free paper). —
ISBN 0-7914-3592-X (pkb. : acid-free paper)
     1. English language—Rhetoric—Study and teaching—
United States.   2. English teachers—United States—
Biography.   3. Women teachers—United States—Biography.
4. Feminism and education—United States.   5. Women
in education—United States.   6. Academic writing—Sex
differences.   I. Schmidt, Jan Zlotnik
PE1405.U6W65   1998
808´.042´071173—dc21
[B]   97-1222
                                                                CIP

10   9   8   7   6   5   4   3   2   1

For Mom, Marilyn, Mary, and Carley—
my community of women

Contents

Preface

> I suspect that female narratives will be found where women
> exchange stories, where they read and talk collectively of
> ambitions, and possibilities, and accomplishments.
>
> —Carolyn G. Heilbrun, *Writing a Woman's Life*

I began working on this anthology several years ago because
both I and the women students in my graduate theories of writing course wanted to read stories about our multiple lives as
writers and as teachers in the academy. At the time, one student, Margaret, aptly represented this multiplicity when she
confessed, "I can't keep the parts of my journal separate—my
personal entries, creative writing, reading responses, and meditations on teaching keep creeping into each other."

As I talked with women around the country about this project, I was struck by everyone's warmth, generosity, collegiality,
and enthusiasm. I realized that I was not the only person
searching for autobiographical visions of our experiences as
women writers and as teachers. There were women, of course,
who suggested that teaching left little time for writing, or that
teaching was a way to fund their work as writers. What dis-
tinguishes the perspectives of the twenty women who have contributed to this volume is that writing and teaching are
envisioned as intertwined, essential ways to construct meaning
in life. The contributors are creative writers who view writing
and teaching as being central to their missions as artists;
women who are active in the field of composition theory and
pedagogy; and women in other disciplines (i.e., educational and
women's studies) who see themselves as writing teachers. We
also are women in different phases of our careers: some of us

are beginning teachers while others are reassessing our work in midlife. The essays represent a range of perspectives across the academy (diverse ethnic backgrounds, disciplines, and roles in the university). This cross-section of points of view broadens the visions presented by the life stories and suggests common themes, issues, and struggles across age groups, cultures, and disciplines.

I hope that this volume will prompt women to take a retro- spective glance—to explore their own life stories, their develop- ment of selfhood, their multiple identities as writers, teachers, and writing teachers. For as Carolyn Heilbrun suggests, we do not grow in isolation from one another: "We can only . . . live by the stories we have read or heard. We live our lives through texts" [*Writing A Woman's Life* (New York: Ballantine, 1988), p. 37]. I hope these essays will create connections among women, conversations about our lives and work, and a collective vision of women—writing—and teaching in the academy.

I owe a great deal to my community of readers. Thanks must go to Pamela Chergotis and Lynne Crockett for our auto- biographical creative writing workshop; to Karen Chaffee for our many enriching conversations about autobiography; to Nicole Boucher, Caren Fairweather, Michelle Ferrante, Candace Frick, Sarah Gruber, and Abigail Robin for our wonderful independent studies on forms of female narrative—and our conversations about women's autobiography that helped me clarify the ideas for this volume; and to Barbara Adams, Ann Dean, Carole Levin, and Patti Phillips for their advice, wise criticism, and many gifts of friendship.

As always, I must acknowledge the friendship and support of the late Carley Bogarad—our intellectual collaboration was rare.

Most of all, I thank Mary Gordon, my trusted friend, reader, and critic of twenty-five years, and my family—Philip and Reed Schmidt, Mae and Harold Zlotnik, Marilyn Zlotnik and Peter Hultberg—for their advice, support, and faith in me. Their love sustains me.

I continue to owe a great deal to Sandra Gildersleeve for her invaluable clerical and editorial assistance. And I thank Can- dace Frick and Nicole Boucher for their generosity of spirit and fine editing. I also owe a deep debt of gratitude to Priscilla Ross, Jennie Doling, and Diane Ganeles of SUNY Press for their in- valuable advice, support, and editorial assistance.

Finally, I thank the teaching assistants in the Graduate English Program at the State University of New York at New Paltz who have enriched my life over the years. This volume is for them.

Acknowledgments

Lynn Z. Bloom. "Teaching College English as a Woman," from *College English* (November 1992). Copyright © 1992 by The National Council of Teachers of English. Reprinted with permission.

Lillian Bridwell-Bowles. "Freedom, Form, Function: Varieties of Academic Discourse," from *College Composition and Communication* (February 1995). Copyright © 1995 by The National Council of Teachers of English. Reprinted with permission.

Linda Brodkey. "Writing on the Bias," from *College English* (September 1994). Copyright © 1994 by The National Council of Teachers of English. Reprinted with permission.

Judith Ortiz Cofer. "Latin Women Pray," from *Reaching for the Mainland and Selected New Poems* by Judith Ortiz Cofer. Copyright © 1995 by and reprinted by permission of Bilingual Press/Editorial Bilingue, Arizona State University, Tempe, Arizona.

bell hooks. "Engaged Pedagogy," from *Teaching to Transgress* by bell hooks. Copyright © 1994, reprinted by permission of the publishers, Routledge: New York and London, and by permission of the author.

Langston Hughes. "Dreams," from *The Dreamkeeper and Other Poems* by Langston Hughes. Copyright © 1932, reprinted by permission of Alfred E. Knopf.

Min-zhan Lu. "From Silence to Words: Writing as Struggle," from *College English* (April 1987). Copyright © 1987, by The National Council of Teachers of English. Reprinted with permission.

Adrienne Rich. "As if your life depended on it," from *WHAT IS FOUND THERE: Notebooks on Poetry and Politics* by Adrienne Rich. Copyright © 1993 by Adrienne Rich, reprinted by permission of the author and W. W. Norton & Company, Inc.

Jacqueline Jones Royster. "Twice Alone, Place Apart: The Role of Spiracy in Using the Power of Solitude," from *The Center of the Web* by Delese Wear. Copyright © 1993. Reprinted from State University of New York Press.

Nancy Sommers. "Between the Drafts," from *College Composition and Communication* (February 1992). Copyright © 1992 by The National Council of Teachers of English. Reprinted with permission.

Introduction

It is late at night, a cool spring evening, and I am reading and grading creative writing portfolios. One student, in a self-evaluation of her work, explains, "Writing—it's more than an escape—it's not an escape; it's part of me, something that keeps me rooted to reality. . . ." Her realization prompts me to ask anew: How did I come to embrace a life guided by a love of words? How did I come to know as a child and as a teenager that teaching and writing together would give my life form and meaning? How did I come to feel that the classroom was a place where at times I felt most "rooted," most at home, most alive?

These recurring questions, these late-night meditations, were the genesis of this volume. Convinced that we brought our whole selves into the classroom—the dramas of our early lives, our relationships with family, with friends, with lovers, our experiences with schooling, our attitudes, values and beliefs—I began including autobiographical creative writing and reflection in my graduate theories of writing course with the hope that the more we learned about ourselves, the more aware we would be as teachers. When I began including autobiography in the course in the late 1980s and early 1990s, I searched for works that meshed personal recollection and reflection, meditations on the writing life, and theories about composition instruction because I felt that these areas of experience were inseparable and enriched each other. I discovered Mike Rose's *Lives on the Boundary* and next searched for complementary works by women writing teachers. I found Nancie Atwell's *In the Middle*

1

and Sylvia Ashton Warner's *Teacher*, which presented compelling portraits of the classroom teacher; however, I did not find works by women that intertwined autobiographical reflection, contemplation of the writing life, and discussion of pedagogy. As I have continued to weave autobiography into the course, I have used several essays that have found their way into this volume; and, since the early 1990s, several autobiographies by women writing teachers have been published.[1]

Although very few of these autobiographical, hybrid works by women have been available until recently, several literary and scholarly developments in the late 1980s have urged the intertwining of the private and public; the autobiographical and the theoretical; the meditative, and the pedagogical aspects of women's lives. There were explorations of the writing life by such artists as Gloria Anzaldúa, Annie Dillard, Audre Lorde, and Eudora Welty. In addition, feminist theory's critique of rational, phallocentric discourse and of the split between the objective and the subjective led to what Nancy K. Miller labels "personal criticism": "an explicitly autobiographical performance within the act of criticism" (Miller 1991, 2). Some feminist literary theorists practiced critical acts rooted in personal passion, emotional connections with subject matter, and theoretical and cultural critique (see, for example, Diane P. Freedman, Olivia Frey, and Frances Murphy Zauhar's *The Intimate Critique: Autobiographical Literary Criticism*). Concurrent with this emergence of "engaged" criticism (Miller 1991, 2) was a developing interest in both autobiography and the personal essay in composition studies. Such scholars as Richard Beach and Linda Peterson[2] investigated approaches to autobiographical writing in the composition class while others like Margo Culley and Cinthia Gannett focused on forms of women's autobiographical writing, specifically women's diaries and journals. Autobiography studies itself, led by such critics as Sidonie Smith and Estelle Jelinek, also emerged as a full-blown discipline, with particular attention paid to contemporary women's autobiography and forms of self-representation for women.

Not only did study of women's autobiography expand, but finally, after many years of neglect, composition theorists began to connect feminist theory and pedagogy and composition instruction. In a 1991 article, Elizabeth Flynn notes that "there can be no chronicling of the impact of feminism on the field of compo-

sition studies because until recently the field has strangely resisted addressing women's issues" (Flynn 1991, 137), and she
asks what would constitute a feminist rhetorical tradition (Flynn
1991, 140–141). Indeed, in the late 1980s and early 1990s, composition scholars began examining writing theory and pedagogy
through the lens of gender, and focused on such issues as male
and female language, curricula of courses, structures and forms
of discourse, and women's processes of reading, writing, knowing, and composing, in an attempt to shape a feminist pedagogy
of composition instruction. Caywood and Overing's groundbreak-
ing 1987 volume, *Teaching Writing: Pedagogy, Gender and Equity*, presents models of feminist composition instruction based
on visions of nonauthoritarian classrooms, collaboration, and
nurturance of women's voices. Janet Emig's and Louise Wetherbee Phelps' 1995 collection of essays—*Feminine Principles and
Women's Experience in American Composition and Rhetoric*—
expands our vision of feminist theory and praxis in composition
studies and considers such topics as the authority of the female
writer in the postmodern age, the need for experimental forms of
academic writing, and a feminist pedagogy that fosters developmental stages of growth for women students.

The essays then in this volume reflect these concerns and
arise out of a need to merge autobiographical reflection, contem-
plations of the writing life, and critical examination of our pedagogical practices in order to comprehend more fully our complex
lives and struggles as feminist writing teachers in the academy.
This collection brings together works by women, instructors of
composition, creative writing, and women's studies, who view writing and teaching as a central way that we have created meaning
in our lives. In our essays, we explore the particular configura-
tions of our pasts, gender, class, ethnic backgrounds, personali-
ties, and cultures that have shaped our personae as instructors of
writing (our feelings, values, and beliefs; our philosophical and
pedagogical assumptions; our stances in the classroom). Autobiographical writing prompts us to lay "claim" to our lives (to use Patricia Hampl's term); to connect past and present; to reflect on and
to re-envision our experiences; and to authorize and to shape our
complex identities as feminist writing teachers.

The essays address certain feminist questions:

- What intersections of past and present experience guide
  women's development as writers and instructors of writing?

- What early experiences—particularly with reading and writing and forms of language acquisition—have influenced women's development as writers and influenced their choices of careers?

- What attributes of literacy stories are apparent in their visions of development of self (e.g., narratives of socialization, experiences of schooling, mentors)?

- How does the hidden curriculum of the schools have an impact on women's coming of age and schooling?

- How do women emerge from silence? shape their voices and stances as professionals? gain authority and power as professionals? balance the private and public aspects of their lives?

- What conflicts and crises associated with gaining literacy and entering mainstream culture as women have taken place?

- How do women constitute themselves as literacy teachers? What forms of literacy and expression and modes of academic writing do women adopt and value? What clashes of culture emerge? How do women cope with what Mary Louise Pratt calls living in "the contact zone"—a space of unequal power relations and authority?

- What characterizes the postmodern sense of self for women writers and teachers? How do women create a language for teaching that captures and interprets the multiple dimensions and the often elusive and fragmented life of the feminist teacher in the class?

- What models of feminist teaching emerge? Are themes of attachment and relational thinking evident (Gilligan 1982)? Is Belenky's (1986) model of "connected teaching" apparent? Do women teachers embrace an ethics of caring (Noddings 1991)? Do they compose a vision of liberatory education (Weiler 1988) and see themselves as "agents of social change" (Weiler 1988, 89)?

Each person's responses to these questions are singular. The essays represent a range of perspectives across the academy (diverse ethnic backgrounds, disciplines, and roles in the university). However, common themes do emerge and point to shared issues, struggles, and visions of language and teaching. I offer these readings as one way to configure the interwoven tapestry of our life stories and urge readers to conceive other patterns in the fabric of these texts.

> I write and rewrite the 'stories' of my life; life's repeating patterns well up in steep banks; I am tossed about in their boiling swells and pulled under by the force of the pounding surf of autobiographical memory; seconds later I shoot back to the surface, gasping, alive. (Ann Victoria Dean)

Ann Dean writes of her need for words, her passion for words that remind her that she is "alive." Indeed, one strong theme evident in these works is the relationship between words and consciousness, words and an affirmation of identity. Words make these writers real to themselves. Witness Elaine Maimon's revelation that being named by her mother " 'Elaine, the fair' " of Tennyson's "Idylls of the King" gave her a confidence that she carried into adulthood: "What was important was that I was named (and deemed beautiful) in a book." Maimon also bestowed through naming a sense of entitlement upon her daughter, Gillian. Or hear Diane Glancy's realization that the desire for words as a child—the desire to "poke through" the veil of a culturally imposed silence—led her to scratch "marks" "on [her] inner thigh," "under [her] arms." Glancy reveals: "The whole universe was trying to blow me away, but the words kept me there." And I think of my depiction of the words and stories read to me by my father as "round glass blown bubbles," luminous moments of sensate and creative consciousness in which I felt most truly alive.

Not only did many of us live in and through words, but we also were children like Pamela Chergotis—outsiders in mainstream culture—who found our place in the world through reading. Lynne Crockett's crayon marks on *The Rise and the Fall of the Third Reich* (a book that she as a prekindergartner could not possibly have known or read) evoke the ways in which reading became an escape, a hiding place, an ongoing drama, a source of pleasure, or a source of power.

Opposing this vision of words as a generative force central to the development of selfhood is the power of social, cultural, and historical forces—the power of the patriarchy—to silence women and to deny them voice and language. Karen Chaffee, for example, investigates her working-class girlhood, a world that demanded "silent submission to God, to husband and father, to nature," and explores how her parents' words—"weapons" used against her—made her feel insignificant. For Chaffee, schooling confirmed a sense of invisibility and powerlessness that she represents in a vision of her locked jaw and hospital stay—a time of total immobility and silence. As I write this Introduction, I realize that I symbolize my fear of annihilation and loss of selfhood in the terror that I experienced in the hospital in the aftermath of an eye operation at age four, a terror rooted in my inability to mouth words: "I opened my mouth as wide as I could and tried to scream. Still no sound."

Sondra Perl also confronts those cultural forces that limited her development as a woman, that prompted her to be the good daughter and then wife right after college, cut off from her own needs and desires. Perl reveals: "Before most of my friends had ever married, I was yearning for something I had not yet experienced and some submerged part of me rose up, remembered art history and literature and . . . left." The entitlement to seek pleasure and fulfillment becomes for Perl a profound act of rebellion. Lynn Z. Bloom, extending the context of this silencing to her life in the profession, juxtaposes her early sense of illegitimacy and marginality (as an adjunct and untenured temporary instructor) with her growing commitment to the field. Bloom contrasts those patriarchal forces in the academy that tell her that her work does not "count" with her efforts to "raise [her] voice" and to create her own "life-saving story" as a writer and as a teacher.

"The difficulty of saying 'I' "

—Christa Wolf, *The Quest for Christa T*

The need to discover the range of our own voices—to gain authority as women, as writers, as teachers—is also central in these reflections. For many of us, personal authority, agency, and authorship are intertwined. Nancy Sommers, for example, explores her family background and her early career in academia to determine the reasons for her dependence on false notions of authority that constrain her voice as a woman, as a scholar and as a teacher. She conceives of a place "between the drafts" where one can feel the "pull" of one's own voice as it struggles to create knowledge in relation to and against other voices. She envisions genuine authorship as a way "to bring life and writing" together and to develop a sense of personal authority. In their essay, Elaine and Gillian Maimon connect authorship with a shared web of three generations of mother-daughter storytelling. In her section of the essay, Elaine Maimon explores how her mother's passion for reading gave her a love of drama and performance that endowed her with a personal sense of authority that she carried into adulthood. In turn, Gillian Maimon demonstrates how her emerging sense of voice, nourished by a legacy of reading and writing, prompts her as a student teacher to challenge the authority of her supervising teacher and to advocate for the "sovereignty" of each child in her classroom. Linda Brodkey also links a sense of authority with her ownership of words (revealed in her census-taking in the neighborhood as a prekindergarten child) and with her mother's ethic of fulfilling labor. For Brodkey and for her mother, work—whether it is Brodkey's writing or her mother's sewing—comes from a union of physical, emotional, intellectual, and imaginative capacities. This ethic grants these women autonomy, authority, and voice.

Gaining authority as women/writers/teachers, however, does not necessarily mean that identity is fixed or that the self is unified. Many of these essays present selfhood as a dialogic interaction of multiple voices created by our class, gender, ethnicity, communities that we are part of, and stances as teachers. Like Gloria Anzaldúa's persona in "To live in the Borderlands means you," we carry these voices "on [our] back[s]" (Anzaldúa 1987, 194) and live in a psychic space without borders—"sin fronteras" (ibid, 195). Many of us wrestle with a state of selfhood that is fluid, ever-changing, momentarily named, and then dissolved.

I think of the many voices speaking within me as I write this essay. Am I the young child straining for words, battling insecurities? Or am I the meditative poet? Or the passionate teacher? Or the more distanced composition scholar? Or the feminist pedagogue? The collision of these voices interferes with my work on this introduction; I have difficulty determining an appropriate theoretical perspective, point of view, and tone. I finally decide to write from a meditative place and space within where these multiple voices converge and enrich each other. In the process of writing, I discover a new, hybrid perspective; I let the writing take over.

Perhaps what is most striking in these essays is the perception that the writing must take over—that we search for, examine, and shape our multiple selves through language. Min-zhan Lu's experience is exemplative. Lu portrays a divided state of identity in her upbringing in Communist China during the Cultural Revolution when she spoke English and a Shanghai dialect of Chinese in her home and Standard Chinese in school until only her school language was sanctioned and she found that she experienced tremendous "frustration and confusion" that she could not articulate until adulthood. Judith Ortiz Cofer experienced similar dislocations in her bilingual upbringing, but she realizes that these experiences taught her to be flexible, to travel across boundaries, and to be a "survivor in language."

Our multiple selves—if often in conflict—do offer possibilities for growth and fulfillment. In *Composing a Life*, Mary Catherine Bateson theorizes that women now lead "lives of multiple commitments" (Bateson 1990, 17), lives of "improvisation" (ibid, 16), and that the convergence of these lives presents multiple opportunities for change and growth. We develop in relation to our students; we nourish relationships with family, with friends, with colleagues; we nurture intellectual friendships; we rely on informal and formal mentors; we search for models in our reading. We create intellectual communities of colleagues. We recognize that those moments when "the seams of life" break down (Sommers)—moments that Jacqueline Jones Royster calls "spiracy"—times of "convergence"—are sustaining. Our multiple lives enrich and support each other.[3]

> I am taken these days by Roland Barthes' image of a seminar as a 'suspended site' where all of us, students and teacher alike, come together to 'write in each other's presence.' He brings to mind a circle in which what circulates is our knowledge, our desire to know, our questions and responses. Barthes likens the circle formed by the seminar to the circle formed by children in the ring game where 'the object is to pass the ring but the goal is to touch each other's hands.' Teaching, to me, allows us to touch one another—what we pass is not a ring but our words. (*A Metaphor for Teaching*, Sondra Perl)

Is the teaching life any more ordered and contained than our personal lives? These essays also portray the world of teaching as multifarious, dynamic, and ever-changing. They envision the feminist teacher as a full human being who lives emotionally, spiritually, and intellectually in the classroom and has the same expectations for her students. hooks' belief that teaching should "foster the intellectual and spiritual growth of . . . students" and teachers is echoed in many of the works in this volume. hooks' vision of "engaged pedagogy" is represented in E. M. Broner's scene of the women in her creative writing class in Israel, combing each other's hair: the physical action symbolizes the physical, emotional, and spiritual bonds that developed in Broner's classroom.

What are the key themes of feminist teaching that emerge in this volume? We envision a pedagogy not of exhortation, not an "assembly-line approach to learning" (in hooks' words), but one in which teachers and students act, as Dean theorizes, as "participant[s]" in the learning process. Maimon's revelation that her students critiqued drafts of her essay for this volume presents a pattern of collaboration evident in many of our classrooms. It is a pedagogy that honors students' complex voices, both past and present. "Always go for the intact part," Mary Gordon counsels. "This is what one must find, first, in all teaching." It is a pedagogy in which teachers value each student's capabilities, creativity, and contributions to the class. As Perl reveals, she wants to convince students that "their words matter." It is a pedagogy in which teachers are receptive, attentive listeners who practice what Nel Noddings calls an ethic of "interpersonal reasoning": an attention to listening, connecting with others, understanding the position of the other, and then engaging in response and dialogue (Nodding, 1991, 160–163). Perl's classroom scene strikingly vivifies this pose:

> I have learned to listen carefully. . . . To look closely at what is in front of me and to listen to what is being spoken. As I meet the challenge to take in what my students say and ask, I am simultaneously called out of myself.

It is a pedagogy that asks teachers and students together actively to create learning communities and to construct knowledge.

This pedagogy creates spaces in which the private and public, the "personal" and the "academic" (Sommers), the classroom and "the world outside" (Bridwell-Bowles) merge. It is a world in which we struggle to craft curriculum that will be meaningful to students, one in which students are urged to acquire not just "tokens"—as Brodkey theorizes—but fundamental aspects of literacy: questioning, critical and imaginative inquiry, and the desire to write and to discover meaning and knowledge.[4]

These aspects of literacy—reading, writing, inquiry, dialogue—are conceived of as fluid, interwoven, and cyclic processes that move students into larger and larger arenas of feeling, thought, experience, and knowledge and give students "ways of knowing that enhance their capacity to live fully and deeply" (hooks). And these processes offer us similar opportunities for growth and renewal. As Dean reveals: "Teaching and writing, writing and teaching, it is the singular rhythm of life."

These essays, however, do not present idealized classroom worlds. Although many of us possess features of Belenky's midwife teacher in that we do nurture students, we do "draw" knowledge out of them, we do "foster" their evolution as thinkers and writers (Belenky 1986, 217–219), we also are deeply cognizant of students' resistance, passivity, and struggle with words. I ask: "Can words fight poverty, loneliness, despair, apathy, violence? Can words ever create a safe space of the classroom. . . .?" We confront differences of race, class, and ethnicity that must be dealt with in the classroom. Storytelling does offer the possibility of bridging cultural difference. For example, E. M. Broner depicts a moment in a women's literature and writing class that she conducted in 1983 in Jerusalem at Hebrew University, in which the Israeli women sensed their differences from what they perceived as their privileged American classmates until the American women told stories of their pain and loss; then, through listening, Broner relates, the Israeli women gained more respect and understanding of their American counterparts. Hephzibah Roskelly, speaking from her perspective as a white Southern woman, also hopes that sharing narratives about the intersections of class, race, and gender will lead students to understand the position of the other: "Hearing these stories may be the most powerful way for students to understand race, class, and gender since it connects and distances experience at the same time. . . . Reading stories, their own and others', brings students an understanding and consciousness of their own and others' contexts that allows them to grapple with the frustrating and painful issues that they have grown up with and have hidden." Roskelly hopes that autobiographical writing and story-telling will help students forge connections with others and become "whole."

These are visions of change. In many of these stories, we hear calls for engaged learning, cultural critique, and cultural transformation. Broner celebrates the roles of the feminist writing teachers in the cultural revolutions of the 1960s and 1970s, reminding us that the drive to "al[ter] language" was a drive to change reality. Lillian Bridwell-Bowles also urges us to "make our classrooms vital places where students learn not only the various conventions of academic writing, but also the power of communication to change things, to transform."

These are hopeful visions. Language invokes an eternal present: moments of reading, writing, teaching, and storytelling that offer opportunities for change, growth, and renewal. As Mary Gordon suggests regarding her work with the elders: It is a source of "something entirely hopeful, entirely loving. A spot of light. Presence and the present. A nest of language for the past." And, I would add, a "nest of language" for the future.

These visions suggest that if we work "as if [our lives] depended on it," if we "write across the chalkboard" (Rich "As if"), we can change our worlds. For the classroom is the place where, as Lynne Crockett suggests, "the past and future meet."

Notes

1. See, for example, autobiographies by Joan Cutuly and Mary Rose O'Reilley.

2. See, for example, Beach, Connors, Peterson.

3. Many of us live in what Gilligan defines as a "web of interconnectedness" (Gilligan 1982, 57) with others.

4. These themes echo recent explorations of feminist composition pedagogy. See, for instance, Ashton-Jones; Daümer and Runzo; Flynn (1988, 1991); Goulston; Hunter; McCracken and Mellin.

Works Cited

Anzaldúa, Gloria. 1987. *Borderlands/La Frontera: The New Mestiza.* San Francisco: Aunt Lute Books.
Ashton-Jones, Evelyn, ed. 1990. "Gender, Culture, and Ideology." Special Issue of *Journal of Advanced Composition* 10.
Ashton-Warner, Sylvia, 1963. *Teacher.* New York: Simon and Schuster.

Atwell, Nancy, 1987. *In The Middle: Writing, Reading and Learning with Adolescents.* Portsmouth, NH: Boynton/Cook.

Bateson, Mary Catherine. 1990. *Composing a Life.* New York: Plume. 1990.

Beach, Richard. 1987. "Differences in Autobiographical Narratives of English Teachers, College Freshman, and Seventh Graders." *CCC* 38: 56–69.

Belenky, Mary Field, et al. 1986. *Women's Ways of Knowing: The Development of Self, Voice and Mind.* New York: Basic Books.

Caywood, Cynthia L. and Gillian R. Overing, eds. 1987. *Teaching Writing: Pedagogy, Gender and Equity.* Albany: State University of New York Press.

Connors, Robert J. 1987. "Personal Writing Assignments." *CCC* 38: 167–183.

Culley, Margo. 1985. *A Day At a Time: The Diary Literature of American Women from 1764 to the Present.* New York: Feminist.

Cutuly, Joan. 1993. *Home of the Wildcats: Perils of an English Teacher.* Urbana, Ill: NCTE.

Daümer, Elisabeth and Sandra Runzo, 1987. "Transforming the Composition Classroom." Caywood and Overing 45–62.

Emig, Janet and Louise Wetherbee Phelps, eds. 1995. *Feminine Principles and Women's Experience in American Composition and Rhetoric.* Pittsburgh: University of Pittsburgh Press.

Flynn, Elizabeth. 1988. "Composing as a Woman." *CCC* 39: 423–435.

———. 1991."Composition Studies from a Feminist Perspective." *The Politics of Writing Instruction: Postsecondary.* Edited by Richard Bullock and John Trimbur. Portsmouth, NH: Boynton/ Cook Heinemann, 137–154.

Freedman, Diane P., Olivia Frey, and Frances Murphy Zauhar, eds. 1993. *The Intimate Critique: Autobiographical Literary Criticism.* Durham: Duke University Press.

Gannett, Cinthia. 1995. "The Stories of Our Lives Become Our Lives: Journals, Diaries, and Academic Discourse." Wetherbee and Phelps 109–136.

Gilligan, Carol. 1982. *In a Different Voice: Psychological Theory and Women's Development.* Cambridge: Harvard University Press.

Goulston, Wendy. 1987. "Women Writing." Caywood and Overing. 19–29.

Hampl, Patricia. "Memory and Imagination." *The Dolphin Reader.* Edited by Douglas Hunt and Carolyn Perry. Boston: Houghton Mifflin, 591–601.

Hunter, Susan. 1991. "A Woman's Place Is In the Composition Classroom: Pedagogy, Gender, and Difference." *Rhetoric Review* 9: 213–245.

McCracken, Nancy Mellin, and Bruce C. Appleby. 1992. *Gender Issues in the Teaching of English.* Portsmouth, NH: Boynton Cook.

Miller, Nancy K. 1991. *Getting Personal: Feminist Occasions and Other Autobiographical Acts.* New York: Routledge.

Noddings, Nel. 1991. "Stories in Dialogue: Caring and Interpersonal Reasoning." *Stories Lives Tell: Narratives and Dialogue in Education.* Edited by Carol Witherell and Nel Noddings. New York: Teachers College Press, 157–170.

O'Reilley, Mary Rose. 1993. *The Peaceable Classroom.* Portsmouth, NH: Boynton/Cook.

Peterson, Linda H. 1991. "Gender and the Autobiographical Essay: Research Perspectives, Pedagogical Practices." *CCC* 42: 170–183.

Pratt, Mary Louise. 1991. "Arts of the Contact Zone." *Profession '91*: 33–40.

Smith, Sidonie. 1987. *A Poetics of Women's Autobiography: Marginality and the Fictions of Self-Representation.* Bloomington: Indiana University Press.

———. 1993. *Subjectivity, Identity and Women's Autobiographical Practices in the Twentieth Century.* Bloomington: Indiana University Press.

Rose, Mike. 1989. *Lives on the Boundary.* New York: Free.

Weiler, Katherine. 1988. *Women Teaching for Change: Gender, Class, and Power.* New York: Bergin & Garvey.

Wolf, Christa. 1970. *The Quest for Christa T.* Translated by Christopher Middleton. Farrar, Straus, and Giroux.

Part I

Silence and Words

Chapter 1

Teaching College English
as a Woman

Lynn Z. Bloom

Prologue

During my first year of doctoral work I spent all my savings on a lifetime membership in NCTE. Already, in my first year as a TA, I knew I loved to teach. Nothing less than a lifetime commitment to the profession I was preparing to join could express that love.

It has taken thirty years to find the voice, the place in the profession, to tell the stories that follow. When the events occurred, I would never discuss them, silenced by guilt, shame, anger, and embarrassment. Like discussing childbirth (which for the same reasons I never did either until a recent reunion with college roommates), it would not have been ladylike. But two years ago at a summer conference, a one-hour session on "gender and teaching," attended by women and men alike, metamorphosed into two nights of telling life-saving stories. And so I tell you what it has been like to teach college English as a woman, to become a member of the profession I now and ever embrace anew. Call me Lynn.

"Teaching College English as a Woman" is from *College English*, November 1992. Copyright 1992 by the National Council of Teachers of English. Reprinted with permission.

My Job as Ventriloquist's Dummy

Once upon a time, as a newly-minted PhD with a newly-minted baby, I got the best part-time job I've ever had, a half-time assistant professorship at a distinguished midwestern university. Unusual for the early 60s, and unique to that institution, my job was created in response to the dean's estimate of an impending shortage of faculty. "It's going to be hell on wheels facultywise around here for the next five years," he said. So I was hired for exactly half of a full-time job: half the teaching load, half the advising and committee work, half the regular benefits. Our second child was born, conveniently during my second summer vacation. Though not on a tenure track, I did have a parking space; it seemed a fair exchange. I taught freshman composition, of course, and sometimes sophomore lit surveys. I even taught in a room that overlooked the playground of our children's nursery school.

During the whole five years I taught there, I never expressed an original opinion about literature, either in class or out. In the course of my very fine education at one of our nation's very finest universities, taught entirely by men except for women's phys. ed. where they allowed a woman to teach us how to develop graceful "posture, figure, and carriage," I learned, among other things, that only real professors had the right to say what they thought. Anyway, in the 50s there were no concepts, no language, to say what I, as a nascent feminist critic, wanted to say. I tried, in a fifteen-page junior year honors paper, "Milton's Eve did too have some redeeming virtues." The paper was returned, next day, in virgin condition, save a small mark in the margin on page two where the professor had apparently stopped reading, and a tiny scarlet C discreetly tattooed at the end. In shame and horror at getting less than my usual A, I went to see the professor. "Why did I get a C?" I was near tears. "Because," he said in measured tones, drawing on his pipe, "you simply can't say that." End of discussion. I did not sin again.

I had majored in English because I loved to read and to write, and I continued to love reading and writing all the way through graduate school. But somewhere along the line, perhaps through the examples of my professors, measured, judicious, self-controlled, I had come to believe that my job as a teacher was to present the material in a neutral manner, even-handedly citing a range of Prominent Male Critics, and let the students make up their own minds. It would have been embarrassing, unprofessional, to express the passion I felt, so I taught every class in my ventriloquist's dummy voice. Indifferent student evaluations reflected the disengagement this approach provoked—"although she's a nice lady," some students added.

Editing textbooks didn't count. Only the other women who taught freshman composition part-time took this work seriously. (Collectively we were known to the male full-time faculty as the "Heights Housewives," as we learned from the captions on the witchlike cartoons that would occasionally appear on the bulletin board in the English Department office.) I had collaboratively edited a collection of critical essays on Faulkner intended for freshman writing courses, signing the book contract in the hospital the day after the birth of my first child. I was working on two other collaborative texts. The English Department invited my Faulkner collaborator, a gracious scholar of international renown, to come to campus to lecture on the subject of our book, but they did not invite me to either the lecture or the dinner for him. The university's public relations spokesman nevertheless called and asked if I'd be willing to give a cocktail party for him, at my expense. That may have been the only time I ever said "no" during the whole five years I taught there.

Freshman composition didn't count. I was so apprehensive about publishing original writing in my own name that when my husband Martin, a social psychologist, and I collaborated on an article about a student's writing process, I insisted that we submit it in Martin's name only. Only real professors with full-time jobs could publish academic articles, and I knew I wasn't one. *College English* accepted it by return mail. "Now do you want your name on it?" Martin asked, "you should be first author." "Yes," I said, "Yes."

My work in nonfiction didn't count. I proudly told the department chair that I was beginning research on a biography of Dr. Benjamin Spock, soon to retire from his faculty position at the same university. I had access to all the primary sources I needed, including Spock himself. "Why don't you write a series of biographical articles on major literary figures?" asked our leader, whose customary advice to faculty requests for raises was "Diversify your portfolio." "Once you've established your reputation you can afford to throw it away by writing about a popular figure." I thanked him politely and continued my research, a logical extension of my dissertation study of

biographical method. I could learn a lot about how people
wrote biographies, I reasoned, if I wrote one myself. And because I couldn't say to the children, "Go away, don't bother
me, I'm writing about Doctor Spock," I learned to write with
them in the room.

Ultimately, I didn't count either. A new department chairman arrived soon after I began the biography. His first official
act, prior to making a concerted but unsuccessful effort to
abolish Freshman English, was to fire all the part-time faculty,
everyone (except TAs) who taught the lowly subject. All women
but one. He told me privately, in person; a doctorate, after all,
has some privileges, though my office mate learned of her status when the chairman showed a job candidate the office, an-
nouncing, "This will be vacant next year." He was kind enough
to write me a letter of recommendation, a single sentence that
said, "Mrs. Bloom would be a good teacher of freshman composition." I actually submitted that letter along with a job appli-
cation. Once.

On the Floor with the Kitty Litter

One of the textbooks so scorned during my first part-time
job actually got me my first full-time job, two years later. The department had adopted it for the freshman honors course, and
the chair had written an enthusiastic review. Then, dear reader,
he hired me! This welcoming work enabled me to find my voice.
After ten years of part-time teaching, as bland as vanilla pud-
ding, I felt free to spice up the menu. Being a full-time faculty
member gave me the freedom to express my opinions about
what we read and wrote, and to argue and joke with my students. My classes became noisy, personal, and fun. Two years
later, I received tenure, promotion, and an award for good teaching. But after four years in Indiana, my husband was offered a
job in St. Louis too good to turn down. I resigned to move.

My voice was reduced to a whisper. I could find no full-time
job in St. Louis in that inhospitable year of 1974 when there
were several hundred applicants for every job. In hopes of in-
gratiating myself with one or another of the local universities, I
taught part-time at three, marginal combinations of writing and
women's studies. I taught early in the morning, in mid-after-
noon, at night, coming and going under cover of lightness and

darkness. It didn't matter, for no one except my students knew I was there anyway. Department chairmen wouldn't see me; with insulated indifference faculty—even some I'd known in graduate school—walked past my invisible self in the halls. For administrative convenience, I was paid once a semester, after Thanksgiving, $400. Fringe benefits, retirement, the possibility of raises or continuity of employment were nonexistent. At none of the three schools did I have any stationery, mailing privileges, secretarial help, telephone, or other amenities—not even an ID or a library card. I was treated as an illegal alien. Nowhere did I have an office, until I finally begged for one at the plushest school, frustrated and embarrassed at having to confer with my students in the halls on the run. After several weeks, the word trickled down that I could share space with a TA—and, as it turned out, her cat, which she kept confined there. This office symbolized my status on all three jobs. It was in a building across campus from the English Department, where no one could see us. It was under a stairwell, so we couldn't stand up. It had no windows, so we couldn't see out, but it did have a Satanic poster on the wall—shades of the underworld. The TA had the desk, so I got to sit on the floor next to the kitty litter. I stayed there, in the redolent dark, for a full thirty seconds.

Then my voice returned, inside my head this time. Its message was powerful and clear, "If I ever do this again, I deserve what I get." I did finish the semester. But I never went back to that office. And I never again took another job that supported such an exploitative system, even though that meant commuting two thousand miles a week to my next job, a real job, in New Mexico. "Go for it," said Martin, and took care of the children while I was away.

Poison in the Public Ivy

Four years later we moved again to eliminate my cross-country commute. Through research support, graduate teaching, directing a writing program, and supervising some sixty TAs and part-time faculty, my New Mexico job had given me a grownup voice. I was beginning to talk to colleagues throughout the country, at meetings, through my own publications and those of my students, and I was looking forward to continuing the dialogue on the new job as Associate Professor and Writing

Director at a Southern, and therefore by definition gracious, Public Ivy.

As I entered the mellowed, red-brick building on the first day of class, a colleague blocked the door. "We expected to get a beginning Assistant Professor and wash *him* out after three years," he sneered. "Instead, we got *you*, and *you'll* probably get tenure." I took a deep breath and replied in a firm voice, "You bet."

"We" contains multitudes; one never knows at the outset how many. Although the delegated greeter never spoke to me again, it soon became clear that *we* meant a gang of four equal opportunity harassers, all men, all tenured faculty of long standing, all eager to stifle my voice. Their voices, loud and long, dominated all department and committee meetings and, word had it, the weekly poker games where the decisions were really made. I could do no right. I was too nice to my students; everybody knows that undergraduates can't write. I was merely flattering the students by encouraging them to publish; that they did indeed publish showed they were pandering to the public. My writing project work with schoolteachers was—aha!—proof that I was more interested in teaching than in literary criticism; misplaced priorities. My own publications, ever increasing, were evidence of blatant careerism. I received a number of grants and fellowships; just a way to get out of teaching. The attendant newspaper publicity, though good for the school, reflected badly on my femininity.

Although I was heard in class and, increasingly, in the profession at large, I had no voice in the departmental power structure. The gang of four and, by extrapolation, the rest of the faculty, already knew everything they needed to know about teaching writing, they'd learned it long ago as TAs. Faculty development workshops were a waste of time. The college didn't need a Writing Director anyway; the students all wrote well, the faculty all taught well, and Southern Public Ivy had gotten along for two hundred years without a Writing Director. Why start now? As a way to forestall my imminent tenure review, this hospitable group initiated a review of the position of Writing Director. If they could demonstrate that there was no need for the job, despite the thousand students enrolled every semester in required Freshman English, not to mention the upper-division writing courses, oversubscribed and with waiting lists, and the initiative in other departments for a writing-across-the-curriculum program, I would not have the opportunity to come up for tenure. Because the review was, of course, of the job and not of the person in it, I, of course, could not be consulted; that would compromise the impartiality of the process. Nor could I discuss the ongoing review with colleagues; ditto. Or the department chair; ditto. Or the dean; ditto, ditto.

The review began in September of my second year. Nobody identified its criteria; nobody told me what it covered; I could not ask. Occasionally a friendly colleague would sneak into my office during that very long fall semester and tell me that he was so anguished by the proceedings he wanted to resign from the review committee; *sotto voce* I urged him to stay on it. A borrowed voice was better than none. Rumor had it, I heard, that I was talking to a lawyer. How unprofessional. Or was I? I whispered. The campus AAUP president heard about the review; write me a letter, he said, outlining what's going on, and I'll send it to the national office. So I did. And he did.

Then, on a clear crisp evening in January, tenure became irrelevant. Our family dinner was interrupted by the phone call that every parent dreads. Come right away.

We saw the car first, on a curve in the highway near the high school, crushed into a concrete telephone pole. Next was the rescue squad ambulance, lights revolving red and white, halted amidst shattered glass. Then the figure on the stretcher, only a familiar chin emerging from the bandages that swathed the head. "He was thrown out of the back seat. The hatchback door smashed his face as if he'd been hit with an axe," said the medic. "I'm fine," said our son, and we responded with terror's invariable lie, "You're going to be all right."

After six hours of ambiguous X-rays, clear pictures finally emerged long after midnight, explaining why Laird's eyes were no longer parallel—one socket had simply been pulverized. The line of jagged-lightning stitches, sixty in all, that bolted across his face would be re-opened the next day for reconstructive surgery. "Don't go out in a full moon," sick-joked the doctor, howling like a banshee, "People will mistake you for a zombie."

Laird had to remain upright for a month so his head would drain, and our family spent every February evening on the couch in front of the wood stove, propping each other up. Every day the Writing Directorship review committee asked by memo for more information; every day I replied, automatically. I do not know, now, what they asked; I do not know, now, what I answered; or what I wrote on student papers; or what we ate, or read, or wrote checks for during that long month.

But I do know that in early March the AAUP's lawyer called me and his message was simple: "A university has every right to eliminate a position, or a program, if there is no academic need, if there are no students in it, for example. But it cannot eliminate a position just to get rid of the person holding the job. If Southern Ivy does this, they'll be blacklisted." He repeated this to the department chair. When the department voted, in its new wisdom, in late April to table the review of the Writing Directorship until after I had been reviewed for tenure, a friend, safely tenured, whispered to me, "You just got tenure." The thick copies of the committee's review were never distributed; I was awarded tenure the next year—and left immediately to become department chair at Urban State University, tenured, promoted to Professor, with authority to have an emphatic voice. The review was never reinstated, says a faculty friend still at Southern Ivy; for six years the Writing Directorship went unfilled.

Escaping the Rapist

Fortunately, even as department chair I could continue to teach, and I often taught Women Writers. One day my class, not only writing-intensive but discussion-intensive, began arguing about Joyce Carol Oates's "Where Are You Going, Where Have You Been?" Some claimed that Arnold Friend, "thirty, maybe," who invades Connie's driveway in "an open jalopy, painted a bright gold," his eyes hidden behind mirrored, metallic sunglasses, is in love with the pubescent teenager about whom "everything has two sides to it, one for home and one for anywhere that was not home." Others asserted that from the moment they met, Arnold's "Gonna get you, baby," signalled the abduction with which the story concludes. Though he does not lay a finger on his victim, Friend does, they pointed out, threaten to burn down her house and kill her parents—scarcely acts of love. After screaming for help into a disconnected phone until she loses her breath, Connie has no more voice and walks sacrifically out into the sunlight and Friend's mockingly waiting arms. "What else is there for a girl like you but to be sweet and pretty and give in? . . . You don't want [your family] to get hurt. . . .

You're better than them because not a one of them would have done this for you."

Such compelling evidence clinched the debate, and I decided to reaffirm the students' interpretation with a life-saving story of my own. "A decade earlier," I began, taking a deep breath. I had never thought I would tell this story to my students. "My husband, adolescent sons, and I were camping in Scandinavia. But it was a dark and stormy night in Stockholm, so we decided to spend the night in a university dorm converted to a youth hostel for the summer. At 10 P.M., the boys tucked in, Martin and I headed for the showers down the hall. He dropped me off in front of the door decorated with a large, hand-lettered sign—Damar. Women. Frauen. Dames.—and went to the men's shower at the other end of the long corridor. As I groped for a light switch in the pitch black room, it struck me as odd that the lights were off at night in a public building. The room was dead silent, not even a faucet dripping. I walked past a row of sinks to the curtained shower stall closest to the window, where I could leave my clothes and towel on the sill.

"As I turned, naked, to step into the shower, a man wearing a bright blue track suit and blue running shoes shoved aside the curtain of a shower stall across the aisle and headed toward me. I began to scream in impeccable English. 'Get out! You're in the women's shower.' He kept on coming. My voice had the wrong words, the wrong language. I screamed again, now into his face, looming over mine as he hit me on the mouth. I screamed again, 'Get out!' as he hit me on the cheek. My mouth was cut, I could taste the salty blood as he hit me again in the head. I began to lose my balance. 'If he knocks me down on the tile,' I thought, 'he'll kill me.' Then I thought, still screaming, 'I don't want my children to hear this.'

"Then time slowed down, inside my head, the way it does just before you think your car is going to crash when it goes into a skid, and the voices, all mine, took over. One voice could say nothing at all for terror. I had never been hit before in my life. How could I know what to do? The man in blue, silent, continued to pummel my head, his face suffused with hatred, his eyes vacant. Another voice reasoned, 'I need to get my clothes and get out.' 'But to get my clothes I'll have to go past him twice.' 'I should just get out.' Still I couldn't move, the whirling blue arms continued to pound me, I was off balance now and afraid of falling. Then the angry message came, etched in adrenaline, 'I didn't ask for this, I don't deserve it, and I'm not going to take it.' I ran naked into the corridor."

The bell rang. "You're right," I said. "Oates's story is about violence, not love." The students, whose effervescent conversation usually bubbled out into the corridor as they dispensed, filed out in silence.

That was on a Thursday. The following Tuesday, an hour before our next class meeting, a student, svelte and usually poised, came into my office, crying. "What's the matter?" I asked. "Saturday night," she said, "I was walking home alone—I live alone— and heard the phone ringing in my apartment. When I rushed in to answer it I must have left the door open. Because after I'd hung up, when I went into the kitchen a man stepped out from behind the curtain, grabbed me from behind, and shoved a gasoline-soaked rag over my face. As he began to wrestle with me, he ripped my shirt trying to throw me down. Suddenly I heard your voice in my head, repeating the words you'd said in class, 'I didn't ask for this, I don't deserve it, and I'm not going to take it.' I ran, screaming, into the street and flagged a passing policeman. You saved my life."

"No," I said, "you saved your own life."

Coda

The computerized NCTE membership card says that my lifetime membership expires in 1999. As the date draws closer, I write headquarters about this. Several times, and still no answer.

I will have to raise my voice. My commitment to teaching English is, after all, for life.

See also my essay "Hearing Our Own Voices: Life-saving Stories" in *Writing Ourselves into the Story: Unheard Voices from Composition Studies*, ed. Sheryl I. Fontaine and Susan Hunter (Carbondale: Southern Illinois University Press, 1992), 89–102.

Chapter 2

Voicing My Self:
An Unfinished Journey

Karen Ann Chaffee

I came to theory because I was hurting.

—bell hooks, 1992
"Out of the Academy and Into the Streets"

I am female. Secondary. Ancillary. Subsidiary. I am voiceless.

I was silenced at birth by parents who reproduced out of anger and frustration: hard liquor plus harsh words equals another mouth to feed. Working-class blues. Laboring in dirty factories for low pay and no dignity. Little money for lots of kids. The Catholic Church. Guilt and pain framed our family values.

I was silenced by authorities: seen and unseen, real and imagined, true and false.

I was silenced by a brown leather belt.

I was a girl-child: a non-person.

* * *

My mother did not want me. Throughout my childhood, I know that I am neither loved nor wanted. My mother either yells at me (Stupid. Dumb. Inferior. Ugly. Can't do anything right. I can't trust you.) or ignores me. My father beats me as she looks on (Don't hit her in the head. You'll make her stupid.). The beating continues until I cry and, then, until I stop crying. I have no explanation for their behavior. I am the second oldest of five.

My mother will say to me in my twentieth year: "I wish abortions had been legal when I was pregnant with you."

* * *

Words were perceived as weapons. Words were used to separate and diminish people, not to connect and empower them. The silent women worried that they would be punished just for using words—any words. (Belenky 1986, 24)

My parents believe that children, especially this child, should be seen and not heard. Actually they preferred that I be invisible. Talking in our home was for adults. I cannot recall any adult entering our apartment and asking any one of us children a direct question. To speak was a punishable offense.

And I had so many questions.

* * *

Kathy runs through the hayfield; she jumps over fresh bales that smell so distinct they defy description. I hear the tractor's rumble, the baling machine's roar, and the shouts of the men working hard and dirty. Kathy turns around, looks at me, and yells, "Come on, Karen."

I know we're not supposed to be in the hayfield, man country.

Kathy laughs as she twirls like an awkward freckle-faced ballerina on top of a bale of hay. She stops, looks up as the sun lights up her chubby face. Glints of sunlight flash off her pink plastic harlequin eyeglasses. Kathy spreads her arms wide as she opens her red mouth and screams. It is a noise that comes from the deepest part of her being. It is a cleansing scream. It is primal.

Kathy has no fear inside of her.

I shiver in the hot summer sun.

* * *

I learn to read in the first grade—Dick, Jane, Sally, Spot, and Puff. Dogs are masculine; cats are feminine. Sally has blond curly hair. Jane wears a bow in her light brown hair. They are always neat and clean. Mother is attached to the house even when she is not in the house. It is a part of Mother. Father arrives home in a big car and everyone is happy.

I love to read. Dick, Jane, and Sally talk and play. No one hits them. No one tells them to shut up. No one calls them stupid and ugly.

See Jane. Pretty Jane. See Sally. Pretty Sally.
No one notices my silence.

* * *

I read. In books, girls are always pretty and smart. Women
are in the kitchen cooking or on the porch shelling peas or in
the parlor mending clothes. They are loving mothers.

I read everything written by Laura Ingalls Wilder, and I fear
her father. From my experience a father is brutal to be avoided.
Laura Ingalls Wilder describes her father's voice as sometimes
being gruff. I fear gruffness. I fear the male voice.

In my existence everything is either good or bad, right or
wrong. I am bad. I am wrong. My mother tells me so.

> The silent women see life in terms of polarities. Everything is
> either big or little, good or bad, win or lose. (Belenky 1986, 30)

That is my reality, so my view of Laura's father has no dimension. It does not occur to me that a human being can be gruff
and loving. In my experience, a father hits and yells. There is no
other dimension to a father.

I want to write stories like Laura Ingalls Wilder. I want to be
an author. I will learn from Laura how to write.

Laura's stories are linear. They follow a logical progression.
She tells her life story from beginning to end without deviating
from the course of action. She does not go back in memory.
Once something is experienced, it is over for Laura. Or so it
seems to me.

* * *

> The ordinary, straightforward, hierarchical way of writing/read-
> ing will be replaced by an agglutinative networking that reaches
> out to include as much as possible, to resonate endlessly.
> Woman's writing will look, sound, feel very different from men's
> writing. (Berg 1989, 10)

I do not see a difference in Laura Ingalls Wilder's writing. It is
much like a man's. She has a story to tell/sell, and she used
male language and male conventions to tell/sell it.

Her character is submissive. She accepts male domination
because that is the way of life on the prairie. It is also God's will.
Is this the role model I want for my daughters?

When *The Little House on the Prairie* becomes a television show, I am astounded at the producer's and writer's creative license. They modernize the story by inserting feminist ideology into the scripts. There was no feminism on the prairie; there was only hard work and silent submission to God, to husbands and fathers, to nature. I know this now.

* * *

My voice remains silent as girls begin to develop sexually and boys begin to notice. I am too tall, too flat, too ugly, too stupid. No one hears me because I have no voice. No one sees me because I am not heard.

In my mind I ask questions. I cannot give voice to these questions.

My head is down, always down, as though lowering my head, looking at my feet, will somehow make me shorter and less noticeable. If I speak, only my feet hear my unused voice.

Sometimes I forget that I am me. Sometimes I begin to trust my voice. The seventh-grade boys and girls meet together in gym class for two weeks of square dancing. The gym teachers assign partners, and I get Neil. And Neil is so cool that he takes my breath away. I watch as the other boys push him toward me. Their derisive laughter bounces off the gym ceiling. He stands next to me, shrugs at his friends, and smiles at me. Me. I cannot speak. My joy is caught beneath my vocal cords. I smile back.

The gym floor fills with squares of couples dressed in gym clothes—bright blue bloomers for girls and red shorts and white T-shirts for boys. We all wear Keds—black high tops for boys. Everyone is awkward. Boys and girls begin exchanging words in the moments before the dancing starts.

"Hey," Neil says.

I am startled. He can't be talking to me.

"Hey," he says again, "this is dorky."

"Yeah, dorky," I answer.

He shrugs his beautiful shoulders. "Well, it won't kill us."

"No, it won't kill us."

Neil smiles, looks around at his friends who are all occupied talking to their assigned partners, and says, "Hey, it might be fun."

And then the gym teacher places the needle on the scratched record, and we square dance: doe-see-doe, swing our partners, join hands, circle to the left, then to the right, promenade. Neil always ends up at my side. He laughs. I laugh. My head lifts up. I start trading jokes about the gym teachers with the other students in the square. Suddenly I am not separate; I am a member of this group of people known as my classmates.

The gym fills with the sounds of square dancing. The male voice on the record calls out commands that we follow as our teachers watch with boredom. Suddenly, the caller shouts, "Now swing the prettiest girl in town."

Neil freezes, looks around the gym with arms outstretched, and shouts. "Where? Where is she?"

Everyone laughs. I stand before Neil completely humiliated. With blazing cheeks and glistening eyes, I try desperately to join in the laughter to minimize the damage. I am separated from the group as quickly as I had been allowed membership.

I notice Neil's white T-shirt is rather gray and his socks have no elastic.

"Knock it off," the boys' gym teacher yells.

I must swallow my anger. When you are tall and sturdy with mousy brown hair and sad hazel eyes, you are not popular. If you are lucky, you are forgotten by classmates: prettier, thinner, smarter, happier. And it seems to me at that particular moment in time that no one has ever felt my pain.

* * *

In my education there are asides, marginal accounts, about women. There is no point of connection for me. When I write book reports, my teachers respond negatively. Their remarks and grades confuse me. I am careful to read the books teachers suggest; then I write what I have learned from the book. Teachers agree that my comprehension skills need development:

> . . . education represses language in woman from her earliest childhood on, and that if by chance this is not the case, she accedes to a language that is not her own, a language of men, by definition alienating. (Herrmann 1989, 23)

It is difficult to speak when words lack meaning. I know about the forefathers, but nothing about the foremothers. Were there foremothers? (My grammar check and spell check have no such word.) How did I come to be here? The teacher assumes the question is sexual and tells me to ask my mother. Classmates whisper and giggle. I am confused by the teacher's response. There was no sexual base to my question.

My questions bother teachers, and I do not know why. My writing bothers teachers, and I do not know why. I am left to conclude that I am indeed stupid (as my mother continues to tell me). I return to my silent state:

> . . . [silent women] see authorities as being all-powerful, if not over powering. These women are aware of power that is accrued to authorities through might but not through expertise . . . In their experience authorities seldom tell you what they want you to do; they apparently expect you to know in advance. If authorities do tell you what is right, they never tell you why it is right. (Belenky 1986, 27–28)

I never know for sure what it is I have said or done wrong; I only know that everyone and anyone has power over me.

* * *

In October 1964 I cannot open my mouth. My jaws are locked. My head throbs. "I don't know," the doctor says to my mother as he removes the stethoscope from my chest, "there is no medical reason for her not opening her mouth."

"Well, something must be wrong. She's been like this for a while," my mother responds.

Actually, I've been like this for more than a while, but my mother hasn't bothered to notice. My entire body has been the home for numerous pains, twinges, and aches. I fear that I am dying, gradually nearing the gates of heaven where St. Peter awaits, holding the book that contains a list of my sins.

The doctor chuckles and asks my mother, "Have you told her lately to be quiet?"

My mother looks at me with those fearsome yellow eyes. She squints, narrows her gaze into my soul, and sneers, "I'm always telling her to shut up."

She and the doctor laugh. He never speaks directly to me. He never asks me what is wrong. My mother never leaves me alone with him. She is having fun flirting with this doctor who pays her compliments.

He puts me in the hospital for tests that will be inconclusive.

During my hospitalization, my grandmother dies. She leaves me without saying good-bye, without assuring me that I will be all right, without considering my need for her. In my hospital bed, I cry. A starched nurse comes into the room and orders me to stop crying.

I am left in the world unprotected, and I am afraid.

I will not speak of my grandmother's death for twenty-five years. I will keep my anger and grief hidden from everyone, especially from myself. I have no words. I have no voice.

* * *

The silent women had limited experience and confidence in their ability to find meaning in metaphors lost in the sea of words and numbers that flooded their schools. For them school was an unlikely place to "gain a voice." For them the experience of school only confirmed their fears of being "deaf and dumb." (Belenky 1986, 34)

I survive the public school educational system. I save enough money to attend a community college about two hours away from home. I rent space in an apartment house for students. My parents do not offer any financial assistance: "Girls don't need to go to college because all they have to do is get married and have kids."

I meet my roommate, June, and fall in love. She is everything that I am not: confident, happy, smart, and cool. June tosses our bedframes into the basement so we can sleep closer to the ground. She staples posters onto freshly painted walls when it is expressly forbidden by the landlord. "Fuck him," she says. June paints directly on the windows, trying to create a stained glass effect. She tells the other women in the apartment, "Don't fuck with me. Don't fuck with my shit. And don't fuck with my friend."

I look around for her friend and discover she is pointing to me. Wow.

June smokes, drinks, does drugs, and sleeps around. Wow.

I become her apprentice.

I follow June everywhere, basking in her shadow, hoping to be categorized as cool simply by association. It works. Everyone at school is tricked into believing that I am cool—hip—freaky—far out. Of course, I know it is all a lie, but I enjoy playing the part.

I apologize to June for being me. I'm too fat. I'm so ugly. I know I'm dumb. I wish I had your voice. I wish I was smart. I'm sorry I'm so slow.

"Hey," June says, "No one talks about my best friend that way. Stop it." She leans closer to pass the joint. "One day, Karen Ann, you will be a bigger hit than Coca-Cola."

I wish I had her faith.

* * *

I begin recording my life, my experiences, my thoughts, in a spiral notebook. Maybe because I see June writing in her notebook every evening. I'm not certain. I only know that I enjoy writing. I enjoy the feel of my pen and paper. I gain a sense of satisfaction after writing a poem.

I begin to be pleased with myself.

I begin to hope for myself.

* * *

I drop out of college and marry Craig. I work; he plays. I go to the local library to check out books because I am tired of television and the idle chatter of co-workers. There has to be something more to life. I find that I enjoy reading poetry. I discover Anne Bradstreet and am thrilled with her expressions of love and devotion to her husband. That is how I feel about Craig.

She writes in the late seventeenth century, and I connect in the late twentieth century. How can that be? We are too different. Time separates our experience. And yet, Bradstreet loves her husband as I love mine.

I walk through my life grateful to the person who chose to love me because I know that I am not worthy of anyone's love. I believe that I am happy (finally) during these early years of marriage. I work while he attends college. I work while he skips class to spend the afternoon getting high with friends. Still, I (silently) thank him for loving worthless me.

It does not occur to me that definitions of love are skewed. I am too grateful to Craig and June for loving me to notice that I am still caught in a web of oppression. My own writing reflects this state of mind. At the time, I do not realize that what I call "grateful" is yet another form of submission.

* * *

I write often. Pages covered with my handwriting are stored in boxes. Someday, someone will read all this and my voice will be liberated. I write poems. I write letters. I write the stories of my life. I think of myself as another Anne Bradstreet writing my feelings. My husband goes away to work for the summer, and I miss him:

> My head, my heart, mine eyes, my life, nay, more.
> My joy, my magazine of earthly store,
> If two be one, as surely thou and I,
> How stayest thou there, whilst I at Ipswich lie?
> (Bradstreet 1973, 75)

Bradstreet feels the same incompleteness that I feel. Without our husbands, we are not whole. My conception of women living in the seventeenth century, especially on this continent, is one of survival. There is not time for love, tenderness, and desire. There is only work. I know nothing of the woman's life in pre-America. My history books gloss over the settling of this continent. People disembark from the Mayflower, touch their feet upon Plymouth Rock, and then set the table for Thanksgiving. How do the women survive in this wilderness? How do they thrive? Why does Bradstreet seem to write about her husband, children, and home, but not about herself? Why is she always connected to others? Why do I feel grief when I read her poetry? She accepts her life as it is constructed by others. But Anne and I believe it is natural to be the way we are.

* * *

> To learn to speak in a unique and authentic voice, women must "jump outside" the frames and systems authorities provide and create their own frame. (Belenky 1986, 134)

When Chelsea is born, I find my voice. I have an audience. Chelsea grows up talking and listening—responding to her world. Just as Chelsea broadens her horizons by going to kindergarten, Sydney is born and my voice stays alive. My daughters speak in a language suitable for their expression. Their voices do not stumble and falter. They have claimed language. I have given them power.

We play word games. We watch Sesame Street. We like the sounds of language. The house fills with our voices as we work and play together. As we grow together. Sometimes we write words on tiny pieces of paper and tape them to the furniture. We fill the house with language—spoken and written.

"Let me read you this story, Mom," Chelsea says as she climbs onto the sofa where I am nursing her new baby sister.

"OK, I'm listening."

She opens the book and points to the words as she reads. When she sees an unfamiliar word, Chelsea stops and looks up at me. "What does this sound like, Mom?" And we discover the sound of this word together as Sydney quietly nurses.

"I have to read to the baby later," Chelsea decides.

So, Chelsea becomes Sydney's teacher. Chelsea comes home from kindergarten to teach her sister. "Look, Syd. What letter is this?"

Sydney stops toddling to stare at Chelsea's paper. "A," she yells proudly.

"Good girl, Syd. You're so smart. Look Mom, I'm a teacher."

From this house, they go to school only to be denied equal access to education because they are female. Their (politely) raised hands are ignored for the boisterous intrusions/demands of the boys in their classes. From this house, I give my daughters permission to assert their voices, to demand recognition, to speak female in a male cultural/educational system/academy.

When will I give myself permission?

* * *

I devote myself to my daughters, especially during the first five years of their lives. This keeps me at home, full-time, for ten years.

I do all the correct mother things: playgroups, library story-times, swimming lessons, pre-school, field trips to museums, daily walks exploring the neighborhood. I read to them. I talk to them continuously. I ask them questions; I answer their questions. Our breakfast, lunch, and dinner tables are full of talk.

On a visit to my parents' house one sunny Sunday, Chelsea and I sit at the kitchen table with crayons and paper while my mother prepares dinner. Chelsea and I carry on a conversation while she draws pictures and letters on sheets of thin typing paper. My mother suddenly turns to me and says, "That's really interesting how you talk to her like she's a person."

I am confused by her observation. Of course Chelsea is a person, and of course I talk to her. How will she become a thinking human being if no one talks to her as though she were a person? Our children need to be heard and read to.

There is a pattern to my life that I have recently discovered. I am always mother, teacher and writer.

* * *

In late August 1991, I begin teaching Freshman composition. I remember my hand trembling slightly as I write my name on the blackboard. My students stare at me in silence as I arrange my notes, books, and roster on the desk. Just buying time until I absolutely have to speak.

I am a teaching assistant in the English Graduate Program at SUNY New Paltz with no experience in teaching, but a lot of enthusiasm and commitment. And, perhaps, that is all that is needed to be a teacher. I have my class plans, syllabus, required texts, and the support of the Director of Composition, as well as the entire department. At the age of forty, I find what would keep me fulfilled as my own children leave the nest—teaching writing.

Am I a mother first and then a teacher? Or vice versa? Do I teach or nurture? Is there a difference? When am I a writer?

* * *

In my classroom I encourage my students to write about anything, everything, and nothing. Often students marvel at how they never knew that they knew so much until they were forced to write down everything they knew or thought they knew. A confusing sentence, to be sure, but I am always delighted with their discovery.

I sometimes assign dialectical notebooks to my students, which can be very helpful for writing responses to texts. Some students eventually enter into dialogues with the texts and/or authors. It is very encouraging. They engage themselves with the texts, and they create their own texts. But even more importantly, they begin questioning.

The composition classroom must be a safe place for students—warm and nurturing, yet challenging and demanding. Students arrive uncertain, perhaps hesitant, and ideally, depart with developing voices.

* * *

Sydney comes home from third grade with a journal. She writes in it, takes it back to school, and places it in the teacher's box. The next day, the teacher writes a response and returns the journal to Sydney. What a great teacher! Sydney spends her time at home writing stories. I save them for her (and for me).

Chelsea comes home from eighth grade and complains about English class. Her teacher has been working on business letters for two weeks. Chelsea is bored. She finds the teacher's assignments limiting. The month before, Chelsea wrote a descriptive essay about a leaf. Every day. Five days a week. The same leaf. Chelsea did not care about the leaf. Chelsea does not care about the business letter.

When I meet with the teacher, she coldly explains her purpose is to prepare the children for a specific standardized state test. The students' performance directly relates to the teacher's professional evaluation.

There is no joy in writing for her students.

There is no joy in this teacher.

I hurt for Chelsea who wants to write, read, learn, explore. And who wants to experience her world and write about it. I fear she will lose her spirit.

* * *

My students consume too much of my time. I spend my summers teaching E. O. P. students and preparing them for college. In four hot and humid weeks I "teach" educationally deprived students to read, write, and think at a college level. Students meet four days a week for over two hours in the classroom, then five evenings a week with a class tutor for hour-long writing sessions. That's fourteen structured hours of writing and reading!

I spend this month with resisting students who would rather be spending their summers back home. They resent the rules and the rigorous schedule. They resent having gone through twelve years of schooling only to be told they are not prepared to function in college. It is a challenge to keep class moving, to keep students interested, and to keep students writing when they prefer talking. They know how to talk; they think that they cannot write.

My expressivist theories are used sparingly, in journal and narrative writing, and perhaps, in composing drafts of essays, but not in writing the final drafts—the academic writing. Here they must learn "correct" grammar and the five-paragraph essay.

I want to allow students time to freewrite in order to find their voices. But they are victims of evaluation—pre- and post-testing. I study their papers for usage errors (articles, verb tenses, subject/verb agreement, spelling) as well as for organization. I look at the mechanics. Many students improve their writing during these four weeks, but I have no proof that these improvements are permanent. And I wonder what exactly students have gained from the experience, other than more verification of their deficiencies. Why is a well-organized and supported essay written in Black English less valued in the academy? If the purpose of writing is to communicate, and if the language used is understood by the reader, then why is it graded down for grammatical errors or language usage?

The best student essays explain the ins and outs of stealing a car, describe the pain and horror of witnessing a cousin's death by shooting, relate the frustration of getting all dressed up for the prom only to be stuck in an elevator for two hours while everyone searches for the super, and tell the story of a young woman's decision to have an abortion. None of these essays are written "correctly," yet every one has a depth of truth and emotion rarely found (or appreciated) in college writing.

I do not want my students, nor my daughters, to suffer the silencing that was imposed upon me—a silence I still struggle to break.

* * *

. . . what is meant by "women." The problem of differences among women has been very prominent in the United States in recent years. We face the task of developing our understanding of difference as part of the theoretical task of developing a theory of power for women. Issues of difference remind us as well that many of the factors which divide women also unite some women with men— factors such as racial or cultural differences . . . We need to develop our understanding of difference by creating a situation in which hitherto marginalized groups can name themselves, speak for themselves, and participate in defining the terms of interaction, a situation in which we can construct an understanding of the world that is sensitive to difference. (Hartsock 1990, 158)

In graduate school, I am surprised to discover that I am (considered) the oppressor of many women—women I have never met. Because I am white, middle-class, and married with children, I am (considered) the oppressor of women of color, working-class women, impoverished women, and homosexual women. This is what I am told by angry women who judge me on appearance, on what they believe is my truth. They do not know my story because they do not ask. Perhaps it is easier to have a target for their rage.

I am made aware of differences between and among women. There must be a point of connection (for me):

> Connected knowers develop procedures for gaining access to other people's knowledge. At the heart of these procedures is the capacity for empathy. Since knowledge comes from experience, the only way they can hope to understand another person's ideas is to try to share the experience that has led the person to form the idea. (Belenky 1986, 113)

I listen to women's voices and concentrate on their stories—from college students to single mothers on welfare to the receptionist for the dentist to the president of a college. It is important for me to understand their experiences. I quietly wait for my turn to speak, to share my experience. But, for now, I continue listening for those silent voices.

* * *

Because I need to know other women's experience, I read their texts: Mary Gordon, Toni Morrison, Rita Mae Brown, Louisa May Alcott, Gloria Steinem, Lady Mary Wroth, Anne Bradstreet, Monique Wittig. Why must I search for women's texts? Why are so few of our texts in anthologies?

I read texts written by students—raw texts, compassionate texts, sensitive texts, bleeding texts, evolving texts. As students engage in their writing process, as female students engage in their writing process, they discover their knowledge.

In everything I read, I see myself, I see all women.

* * *

It occurs to me that Anne Bradstreet is often anthologized. Why? Is it because she submits to the patriarchy? She praises man and glorifies her secondary status. Has she bought into the lie?

> The lie of the "happy marriage," out of domesticity—we have been complicit, have acted out the fiction of a well-lived life,

until the day we testify in court of rapes, beatings, psychic cru-
elties, public and private humiliations. (Rich 1979, 189)

Anne Bradstreet is a good wife and mother—a good woman. But
where are her dreams? I cannot find her dreams:

> Woman does not dare to dream for herself. She has been con-
> demned to dream of love or to share the dreams of men. She is
> forced to imitate; if not, she will not be understood or else "she
> will cease to be a woman." (Herrmann 1989, 79)

Are my dreams false?

I wanted to be a wife and mother and to live in a big house
with lots of nice furniture. I wanted to stay at home and care
for my children while my husband went off to work each morning. I wanted to be the perfect wife and mother. I wanted to believe that such an existence was natural—that I was born this
way:

> All knowledge is constructed, and the knower is an intimate part
> of the known. (Belenky, 137)

I am just beginning to accept the reality of my construction
as a woman, mother, wife, teacher—all of my constructed roles
that I play so well. My awareness of my construction is the first
step in reconstructing myself. But who do I want to be?

Every day I read and write and read some more. As I wait in
line at the grocery store on a busy Friday night, I pull a book
out of my heavy black purse and read. In the waiting room at
my daughter's orthodontist, I open my notebook and scribble
across pages, making lists, developing class plans, posing questions, considering alternatives. With a cup of steaming tea in my
hand, I grade papers at 6:00 A.M. While taking my daily walk, I
review my purpose in the classroom and think about more effective ways to "teach writing." And sometimes, if I am very
lucky, I write another poem or piece together one more short
story because maybe, just maybe, one day, I will have the time
to be a creative writer.

I do not dream for myself. I dream for my daughters who are
not silent/ silenced. I dream for my students who are moving
forward in an exciting and a changing world. I pick up another
book written by yet another woman, and I immerse myself in

her difference. I read another student essay and marvel at the knowledge embedded in the chaos.

Just as I encourage my daughters and students to resist being silenced by their society, so do I. My voice comes to me slowly; since I am unfamiliar with its sound, I have trouble hearing it. I do not always recognize its cadences, but I will.

* * *

Once a woman has a voice, she wants it to be heard. (Belenky 1986, 146)

Works Cited

Belenky, Mary Field, Blythe McVicker Clinchy, Nancy Rule Goldberger, and Jill Mattuck Tarule. 1986. *Women's Ways of Knowing.* New York: Basic Books, Inc.

Berg, Temma F. 1989. "Suppressing the Language of Wo(Man): The Dream as a Common Language." *Engendering the Word.* Edited by Temma F. Berg. Chicago: University of Chicago Press, 3–28.

Bradstreet, Anne. 1973. "A Letter to Her Husband, Absent upon Public Employment." *American Literature, The Makers and the Making, Vol. 1.* Edited by Cleanth Brooks, R. W. B. Lewis, and Robert Penn Warren. New York: St. Martin's Press, 75.

Hartsock, Nancy. 1990. "Foucault on Power: A Theory for Women?" *Feminism/Postmodernism.* Edited by Linda J. Nicholson. New York: Routledge, 157–175.

Herrmann, Claudine. 1989. *Les Voleuses de Langue.* Translated by Nancy Kline. Lincoln and London: University of Nebraska Press.

hooks, bell. 1992. "Out of the Academy and Into the Streets." *Ms. 3.1* (July/August): 80–82.

Rich, Adrienne. 1979. *On Lies, Secrets, and Silence.* New York and London: W. W. Norton & Co.

Chapter 3

Sailing Back
to Byzantium

Pamela Chergotis

My life has been a progression from dark to light. I have come from the dim chambers that enclosed my young life, furnished with my mother's heavy carved tables and upholstered sofas and shroudlike drapes and valances of dripping fringe, to teach in classrooms bright with hope and activity.

I often dream that I am back home again, in the house of my childhood, the old foursquare in Bayonne with its pink concrete steps and three stories of unblinking windowpanes. Home is still those five rooms within which my personality was forged. In my dreams I creep along the walls of those rooms, as I must have done as a tiny child, and I see clearly the contours of the molding, and where the pieces are imperfectly joined, and where they are gummed with paint. I can point to the small square recess in the wall of my mother's closet, where she stored her diaphragm. I see the cameo of the aristocratic lady stamped in the thin metal cover of my hissing bedroom radiator, her decolletage and pearls still discernible through layers of paint, the easy lift of her head hinting at a whole leisured society of cultivation and refinement.

Having gotten to know those rooms in a child's slow time, I know them better than I have known any rooms since, though I have shuffled my possessions from apartment to apartment, and finally to my present house, which I built with my husband. But although I know even what is behind the walls of my house, having lifted them into place and joined them with plaster and covered them with paint, still, I cannot say that I know this house as well as I knew the first. In my dreams I go back to all the early places, dark and distant though they are, yet vivid and sharply delineated.

* * *

The church my family attended was pervaded by a gloom that crouched like a living creature in the corners; the only sunlight that seeped through to the interior was dyed red by the wounds of martyred saints frozen in stained glass. The thick walls shut out all vagaries of season or weather, the most violent storms acknowledged only by the tremor of the saints' knees. As a child, I was impressed less by the church's austere dignity than by the poverty of the worshippers who could derive hope from a day passed in that place.

We went to church every Sunday. On the way we picked up an ancient lady who smelled of chickpeas and wore a queer dress so black it sucked up all the surrounding light, making it impossible to tell where the dress began and ended, even on a sunny day. The skin on her hands fell in long, soft folds that she encouraged me to pinch and pull, as a form of diversion, as we rode in the back seat together. The lady was too poor to buy the candy and trinkets that adults bestow to curry a child's favor, so she would extend her frail and spotty hand, enticing me with a smile and a twinkling of gold teeth, and pulling up the skin to show me how. Her smile was so kind, and radiated such gentle benevolence, that she cut through the resistance of my child's selfish heart, which otherwise would have led me to withdraw to the furthest corner of the car.

Still, it was with resignation that I endured the trip to church because it took me too far from my sunlit schoolgirl's life. The clamor of the classroom, the hand-scissored decorations taped to the windows, the wisecracking teachers, the books and pictures and jars of sticky paste and coffee cans crammed full of crayons assumed an air of unreality here, in church. The old lady with the spotty hands melted into the shadows as soon as we passed through the church doors; she belonged here, but not me. Everything, from the mournful antiphonal droning of the deacon and priest, to the acrid sting of incense, conspired to murder lightness.

Once inside the church, I observed the changeless protocol, stopping in the narthex to kiss first one saint's icon, then another. I crossed myself and touched my lips to their tormented brows, unfairly caught at the peak of martyrdom.

"Constantine," I might hear my brother, Nicholas, declare in a low snort as I stood before that saint's icon. "He had his eldest son slain and his wife suffocated in her bath."

I would drop a coin into a tray and retrieve a slender yellow candle which I jammed into the sand without a prayer. Then I would pass into the nave, eager to avoid the old ladies whose whole vision was filled by the specter of death. They worshipped so vigorously: they always kneeled, rejecting even the cold comfort of the hard, worm-eaten pews; then, as if in the grip of some terrifying compulsion, they bent forward until their bony foreheads struck the floor with an audible crack. All the while, they crossed themselves over and over, singing the liturgy in a low voice. On most Sundays I proceeded directly to the basement Sunday school by descending a crepuscular stairway overwatched by saints in their icons, each austere face split by a great hooked nose and fiercely downturned mouth, and illuminated by a small red bulb that barely pierced the gloom.

In the sunlit schoolroom, our study of world history began with the Greeks. We learned it was with them our civilization began. The Doric people walked into the Greek peninsula from the north, and, enchanted by its brilliant sunshine, decided to stay. There, we learned, great philosophers, kings, builders, and poets established the ruling principles of the West: clarity and unity, reason and logic, balance and moderation, restraint and decorum. I was proud to learn this, but then Nicholas pointed out that our true progenitors were not the classical Greeks at all but rather the Byzantines—like the Empress Irene, he said, who, mad with ambition and aided by perfumed eunuchs, killed her only son by putting out his eyes. I had to admit that, when I looked around my church, I saw nothing of classical Greece and everything of Byzantium, which I did not understand. We in the schoolroom skipped one thousand years of Byzantium, moving directly from the fall of Rome to the feudal West. All the rest my teachers dismissed as darkness.

My knowledge of Byzantium, then, entered the rooms of my consciousness not through my head but through my senses. One Sunday, as I vacillated between a stupor of resignation and a delirium of boredom, I fixed my gaze on a life-sized icon of Saint George, painted with a hand that conceived him as beautiful and sensual. He was unlike his attenuated brethren, the other angels, prophets, and apostles that looked out from the *iconostasis* with eyes contorted by pain or fury. Saint George was poised and elegant, wearing the dress of a Roman centurion that exposed the full length of his powerful legs, idealized, but with flesh warmed by blood that pumped just beneath the paint. The point of his slender spear pierced the head of a fat snake that had wound itself around his body, and he wore a faint smile. He had just won a battle for the soul of the church, but he showed no sign of struggle. The first wave of sexual desire I had ever felt came over me just then—as I gazed at the icon and breathed incense and attended to the mournful song of the deacon—and so my burgeoning desire became confused with religious feeling. A silent sob of frustration rose suddenly in my chest; I squeezed my legs together and my hair went damp. A lonely teenager who had finally found a feeling to which she could attach herself, I joined the choir soon afterward, glad for any chance to practice my piety. From the choir loft I took in the grand design of the nave in one sweep—the altar piled with gold, the encircling *iconostasis*, the rows of curving pews.

* * *

Upon my return to the profane world, I often went to the Loew's Theater on Journal Square, a place where the working class went to see movies and to feel grand. Its architecture offered complete escape. Originally a vaudeville house, the Loew's was frosted with whipped molded plaster of a wildly rococo design—a "set" for moviegoers not unlike the sets against which actors played. Cherubs strung garlands in the overhead friezes, and baskets spilled over with fruit; statues stood in niches molded like scallop shells; and a wide, red-plush staircase swept in a spiral from the lobby to the mezzanine. During those years, these elements formed the backdrop of my imaginative life. I would trail my hand lightly on the marble balustrade while imagining myself a movie star or royal princess, which meant having to squint to fudge the forms of my brown-coated parents climbing the steps just ahead of me.

My uncle George loved the Loew's and copied its theatrical baroque for his beauty shop. I spent long days there, squirming on tufted cushions, big pink billows anchored in the middle by gold-and-white statuary, while waiting for my mother to get her hair done. Hour upon hour I attended to a ceaseless stream of gossip as my lungs stiffened with hair spray. I fought a feeling of choking suffocation, as well as a gathering fear, which overcame me as I contemplated the ideals of beauty realized in George's shop. Ladies of all types—even dark ladies, even Chinese ladies—walked out with helmutlike hairdos of gleaming platinum that constituted an abnegation of their true selves. They were always delighted. My mother led me to understand it was nearly time for me to start shaping my own beauty. Within the circle of her chattering friends, my mother would pause to lift a hank of my limp, dark hair, which she would let drop with a sigh and an aggrieved look. I would struggle away, escaping to an empty station, where I would sit between facing mirrors and stare, with fascinated horror, at my trapped and flattened image, framed by a graceless tangle of smutty hair, copied over and over into infinity.

I felt that I was locked in a forever-adolescence. How did teenagers become the adults who raised wolves in the Arctic or cooked Cajun food in the French Quarter? Like the subjects of an oppressive regime, the oddballs among us—whose strangeness would flower only later, as adults—kept silent, rarely disclosing ourselves, even at the cost of loneliness. Our association would serve only to confirm our general unfitness, and so we glumly flocked to shopping malls to buy yet another pair of too-tight jeans and platform shoes. These effects did us little good, however; and so we squirmed and tottered back to our bedrooms for yet another Saturday night of pacing and sighing—and reading.

In books, the misfits revealed themselves to me, and they were the first to unlock the prison of my loneliness. They vouchsafed comfort and fraternity and wisdom. They helped me to belong, to become part of a body I could recognize. During my passage from infancy to adulthood I felt contrary tugs: the desire to attach and assimilate, and the desire to break free and find the wider world. Reading satisfied both needs by providing connectedness and the world, at once. When there, I felt happy and strong, and fostered a love for humanity that few people who have moved in the orbit of my actual life have been able to do, closed as we are to each other by convention, by our own skins.

* * *

During this time, when my desire for connection seemed to make impossible such a lonely life, I decided to retreat with books until I should finally be grown. I held desire under a tight rein and at the same time expanded through reading. I took as my example the Christian martyrs, who disappeared into the desert to pray, subsisting on a diet of honey and locusts, before they emerged, strong and powerful, many long years later. When choosing a college, I cared only about the character of its library as the backdrop for the transformation for which I was preparing myself. It was necessary that the library be Gothic, and gloomy, and absolutely quiet, with long polished tables that reflected pools of light cast by shaded lamps, and chinks that turned every blast of wind into a baleful moan.

I arrived at the library with a light heart on the first day of classes, happy to have gotten my first assignment. Opening the heavy wooden door, I stepped from bright sunlight into a gloom that neither September 1 nor May 15 could penetrate, then climbed the shallow stone steps to the main reading room hung with tapestries and paintings featureless in the shadows. I paused in the doorway, breathing the musty smell and adjusting my eyes to the perpetual dusk. This was not a place to stop for an hour or so, but a place for total immersion. Day after day my spongy brain soaked up Aquinas, Aristotle, Joyce, Woolf, Aquinas again, Moliere, Euripides, Baudelaire, and more Aquinas still. (It was a Jesuit College.) In the hours I spent with them, although I understood them very imperfectly, I forged a deep and personal connection. I was desperate to know the secrets of the world, but I knew nothing except that these secrets were contained in the books I held open before me, and they did not give up their secrets cheaply. I had to approach them with humility. I had to tell them, "I am yours for today, and tomorrow, and tomorrow"—and only then, slowly and reservedly, did they open up to me.

* * *

I spent my first summer out of college working at a bank. It was an imposing monument, shored up by old Hoboken money. The walls and floors were marble, beautiful if your eyes locked into its rich, gold-flecked swirls of deep green; but its crushing weight, piled on the earth without regard for human scale or frailty, pressed all the life out of me. I felt small and raw and exposed, like a tiny crab waiting to grow back its shell. I furrowed into the building's interstices, where there was as yet room enough for predators to follow.

Old Hoboken money never got older than it did in the trust department, where I worked. Remittances dripped out of our office like drops out of an IV bag. They went to nursing homes and even to cemeteries, where grave markers needed to be polished and repaired. The living clients, those in the nursing homes, were old during World War II, dry and insensate as sticks in 1980. The bills for their upkeep came regularly, pages of detailed line items for medicines and rubber tubing—not even for an occasional curl-and-set, because the ladies were bald as newly hatched chicks; not even for gifts of slippers, because their feet and legs were useless, curled like dried leaves under papery-light bodies. In one case, represented only by a yellowed index card on which strings of tiny pencil marks checked off remittances mailed, a grand dame who lived too long faced destitution while lying in her nursing home bed, as helpless as a grasshopper.

* * *

The air in the mausoleum was so dry that I imagined I would turn into a small cone of fine, powdery dust if I stayed there too long. I was in my twenties, still waiting for my real life to begin. I sat on a bench alongside my godmother on her first visit to the site of my godfather's interment, and we were each filled with our own thoughts—or maybe the same one, a meditation on the final sterility of existence. We were both where we had expected to be, and, this afternoon, no extended path was revealing itself to us. My godmother leaned back to commune with my godfather in the uppermost row; perhaps she was thinking that, for the first time ever, she knew, definitively, where the whole of her life was ultimately leading her. She would lie in that narrow space alongside my godfather far longer than the whole term of her life, hundreds of times longer, thousands—as long as the great state of New Jersey was not razed by conquering civilizations, shaken by earthquakes, or swamped by tidal floods.

I detected a current of air; it did not blow briskly, as from an open window, but made faint eddies everywhere. This cool, dry air was being circulated by some invisible construction. It had no smell, not even the sweetness of flowers, which hung in tidy nosegays here and there on the tombs. I felt as though I were on a stage whose mechanics were hidden to preserve illusion. What if all were turned inside out? What if the drawers suddenly were yanked open and the walls fell away? It would be a scene of surpassing horror. Our minds cannot help but light upon, and turn away from, what lies behind the sharp marble squares. A whole city of the dead—not turning back to soil beneath our feet, but rising up on either side of us, dressed in their Sunday best, drying politely on their slabs like apple rings on a windowsill, their drawers neatly sealed and labeled. I had done a lot of sealing and labeling myself at the publishing house, and I imagined the horror of living one's whole life that way, sealing envelopes and labeling files while dreaming of becoming a nightclub singer or lumberjack, but dying before realizing the dream, and then being laid down in a sober dress and office pumps, labeled, and filed away.

* * *

My friends said I should go to the woods and write. That is not how I came to build my house in the woods, although it may have been considered part of a larger scheme, which was to embark on a new life. Indeed, life in the country bore no resemblance to that which had gone on before.

My husband, Tom, and I built our house with lumber so fresh and sticky-green the sap seemed still to be running through the planks even as we nailed them up. The soft pine, luminously blonde, could be dented with a fingernail, yielding readily to three-penny nails and ripping like paper under the teeth of our rickety table saw. The lumber was not yet separated from its forest life; the house seemed to sprout from the trees that crowded it, though the boards were carried from a distant mill.

The first thing I carried into the house, before there were inside walls to conceal the skeletal frame, was an oil lamp. We had arrived from the city at dusk on a Friday with duffel bags stuffed with clothes and blankets for the weekend. We were still intoxicated by the sweet air of the country, our heads flushed into sharp lucidity with the sudden rush of oxygen. The elaborate constructions that pass for thought in the city seemed suddenly convoluted, as clarity struck the brainpan with the force of revelation.

I set my lamp down on the basement floor, a slab of cold, freshly set concrete that formed the foundation of our new house. The light flickered through the joists of the main floor and up through the rafters to the roof, casting striped shadows everywhere. I could at a glance take in the whole structure, every corner of the box that would contain my new life. There, in the southeast corner, was the frame of the bedroom where I would sleep and dream. In the corner opposite was the kitchen, its naked copper pipes connected to the tap but not yet to the well; there I would fill up pots of water in which to boil spaghetti. That we could sustain life in this place, that we could have heat, food, and water here, seemed improbable then.

The roof soared to a peak, as in a Gothic cathedral. I was overtaken by a hushed awe and reverence, an effect intensified by the deep shadows cast by the flickering lamplight. It was not solitude that held me to this place, because, once alone in my house day after day through the seasons, I became aware of the sentient life that surrounded me, and of its struggle to get food and bear young and weather storms that was every bit as raw and vigorous as the struggle of humanity in the city. Nor was it the quiet that held me, because my ears, once they had stopped vibrating from the din of the city, were full of sound— the rush of water during a thaw or the whoosh of drifting snow, the caw! caw! of cowbirds swooping into the bird feeder. These sounds informed me more than the clang of subway trains or the wail of sirens.

What held me to this place was the turning of a corner into a new life. I carried my mother's heavy carved tables with me as I moved from one apartment to another, giving away a few pieces with each move until my load was light. In my new house I have no drapes at all; the air and sunlight pass freely to the interior, and I pass easily outside. The outdoors became another room, the grandest of all. In the middle of writing a line I can push back my chair and within seconds be moving down the rocky trail to the lake, filling my lungs and clearing my head.

I needed to write about my old life but could not do so while my consciousness was centered in the old rooms. The moment I carried the lamp into the open skeleton of my new house was a moment that divided my life, but that unified it as well. The separation from my old life brought me, through memory and writing, closer to the old life. The separation from people, here, alone, in the country, brought me closer to people: I decided to join the world truly, and not just through imagination. I would share what I had stored up during my years of waiting. I decided that I would teach.

* * *

My students had just left the classroom after writing their final exams. They each in turn had whispered "Merry Christmas" as they dropped their booklets on my desk and filed out. My first semester of teaching was over, and I felt a rush of longing for my students, and for the fleeting weeks just passed. We had been a community of writers, and now that community had disbanded and would never come again, except in memory. Those memories would be framed by this classroom, which had witnessed my transformation into a teacher. It was bright with whitewash, built to human scale: I could easily reach the top of the chalk-impregnated blackboard, and I was close to all of my students when we drew our chairs into a circle.

I was alone in the classroom for the first time since I had started teaching, and I was shocked, now that I had no students to focus upon, to discover just how grand the view was outside the windows, with the Shawangunk ridge rising dramatically in the background. The windows let in the sun, the air, the mountains. Yet, I never dreamed out the window during a lesson; I might have done so, but I never knew the mountains existed, so completely was I absorbed with my students from the moment they first slid into their chairs. I walked through walls of resistance and discovered in each student's mind a different world, vital and rich. Each connection, as it clicked into place, was a surprise to the soul. The writing produced in the classroom was a path to new minds and new worlds.

I did not know how to teach. My absorption was that I was learning intensively, learning more than my students did, learning from them. I was new to teaching, and they were new to college. Some were new to writing, and I felt, as I stood before them in the classroom, that I was, too. We were together on a journey of discovery. I may have had more knowledge to give them were I more experienced, but I could not have given more of my attention. I wanted to trace back to their imaginations the origins of each word they wrote, to understand the heart and mind that conceived it. It was a connection almost excruciating in its closeness.

Rita, brilliant and sensitive, was a young mother. The journal entries she wrote late at night, after her son was asleep, conveyed a sharp anger at the homework that kept her from him. She always felt that she was falling through space, she wrote, as her words dropped down the page. Then she drew a series of shapes, rounded blobs that became sharper and more defined as she went, accompanied by quickly drawn notes that echoed in her next paper: "Amoebas are pseudopods that move by changing their shape. Paramecium are flagellates. They move by means of a whiplike appendage, which propels them through the water like a spinning football."

Anthony, living away from home for the first time, was homesick, a feeling that hit him in the gut like nausea. He pined in his strange new surroundings; he wrote that he felt like a lonely balloon cut loose from its moorings. English was not his first language; and yet, he described his bedroom at home and his mother and father so vividly that I could see them before me. We sat together in my office, and I asked him about the home he had described. The tension and sadness in his face fell away, as he realized that through writing he had created an alternate reality to supplant the present and painful one.

So much of our class was centered around memory, which proved soft and mutable as we shaped it through writing and revision. I asked my students to reach far into their pasts—to record their earliest memories, to describe the important people, to draw the line of demarcation that separated them from their childhoods. I asked them to write about the sudden present, quickly—what they were thinking and feeling in the moment. And I asked them, "What does your future look like? What will you be doing ten, twenty, fifty years from this day?" Jay wrote an angry response in heavy block letters, accompanied by a sketch of himself as an old man, caved into an armchair, a can of beer in one hand and in his mouth a cigarette flaking ashes onto a dirty T-shirt.

I asked my students these questions, and then the room would fall silent as they bent over their notebooks, writing their responses. I wrote along with them; these were some of the best moments: I would look up occasionally to watch them intent on their work. If they were recording the present, a shout from the next classroom might make its way onto the page and there trigger a memory, or a fear. My students' writing showed me how past, present, and future move fluidly together; and it was with this realization that I began to be a writer myself.

As the semester was ending, Truman asked, in one of his last journal entries, "What will happen to us all after the semester? What will happen to English class?" Then he answered his own question: it would always exist, time out of mind.

This little notation in Truman's notebook taught me more about the freedom of imagination than I have ever learned through books. I learned to free myself from the prison of memory through memory itself; by unlocking the rooms that enclose my past, I can move in and out of them easily, and use what I have stored up in them to inform my teaching and writing. The old dark past no longer depresses my spirits as strands of light weave with the dark to create a new and textured fabric that is myself. I am freed from the paralysis of loss: the students I have taught have stayed with me a little while and then passed out of my life, but I can even now see their faces before me, and their words continue to echo in my ears. I am still, too, in my childhood bedroom with the hissing radiator, and I am still in church with Nicholas behind me, whispering. And I am still in the whitewashed classroom, still teaching, and my students, gathered into a circle, are right there with me.

Chapter 4

She-ro-ism

Diane Glancy

I'm not sure what made me choose writing and teaching as a career. I'm not sure I even chose it. My childhood was full of aloneness, isolation, and the numbing sameness of a mother who both loved and hated routine. She worked to establish and maintain it, then raged against it when she achieved it. I heard those two poles from my room, trying to stay out of her way. Knowing whatever I did would bother her. Sometimes doing it anyway. I remember wanting to run, yet having nowhere to go. You know as a child you don't. I remember having a little desk and one book, *Neighbor on the Hill*, which I wanted to write in but was told not to. But I remember making marks somewhere— Maybe on my inner thigh. Under my arm. Inside my mouth—on my largest molar. I remember words as something I didn't have. They moved outside the edges of my room. With my pencil I poked holes in the curtains, the window glass, the house itself. Trying to get to the words. I think I would wake sometimes grabbing for them, thinking I held them in my hand, but they were gone. And in school I was unable to speak, unable to perform in any way other than endure. I remember wanting attention. I remember the schoolroom with its high ceilings and teachers also far above me, always out of reach. I was certainly outside their recognition, except for their irritation that I was there.

I was other than what they were. I was left out. An invisible erasure that somehow still existed. What was wrong? I still can't say I know. My father and mother were of different backgrounds, different races actually (My mother was English and

German, and my father was Cherokee). They married, and I was both of neither. Maybe it was neither of both. I was small and dark and somehow unacceptable. I remember the years of self-hating.

I went to college. Married. Had children. Was divorced after nineteen years. I had to earn a living, and I could do nothing. I was a writer who was not much published, and I finally traveled, teaching creative writing for the State Arts Council of Oklahoma.

But I was born in the heart of the Bible. The Bible Belt that is. And what I had in the middle of it all was the Bible. I went to Vacation Bible School. I went to church. Jesus was the word. Jesus loved the lost sheep. He had a tongue that was a pencil and in the night you were his paper. That's the way I understood it. He gave me his hand, moving over my hand, showing me how to write until the words I wrote were angels flapping their wings. I had to brush the hair out of my face because they were beating the wind, and I had to hold onto the paper too. The whole universe was trying to blow me away, but the words kept me there. After those holy visitations, the years followed my car on the road going over and over Oklahoma in stifling classrooms where I faced the stillness, the nothingness I remembered in school. But there on the board, the little trail of white that came from the holy chalk like a vapor trail in the prairie sky.

Inside their coats the angels had more words. Stacks and stacks of words. There were words without end. I can't remember how I got the money for my first word processor. When it stopped working, a friend in Oklahoma, Bud Hollingsworth, sent me another. I've had help from friends in the past. And fellowships and grants.

I think it was in 1986 when I was forty-five, I met Gerald Stern at a writer's conference. He said that I should apply to Iowa. He got me an Equal Opportunity Fellowship. I rented a Ryder truck that a neighbor and a friend helped me load, and I drove from Oklahoma to Iowa City with my cat. I was there for a year when one Sunday afternoon I was sitting in the farmhouse I rented and Alvin Greenberg called from St. Paul to ask if I would come to look at Macalester College. The next fall I commuted between Iowa City and St. Paul to finish my MFA and teach. I was at Macalester six years when I went through a strenuous tenure review, which lasted from June, when I handed in my materials, to the following January. I had to present three copies of my books and manuscripts and works-in-progress for outside reviewers, letters of support from students and colleagues, and my own nine-page single-spaced statement of why I should be considered for tenure. Out of seven going through tenure only three received it. In fact, it was the third week in January before we heard. We were waiting and holding onto the thought that we would have a job for life, or we would have none. All of this on the ice field of a Minnesota winter. I had even attended the Modern Language Association, wondering if I should be looking for a job. But now I have tenure and was awarded a year's sabbatical with pay because of some writing projects. I have a whole year without grading papers, preparing lessons, and attending department and faculty and committee meetings of every description, when I would much rather be working on my own writing.

I am not a natural teacher. I can't walk into a classroom talking like I remember Gerald Stern doing at the Iowa Writer's Workshop, but I struggle for words to say in class. I struggle for a connection to my students. I move in a different place in my head for teaching than I do for writing. I need more time to reach teaching. When I'm discouraged, I think at least that teaching is a living because I can't earn it through writing, but that's not true either because I like teaching and want to continue. I teach only five classes a year but that's not as easy as it sounds.

I still have that hunger for words to write—to reach *my neighbor on the hill*. And I can get a lot done. My children are grown and I'm not married and I have that time I used to spend with them. My son is a teacher in Texas and my daughter is a lawyer in Missouri. I have a companion also, but he lives his own life and we meet for dinner. I don't even cook much anymore. My house is small. I clean it myself. I mow my own lawn. Shovel my own walk. I have trouble not letting the house get overrun with papers. Often the dining room table in my kitchen disappears under them.

During the sabbatical, I'm going to catch up on my reading. There's a renaissance in Native American Literature. I'm going to some conferences. I'm going to organize my house, which I've neglected for the six years I was immersed in teaching. But mostly I'm going to write. Going over it and over it until I don't snag. I'm working on a second novel, *Flutie*. I'm still waiting on a contract for my first. I've been waiting for months. I'm working on a third collection of essays which doesn't have a name yet.

My second collection, *The West Pole*, has been around the circuit and was just accepted at the University of Minnesota Press. It's a mix of personal thought and papers and lectures on Native American literature and writing. Fragmented. *Choppied.* I like to make up words to fit the broken disenfranchisement I feel. The manuscript also moves between traditional writing and the experimental. I will spend part of my sabbatical proofing that manuscript.

I also have stories circulating. And poetry. A file cabinet drawer of poems. May they find their place too. Though I often think—Nobody wants my work. No one reads me. No one asks me to read. No one comes to my readings. I am no one. Nothing I do matters. I will stay in my room forever. The bats can come and stick to my hair. What does it matter that I've tattooed my whole body with words? That I've tattooed my heart—and inside my head—

When I feel my failures and the hard edge of frustration over the difficulties of getting published, I also remember the student evaluations that have hurt—to make myself feel worse. One, I remember, said, "She's a better writer than a teacher." Bless whoever's heart said that. That may seem true when I come into class and I've been working on a poem or story, which also is calling for my attention. Or I've been answering mail and sorting through teaching responsibilities and community work and conference panels and travel arrangements—all competing for my time and attention, like children.

Sometimes I have not had my full attention on the class I was teaching. Sometimes I cannot give my all. Talking about something like using detail in writing, talking about the elements of fiction or poetry, trying to lead a discussion about a story I realize not many have read. And, sometimes, when I get back to my own poem, I can't find again where I was going.

But there's also the flowers I received from a student. I had worked with her on an honor's project and she said, "Thanks for your strength and support." There are many students I still hear from.

I've had a blessed career. I've had a lot published now. At the same time, I get more rejections than acceptances. But somehow there was an opening in the wall of the house. At least I poked a way through. Surrounded by different worlds moving together simultaneously, I can move through them all. Maybe that's what I found as a child, feeling disconnected yet somehow surviving. Remember Jesus my redeemer and lamb chop? I've been able to emerge from silence and the backroads of Oklahoma to a strenuous academic life with many demands, though it took me a long time to know I had a voice, and it took me awhile to learn how to teach.

Mostly I feel I deal with personal mediocrity and failure and staying on top of the demanding, every-minute work at school without ever having it all *zippied up*. I think of the students who have kept books I loaned them. Students who never gave of themselves in class. I still deal with the feelings of marginality. In my dark moods, I still feel unacceptable. Yet I know the center of being when I'm writing something I like—or when class discussions go as they should—and you feel exhilaration from teaching the rest of the day. Sometimes I get stomped on—yet I go on. I know the poles of strength and discouragement. I know them often. My polarities are different than my mother's, yet I have them too.

But I woke up this morning and picked up my pencil and began writing. Here in my writing room where I face the wolves and know I am a sheep, but the shepherd is there, you better believe it, and I have come through the prairie and I have come through the wind that could erase the toes from your feet and I have novels and short stories and poetry and essays and plays which I send out and get back and I will keep on because it's my survival. My life. I write through the aloneness that fills the house, much as it did when I was a girl, hitting my pencil to find a hole. A way through.

Chapter 5

The Story of a Woman Writing/Teaching: "The Shining Elusive Spirit"

Jan Zlotnik Schmidt

I

Like Penelope, each night I unravel a skein of memory, and each day I weave the thread again. How do I see myself as a woman? as a writer? as a teacher? Which patterns seem most real? Which ones most truly false? Which threads should I not unravel? Which patterns persist? Which are products of my need to mythologize my past? to verify myself? to give myself that legacy I deeply want? to be an active woman, writing and teaching? To feel entitled to name myself a writing teacher.

Is it too self-indulgent to write about my life as if it existed, as if I have mattered? I imagine that I look into a dark pool of water, a stopping place, and see my face obscured, wavering swatches of mildly ruddy skin, a fleshy patch of cheek, almost invisible lines that are my lips. This mask seems not to make a face, not to be me. Where do I begin?

Do I need certain images to authorize myself? Example: I have always thought that I was a quiet, inward child. The child in kindergarten who stacked blocks and didn't utter a word and wet herself for fear of standing out, for fear of making a commotion. I was the kindergarten child who remembered with dread the way to school: the tall cement buildings with looming mouths . . . and I took in all that concrete and blank sidewalks and was sad most of the time. Or so I thought. Then one day last year, at forty-five, I saw old home movies of myself at ages four, five, and six. There was no sound. But I clearly was laughing, mugging for the camera: sticking my tongue out, careening in cartwheels, shoving my Buster Brown haircut into the camera lens. I was obviously happy, obviously chattering. Was I less introspective than I thought? Was I acting for the camera? Was childhood more joyous than I recall? Do I need to forget the laughter? Do I need to forget in order to create my childhood precursor, my childhood ancestor? Did I create the image of the shy, inward child to give myself the start of the suffering artist? The voice of the silenced child?

II

She is on a front step; the cement is cold, grainy. She is very small and by herself. She hears children playing in the street. She hears the familiar shuffling, clicks and cries of games: stoop ball, hide-and-seek, kick the can. She counts the smacks of a punchball against a wall. She knows there are people around her; people pressing their weight down into the ground. Their heft bears down on her. She is the quiet one. She holds the quiet gingerly, carefully, like a fragile glass bowl. It is her trophy. Everything outside is milky, wavering, murky. Everything outside is echoing, thundering. Are the words inside her head real?

III

It was the lack of sound and color that she remembered. She wanted arpeggios, minor chords, lilting words that took her in, that meant savory Italian smells—basil, oregano, tomato sauce, stews on the stove. Open arms. Fleshy pleasant arms. Sounds and smells that she associated with a hearty laugh and crusty bread.

She wanted words that meant vibrancy, color. Instead, in her house, she had perfect syllables in English, not the lilt of Yiddish. The lilt that she associated with her Russian grandmother's kitchen, with chicken simmering on the stove, broth bubbling, red-orange cabbage rolls in a sweet tomato brown sauce, or the Russian dark bread that came with the hated borscht and shav that looked like dripping green seaweed.

These words were tantalizing, repulsive, unsavory. Yet she desired them. She wanted limitless words.

IV

In the grey room with shadows she was read to. At twilight, dust specks scattered into the air and settled on the wooden table, chairs, and easel. Shadows haunted corners, and against one wall witches and goblins, their bodies flattened by dusk, were ready to set upon one small child. Her father sat in a hardback chair, his posture erect, his hands turning pages. And she lay in bed, long-limbed, thin, listening—her cheek turned toward the cool white pillow. Her body in memory disappears. All that she remembers is a little girl's eager face—listening.

The words were like round glassblown bubbles in the air—cardinal red, fir tree green, cobalt blue, thinned and shining in the night.

> Wynken, Blynken, and Nod one night
> Sailed off in a wooden shoe—
> Sailed on a river of crystal light,
> Into a sea of dew.

She could see the river of light glowing, the dew luminous, like the first sparks of frost on the lawn. And she was in the wooden shoe in the stars, peering down over the edge of the world.

And her father would tell her stories of the shiny, copper penny which went from gum machine, to pocket, to auto center, to a crack in cement, only to be found by a young girl named Sarah, who very carefully took it and gave it a home in the pocket of her corduroy jacket. She was that vagrant traveler. She wanted to be in the soft pocket of home, but she also wanted to be that coin on a current, rolling dangerously down a river, flipped upside-down on the sidewalk, perched in the air ready to fly down the chute of the gum machine.

The end of the storytelling was marked by the birth of her sister, her grandmother's illness, her transformation in the middle years from a child to a young girl. The end of those years comes with another Eugene Field poem, "Little Boy Blue": a work about toys that wait quietly for the return of the dead master,

Little Boy Blue. On Brownie night, she had to show her talent, and since she didn't know how to carve soap, to knit, or to build bird houses, she decided she would recite her favorite poem. Now she realizes that it was an odd choice for a young child.

Why did she choose it? She knew that she didn't want to die, and she didn't want anyone else to die. She felt as if she were one of those toys, waiting, waiting for the boy who would never come.

V

She remembered moments without speech. They were the ones that terrified.

She was in a hospital for an eye operation. Her parents had tried to prepare her. They had told her about the stiff white robes, the needle, the drifting into sleep. But they hadn't told her everything because they couldn't possibly know. All the things her parents couldn't know:

1. The prick of the needle when they took blood and the smearing of the red fluid on the test tube slides.

2. The suffocating, sweet choking of the ether. The fear that she couldn't breathe when they put the cone over her nose.

3. The terror when she woke up, and she couldn't move.

She woke up—her hands and feet tied. She was only four years old, and the nurses didn't want a child to rip the bandages off her eyes. And she couldn't move. And she couldn't see. She wriggled from right to left, her limbs paralyzed.

She could think. And she thought that this must be death. To be just a body—heavy, immobile, immovable, and an inner voice talking. Talking and thinking separate from the body. Just a blackness, a voice thundering inside her head in this blackness. She thought that this must be death: to be a voice separate from a dead body.

Then the voice and body took over. Fear. She wanted to scream. She could not. All that came out were animal gurgles, grunts. Harsh, guttural sounds came from her stomach, into her throat, into her mouth. She opened her mouth as wide as she could and tried to scream. Still no sound.

Finally, she must have begun to scream because a nurse arrived and untied the straps binding her to the crib.

VI

She always pretended to teach. Determined, she would stand in front of the room and lecture about books she read: "Sally if you were Jane Eyre, would you have left Mr. Rochester? Tell me. . . ." And this image of herself at a blackboard merges with the one of her Aunt Evelyn at the age of twenty-five: tall, thin, exotic-looking. Dark, thick black hair. Later, Evelyn reminded her of Hester in *The Scarlet Letter*. She was a stranger to the young girl because she died of stomach cancer when the girl was two.

But she was a sign of what the girl could do: She had gone to Antioch, Wisconsin, had married a non-Jew, had become a journalist, a writer. When she married, her father had disowned her, had sat shivah for her. She had dared and paid the price. She had made those choices. Or so it seemed later to the teenager observing the facts of her life.

As an adult, she still has a barrette that her father had given her which was her aunt's. It is a Navajo design. Thin calligraphed birds fly off the edges of the burnished silver. In the center is an oval, green turquoise, green like the light green jade of early times. There are veins in the stone, like cracks in a dried river bed.

During this same time when she idolized her Aunt Evelyn, she worshipped Amelia Earhart. There was secret pride for the teenage girl in thinking of these women. She didn't have to be ashamed that she wasn't pretty, that she didn't attract boys, that she never had dates, that she didn't roll her hair in pink curlers and go to a prom. She had different precursors.

She imagined what Amelia felt as she fell into oblivion. Did she die in a blue mist? A speck in a white wind and white sky? Did her plane explode, scattering wreckage across the South Seas?

VII

In the still quiet, she roams through the house listening for breathing. Pacing, she can hear her grandfather turning in bed, her grandmother snoring in the next room. She can feel the dampness of their bodies on the sheets, the warm places where their bodies were—are, where the curves of flesh burrowed into sleep. She walks down the hall, slowly, carefully, listening for a rustle, a sound that would splinter the silence. A sound that would indicate that they were awake. Nothing. Then she knows that she would have a soul. And she, a small thin figure, would live with the ghosts and tell their tales. She wouldn't die. Not yet.

VIII

How do I understand my own silences? I am seventeen in an advanced placement English class. And the teacher keeps telling me, "You're going off track. You need to be more objective. Avoid sweeping statements. You need to be more precise and look for the facts. Don't use I. Use one." I examine my work, trying to figure out how to relish the small, fixed detail of the poem rather than the feeling the poem created in me. I don't remember one work we read all year, except William Blake's "The Tyger."

In my freshman year of college, I take a seminar in Russian literature. A male professor who resembles a gargoyle loves my essays (outrageous comparisons—Raskolnikov in *Crime and Punishment* and Heathcliff in *Wuthering Heights*). Leaps of connection and intense discussions of Gogol, Tolstoy, and Dostoevski. Next, I have a woman professor who tells me that my style is turgid, thick, and that I need to outline. I try my best; I switch majors.

A student in a creative writing and autobiography class, who, when required to use a fairy tale as a jumping-off point for a myth or a fable about her own life, suggested that she was Rapunzel. Everyone in her family had loved her long, flowing blonde hair. "Hair like wheat," she said. When she announced that she was cutting it off, her family and boyfriend cried. She cried, "F— this!" and fled the town. She left behind their views of her, her role as an obedient daughter and a lover. I am Rapunzel and my student as I write about language and its constraints, about my anger and my swallowing of my own anger as a dutiful female graduate student, about my confusion—I didn't realize during those times that there were reasons for my vulnerability, insecurity, and rage.

I am in graduate school in Wisconsin, in an Alexander Pope seminar. The professor keeps asking me to go to Chicago with him and keeps telling me that I'm the smartest one in the class, yet I keep receiving the lowest grades. Finally, he calls me into his office and suggests that I go back East, marry a doctor, and give up graduate school. "You haven't got it," he says. When I begin to weep and am mortified that I am losing control, he compassionately cajoles, "Don't jump out a window over this." I glare at him and emphatically state, "No. I'm not a suicidal woman."

I am in a Ph.D. program. In a seminar on Melville and Hawthorne, my male professor twirls paper clips and puts out cigarettes in cups of coffee. I imagine the butts bobbing in the steaming brown liquid. The image breaks up the boredom. Periodically, he complains that his left side is paralyzed and that he has to take a break. All the graduate students roll their eyes. At appropriate intervals, I inject a remark. His response is "Uh, huh." One of my male fellow students rephrases my point. The professor comments: "Quite good. Quite good. Yes." The men in the class laugh and tell me to keep on talking.

I do have a mentor: a professor who teaches new courses every year, who does not want to publish, who relishes the interplay among ideas, self, and the world, who teaches as if he must, as if his existence depends upon this passion for language, for ideas, for insight. Unlike Wallace Stevens's small, circumscribed yellow globe of the world, this man's world is Whitmanesque, bounteous. I remember the broadness of his back as we talk about my dissertation. It is a relationship that surely had some unstated sexual dimension, but it also is a love that embraces a way of being in this world. He gives me a sense of exuberance and possibility.

IX

I smile when I think of my early years in the classroom. I am an impassioned, eager teaching assistant, aware of the sweep of my long flowered skirt, of the sway of my long black hair. I am at a blackboard drawing diagrams that illustrate the reversal of roles in Edward Albee's *A Delicate Balance*. I demonstrate how the uninvited guests become the other couple; the other couple, the outsiders. Are all teachers outsiders yearning to be invited to dinner? We are the eager guests, not the reluctant ones, at the supper table. And we sit quietly, listen to the conversation, and hope for a sumptuous feast.

Another moment intrudes: I am teaching "The Dead" to a freshman composition class. I yearn for the students to experience Gabriel's despair and loneliness, to feel "the snow [that] was general all over Ireland . . . falling on every part of the dark central plain, on the treeless hills, falling softly upon the Bog of Allen and, farther westward. . . ." I want them to know Gretta's secret world, to be part of her secret life. I ask: "Don't we all have hidden desires, secret passions?" I hope that the classroom becomes a place for these secrets to be revealed: a green, safe space, a space for disclosure, for growth.

It is a dark, late afternoon in our tiny graduate student lounge. My student, Mark, begins hesitantly: "I was drinking too much. My father drinks too much. It is my story and my father's. See here about the accident that wrecked my car, my friend's back. It was my fault. How do I fix the paper?" He is bent over the page, elbows on his knees, chin against his knuckles. "How do I fix it?" I know he doesn't mean the paragraphing, the organization, the run-on sentences. But we talk about the paper. That is where we begin.

"In this green, quiet place we share, we live, we grow." I have deleted this passage from an earlier version of this essay— thinking it too sentimental, too much a part of my untested, naive younger self. Now it has found its place. The younger me wanted students to have words that would transform them into more emotional, empathic people, words that would lead them into new worlds, words that would give them richer places to live. Words that would lead them to see, to be, to live, to experience, to question, to know. Later, I read Wittengstein's reflection: "The limits of your language are the limits of your world." And I know that it was my maxim as a young instructor of writing. It still is.

Yet I have become a more chastened teacher; the world has become progressively more complicated. I move to a small town in Kentucky. There I am barraged: "Why teach me these words? I'm going to grow tobacco. I'm going back to the farm, to the holler, to the coal mine." I realize that the earth is filled with lime, that the grass has a blue-green sheen that drenches the land at twilight, that the meadows float in a blue-green mist, and that words are quite beside the point. Who needs words?

One student at the end of class quietly hands me a rolled piece of parchment. As I flatten the sheet, a charcoal etching of a woman's long bony face (like a Dorothea Lange portrait) reflected in an iron is revealed. She tentatively offers her present: "Here, this is for you. I hope that you like it. It's my response to 'Jury of her Peers.' "

Another dares me: "I hate this s—. Why do I have to take this course?" He scrunches his essay into a ball, aims it at a wastepaper basket, and shuffles out of the room. I have to race after him and firmly tell him that his behavior is inappropriate, that he is rude and has been surly throughout the semester, that he can think and write if he cares to. I know that he curses me as he struggles with words that he hates.

Many other stories: A man weeping, "My girlfriend's pregnant. I got to go home. Back to Hindman. Back to the coal mines."

Another woman admits, "It was my uncle. By the time the others came to search for me, it was too late."

A young girl, tall and thin with stringy, greasy hair, confides in me, "I won't be in class. My aunt she want to commit suicide. We each sitting and taking turns by her bed. She can't be alone."

The ethics of possibility is not enough. The force of the world is dark, bleak, unfathomable.

These are the stories of my teaching lives. I move to New York State. There is Ricardo whose brother, a drug dealer, is murdered on the streets of New York, or Christine who is taking care of her sister while her brother is in jail. And Samantha who struggles to be an actress and rebels against the father who wants her to be a teacher. And Rachel who writes about a father whom she's never met, who won't see his kids until she sends him a story she has written about him; then she calls him from the Port Authority, and he says that he will meet her. And there's John who wants to be a packer at Lechmere, but whose father says that he's got to have a future. All that John wants is to be a World War II fighter pilot, or if he can't do that, he'll be a couch potato instead. He keeps telling me that he's bored, totally bored. He keeps looking out a window, folding his arms and yawning, and I keep giving him D-'s, urging, then requiring him to revise his essays. He keeps refusing. At the end of the semester, when he receives his Final D-, he complains that I wasn't hard enough on him, that I wasn't tough enough. "You should have screwed it to me," he advises. Or there's Tom who argues that women's lib has ruined the nuclear family and that the decline of the nuclear family is causing the ruin of America. And there's Jing Mei who angrily insists that English is her prison, that she's never going to learn it and never going to get out of school.

She still believes in the power of words, but an insistent voice questions: Can words fight poverty, loneliness, despair, apathy, violence? Can words ever create a safe space of the classroom, provide a shelter from the conflicts, malevolence, and terror of the larger world?

The world is darker, more complex, more dreadful than she ever could have imagined when she began teaching. And she is older, much older.

One February day she is late for work. Her son has had a $102°$ fever, her car has died, and she has dropped all of her papers in her snowy driveway while waiting for a taxi. She scrambles into class, heaving, out of breath, completely frazzled. Karen, noticing her teacher's frantic state, places her hand on her teacher's shoulder, and gives her a welcoming pat: "It's O.K. It's O.K. Sit down. What do you want us to do?"

The warmth of her hand makes the teacher yield inside. The little girl in her accedes to her student's demand. She is taken care of.

She must embrace this ethics of hope, of possibility, of caring. And now the challenge for her is to love the students beyond themselves. Karen is easy to love; others are more difficult. To love them despite their passivity, their resistance, their anger. To believe in them more than they believe in themselves. To accept them and give them more than they believe is possible. The challenge for her is to take a leap of faith and still believe and convince her students that words are potent, that words give us back our selves, that words lead us to larger worlds. That using language, as Audre Lorde believes, "is not a luxury but an act of survival." She must move beyond despair, apathy, and love; otherwise, she feels drained, like the startling grey of a winter twilight.

X

When did I realize that I needed to climb out of my tower? cut my hair? Maybe I haven't because I still am in academia? Maybe I did many years before when I saw that reading literature could be an adventure? that teaching could be a journey fraught with both riches and peril?

When did I realize that the words weren't mine? But that the anger was. I don't know exactly when I began to understand my own silence and rage. I wasn't stupid, incompetent, or boring.

Maybe I began to understand in the early 1970s, when the women graduate students organized, despite vehement protests from the men in the department, a colloquium on women's poetry? Perhaps it began when I started teaching basic writers and colleagues asked me why wasn't I teaching real courses, why was I being a nursemaid, pure woman's work? Maybe it coalesced when I started teaching creative writing courses at night in the Kentucky mountains to returning women in their forties, fifties, sixties, and eighties? Perhaps the rage became stronger when I came to a department where a few faculty members treated me as a second-class citizen because I was a composition specialist. The insistent voice kept repeating, "Climb out of your tower, cut your hair, speak your mind." Or perhaps it came early. Out of a knowledge of death and sickness? Or of wanting to be the defiant one, yet being the acquiescent child, the good girl?

One image remains. A student tells her story: "I lived in a small mountain town in Kentucky up a holler with my sister and brother and parents near my grandparents. Every day my father beat us up. Everyone in the town knew. But we were a good family, a family with a good name. No one told. No one called the police. Finally, at fifteen, I couldn't take it any longer. I moved into a little cabin on my family's property. I lived alone for the rest of my high school years. And every day another neighbor would leave me dinner: green beans, fried turkey steak, hamburger pie, ham with mashed potatoes and red eye gravy. Every day another meal. Every day till the day I graduated from that high school I had dinner. But no one told. The day of my high school graduation I left that town and never came back."

I know this woman. I have tried to leave that rage behind. And yet I don't always know where to go. I burn with rage, but I don't want to be consumed. I don't want to die. I don't want my words to die. I want my students to have words, to live in spaces where their words matter. Where *they* matter. I want to move beyond.

Muriel Rukeyser writes about Kathe Kollwitz. In the poem, Kollwitz speaks: "I am in the world/to change the world. . . ." Like Kollwitz, I feel as if I am in the world to change it. But I am not at all certain that I have changed anything or anyone.

How do yesterday and today become now and the future? Where does memory lead? I am that little girl who is afraid of the dark, who swallows fear each time she is in a dark room, who feels yearning when she walks into a new class and sees the steely, blank, or anxious eyes of each new group of students. She wants to be loved. I also am the teenager who keeps the world at a distance. She would smile to herself, read Jane Austen, and imagine tales for people on the subway. She would go to coffeehouses in the Village, smoke cigarettes, wear white lipstick and peasant blouses and dare to imagine that she could have a rich Bohemian life and be a poet. And when she goes into the classroom, she knows that she still wants the class to become a romance, a romance with language, with words, with dreams, with desire. And I also am the teacher who wants to wait and to watch. I do consciously fight against the desire to be at the center. I always have been on the outskirts; it is a place that suits me. I want to let others step forward and take over. It is their world—not mine. For the journey is unpredictable, enriching, chaotic. And never mine.

XI

In eighth grade, I compose a story that I love, but the teacher whom I don't remember doesn't think it remarkable or even worthy of notice: In an unnamed African country, in another century, a young woman who resembles a thin, curved, mahogany Modigliani goddess must sacrifice her girl child to save the tribe. She takes the child half way up a hill, and arms outstretched, turns her thin face, marked by tears, upward to the sky. Frozen in that gesture, the woman provokes my questions: Did I identify with the mother? with the unnamed child? Was I both mother and child witnessing my own complicity in my own death?

I knew as surely as Pandora intuited what would come about as soon as she struggled with the heavy metal lid or sharp iron lock or rusty chains or leaden rotted logs. She knew that she would open a cavernous darkness and that spirits— elusive phantasms with terrible powers—would twist and knot about her and that she would pull herself apart and yet be consumed. She knew that life would wait, dangerous, threatening, disturbing, and dark. And hope would be the only possibility.

And in me there is that same quiet yearning: a place inside, a great hollow. A cavernous place that no one knows, that I don't know, a place that is quiet, green, and sad. A voice says, "I am lonely, so lonely." I listen and imagine there are other voices to be heard, other voices to be desired. And then I turn to my students. For teaching is, as Willa Cather suggests in *The Song of the Lark*, about the broken pottery that the ancient women have fashioned, an "art . . . an effort to make a sheath, a mould in which to capture for a moment the shining, elusive element which is life itself—life hurrying past us and running away, too strong to stop, too sweet to lose."

Part II

Authority and Authorship

Chapter 6

Writing on the Bias

Linda Brodkey

One of the pleasures of writing that academics rarely give themselves is permission to experiment. I have broken with tradition here because I wanted to document the experience of being my own informant as well as tell a story about a white working-class girl's sorties into white middle-class culture. I began working on the narrative in an effort to recall my childhood and adolescent experience of literacy, and kept at it because the more I wrote the more uneasy I became about having forgotten that I had learned to read and write at home before I started school.

"Writing on the Bias" was written under the influence of all that I remember of what I have seen, heard, read, and written over the years. Yet not one of the thousands of texts that has influenced me is appended in a list of works cited, since no textual authority was summoned to underwrite the telling of the narrative. While I may not have depended on published texts, I prevailed mercilessly on the generosity of family and friends, whose support I gratefully acknowledge here and whose advice contributed to none of the shortcomings of this text: my son Jesse Brodkey, my sister Mary Archer, Mark Clark, Michelle Fine, Patricia Irvine, Sara Kimball, George Lipsitz, Robert McDonell, Susan Miller, Roddey Reid, and Barbara Tomlinson.

If you believe family folklore I began writing the year before I entered kindergarten, when I conducted a census (presumably inspired by a visit from the 1950 census taker). I consider it a story about writing rather than, say, survey research because while it has me asking the neighbors when they were going to die, in my mind's eye I see myself as a child recording their answers—one to a page—in a Big Chief tablet. As I remember, my mother sometimes told this story when she and her sister were of a mind to reflect on their children's behavior. Since in my family the past provided the only possible understanding of the present, the story was probably my mother's way of talking about her middle daughter's indiscriminate extroversion and perfectionism. On the one hand, these inborn traits would explain my performance in school, for teachers like gregarious children who approach all tasks as worth their full attention. On the other hand, my mother, who claims to have found me engaged in conversations with strangers on more than one occasion, would have been worried about such wholesale friendliness. Innocence was not first among the virtues my mother admired in her children. That I view the census story as my mother's does not erase faint outlines I also see of myself as a little girl who leaves her mother's house to travel the neighborhood under the protective mantle of writing.

Writing was the girl's passport to neighbors' houses, where she whiled away the long and lonely days chatting up the grownups when the older children were at school, and otherwise entertained herself with this newfound power over adults, who responded to her even if they did not also answer her question. As naïve as the question may seem, as startling and by some standards even unmannerly, a child asking grown-ups when they were going to die was probably considered a good deal less intrusive in the white, working-class neighborhood in the small midwestern city where I grew up than the federal government's sending a grown man to ask questions about income, education, and religion. Forty-some years later, stories are all that remain of that childhood experience. I remember nothing: not if I ever met an official census taker, not if I believed grown-ups *knew* when they would die, not if I was a four-year-old preoccupied with death, not even if I took a survey. And while it seems to me of a piece with other family narratives explaining human behavior as inborn, whether it is a "true" story interests me a good deal less than how it may have affected me and my writing.

I would like to think that the story of my pre-school experience sustained me through what I now remember as many lean
years of writing in school. Yet when I look back I see only a
young girl intent on getting it right, eager to produce flawless
prose, and not a trace of the woman who years later would write
that school writing is to writing as catsup to tomatoes: as junk
food to food. What is nutritious has been eliminated (or nearly
so) in processing. What remains is not just empty but poisonous
fare because some people so crave junk food that they prefer it
to food, and their preference is then used by those who, since
they profit by selling us catsup as a vegetable and rules as writing, lobby to keep both on the school menu. Surely a child possessed of a Big Chief tablet would be having a very different
experience of writing than the one who keeps her lines straight
and stays out of margins, memorizes spelling and vocabulary
words, fills in blanks, makes book reports, explicates poems
and interprets novels, and turns them all in on time. In the
neighborhood I was fed food and conversation in exchange for
writing. At school I learned to trade my words for grades and
degrees, in what might be seen as the academic equivalent of
dealing in futures—speculation based on remarkably little information about my prospects as an academic commodity.

Lately I seem to have come full cycle, for I am sometimes reminded of the little girl whose writing seemed to make food appear and people talk when something I write appears in print or
when I give a paper. I never think of her when I write annual reports on my research and teaching or revise my curriculum
vitae (that's school all over again), but when someone writes
back or talks back, I'm in the old neighborhood again, back
where writing is playing is eating is visiting is talking, back
where the pleasures of writing are many and school just another
game I played. While the census may have taught me *to* write,
taught me that writing is worth doing, I learned things about
how to write in school. That some children who already see
themselves as writers can appropriate skills which when presented *as* writing would arguably alienate most children from
writing should not be construed as a testimonial for teaching
writing as skills. Well into graduate school, I despaired of becoming a writer whenever a grade or comment even hinted that
I had not learned and meticulously followed all the rules of
spelling, punctuation, and grammar. To this day, when a copy

editor invokes an in-house rule I feel shame, as if my not having mastered a rule that I could not have known even existed means I must not be much of a writer. As a child I trusted teachers and distrusted myself, as girls are known to do. And to make matters even worse, I was a child who lived by rule.

I suspect I loved rules because I loved the idea of controlling events. Step on a crack and break your mother's back. Hop over it and save her. You are safe from all harm as long as you cross only on green. Say a perfect act of contrition immediately before dying and you will go directly to heaven. Say it too fast or too slow, misspeak a word, forget one, or remember something you should have confessed, and you will go directly to hell or, worse, languish in purgatory. Better yet, live such an exemplary life that confession will be moot. The new rules for spelling, grammar, and punctuation were simply added to injunctions against stepping on cracks in sidewalks and crossing against the light, not to mention the rules for saying a perfect act of contrition. Write perfectly spelled and punctuated grammatically correct sentences and you are a writer. I fetishized the rules of grammar, spelling, and punctuation as I did the others, believing that if they governed me they also governed reality/eternity/writing.

Over the years, I have thought a good deal about why I succumbed so readily to what I now recall as senseless hours of tedious exercises, distracting at best and debilitating at worst. To this day, I police my own prose with a vigilance that ought to be reserved for writers who set out to deceive—say, for spin doctors who write off the indictable crimes of their bosses as peccadilloes. A tendency to fetishize rules at once fueled my childhood enthusiasms and threatened to extinguish the pleasure of the most powerful of my desires, to be a ballerina. My long affair with dance began where all my childhood enthusiasms with Art began—in the children's room of the public library, where in the summer of the fourth grade I found the holdings, as I now say, on dance. As I remember, these included biographies of dancers (Anna Pavlova and Maria Tallchief) and probably choreographers, and at least one illustrated book, which I studied and as a result forced my body to assume the positions illustrated until I could complete with relative ease my rendition of a *barre*. Above all else, what I seem to have learned from those hours of painstaking and excruciating self-instruction, in addition to a number of habits that later had to be just as painstakingly unlearned, is that dance is discipline, and discipline a faultless physical reenactment of an ideal. Perfect *barres*, perfect acts of contrition, perfect sentences. Without diminishing the importance of the *barre* to dance, prayer to religion, or grammar to writing, the danger of making a fetish of rules is in the illustrated book of ballet, the Baltimore Catechism, and English handbooks, in codifications that purport to instruct, but as often as not ground a ritual fascination with rules, the perfection of which is in turn used as a standard against which to measure someone's devotion to dance, religion, or writing rather than their performances as dancers, *religieuses*, or writers.

In the mid 1950s when I was checking ballet books out of the children's library, I had seen ballet performed only on the *Ed Sullivan Show*, that is, seen tiny dancers flit across a snowy screen. Other than that, there was the seemingly spontaneous, effortless, and flawless dancing in movies. But the dance I tried to recreate from the photographs in the book little resembled these professional performances or even the amateur recitals staged by local dance studios. Others who grew up in small midwestern cities (Quincy, Illinois: population 41,450 according to the 1950 census; 43, 743 according to the census taken in 1960) may have also attended recitals where top billing was given to adolescent girls adept at toe-tap, origins unknown to me. I consider it still a quintessential spectacle of white lower-middle-class female sensuality. The girl danced solo, and the din created by the plates on the points of her toe shoes was as riveting as it was raucous. For all I know, the plates were there to warn the weary women who usually operated dance studios that a child was not *en pointe*. Or perhaps since toe-tap recitals are as noisy as they are vigorous, the taps, which would disguise the noise of moving feet and creaking bones, were there to distract audiences and dancers alike from the painful reality of being *en pointe*, which is not unlike that of running in five-inch heels. I secretly admired the girls I publicly condemned, and in my mind's eye I see them flaunting their sexual independence before a captive audience of family and friends. As wildly different as toe-tap is from ballet, they are nonetheless alike in being performing arts, even if the flagrant sensuality of the one now seems to me a burlesque of the sexual sensibilities of the other. By contrast, the book I read illustrated ballet as a set of discrete skills to be learned and then routinely deployed in seemingly endless and sexless reenactments of tableaux—bodies transfixed in rather than moving through space.

When I finally studied dance—with the only teacher in town who disdained toe-tap—I learned the rules and followed them religiously. I loved the discipline of ballet with all the fervor of an S&M enthusiast, for I can recall making no distinctions between pleasure and pain. I cherished the grueling daily routine that disciplines students not to cut classes for fear of permanent injury; I learned to trust bloody toes and aching muscles as proof of progress; I fasted and dieted routinely, all so that I could, every once in a while, fly. Not incidentally, I also acquired the arrogance that dismisses toe-tap as shameless artistic pretense and that places New York City at the center of the cultural universe and displaces Hollywood to the hinterlands (this even though "my" New York was created by Hollywood). Inasmuch as ballet is discipline, I learned to be a reasonably good dancer. If I didn't fly as often as I wished, perhaps it was because I was a good Catholic girl who translated the discipline of ballet into ritual enactments, for my understanding of religion and dance alike was radically diminished by my experience of, and faith in, the absolute power of rules.

A child's confusion of discipline for dance is understandable, for it can be traced to the order of things, an ordering produced by her reading, which represented dance as a natural progression from the *barre* to the stage. It's not so much that the child misunderstood the illustrations, but that she misread the book, which was not a manual for dancers, but one from which children who attended performances were to learn to appreciate ballet. Fortunately for me, my autodidacticism was modified enough by performance that I gradually revised my understanding of dance. And fortunately for me, my mother's narrative of my preschool writing as a social performance worth remembering and telling probably enabled me to learn rules and eventually to resist mistaking them for writing. Over the years, the schools have probably quelled a desire to write in a good many children by subjecting them to ritual performances of penmanship, spelling, grammar, punctuation, organization, and most recently thinking. Every generation mixes its own nostrums and passes them off as writing. The fetishes may change but not the substitution of some formal ritual performance for writing.

When I was in elementary school, before children were allowed to write, they were expected to learn to read, write cursive, spell, diagram sentences, punctuate them, and arrange them in paragraphs. The first writing assignment I remember was in the fifth grade—"Write about your favorite country"—and my essay on "Africa" was a compilation of sentences copied in my own hand from encyclopedia entries. Apparently neither the teacher nor I knew that Africa is not a country. And apparently neither of us noticed that the Africa in the encyclopedias was populated by precious goods and wild animals, not people. I would have produced that essay around the time that I gave up on the novel I was secretly writing, featuring the heroine Susan Saint, because while I wanted her to drive away in her roadster (she bore a striking resemblance to Nancy Drew), she could not because I did not know how to drive. By the time I learned to drive, however, I had already learned to write fluent essays and to keep Susan Saint and her problems to myself.

I am sometimes reminded that I nearly became a reader rather than a writer in a vivid memory of myself as a young girl slowly picking her way down the stairs of the Quincy Public Library. I know I am leaving the children's library and am en route to the rooms reserved below for adults. The scene is lit from above and behind by a window, through which the sun shines down on the child whose first trip to the adult library saddens me. On mornings when I wake with this memory, I am overcome by sorrow, even though I know the actual trip to have been a childish triumph of sorts. I literally read my way out of the children's library in the summer of the fifth grade.

This memory of myself is carefully staged. I can be looking only at the loss of innocence. A young girl. A descent. Away from the light. That I set the scene in a library suggests a loss specific to literacy. Yet here is a child who reads so much that the librarians have declared her an honorary adult and sent her to the adult library where there are even more books than in the children's library, some of them not suitable, she hopes, for children. She should be dancing down that stairway, as I may actually have done, full of herself and in full possession of the tangible proof and token of her recent enfranchisement—a card good for all the books in the adult library. Indeed there were more books there, so many more than the child imagined that she found she could not read her way out, not that summer, not soon, not ever. I can see the girl is on the brink of learning that the books are not hers, that books, even children's books, are copyrighted, someone's property. And, since she already knows that some properties are more valuable than others, before long she will confound their imputed value and her desire, and want only the best books.

I must have suspected even in the children's library that *someone* wrote the books I read. But they were my stories: I lifted them off the shelves, checked them out, took them home, read them, and returned them a few days later in exchange for more. In the child's economics of literacy, the cycle of exchange depended entirely on *her* reading. It is a childish and even a dangerous view of literacy, for it entirely ignores the labor of producing books (with the possible exception of the material facts of books themselves), and yet it is one that libraries and schools promote when they base children's experience of literacy solely on reading.

Finding out that every book belonged to an author made the adult books different from the children's books I had regarded as public property and treated as I did the equipment on the school playground or neighborhood park. I didn't think I owned the swings, but I believed they were mine while I used them. I read the children's books seriatim—fiction and nonfiction, off the shelves, one after the other, section by section, top to bottom, left to right. There must have been a card catalogue, but I remember no one suggesting I check the catalogue. Shelves rather than Dewey guided my reading, aided and limited by my height and what my mother called my "boarding house reach," since I was, as they say, tall for my age. What I could reach I read. And at some point, the librarians decided that I had read them all, or more likely that my grasp exceeded my reach, and sent me downstairs. Or more likely still, they probably ran out of prizes, having rewarded me for the most books read by a child in my school, my age, in a week, a month, over a summer, during a year.

Things were not the same in the adult library. Not just the books but the place. It smelled the same (of paste and glue and paper and must), but it neither looked nor felt the same. The books were tightly wedged on shelves, lined up like the aisles of supermarkets. There was just enough room between shelves to make a selection, but not enough to linger, and nothing like enough to stretch out on the floor and read. Truth to tell, I never felt I really belonged in the adult library, and I wonder now if that's because the loss of human space figured the even more important loss of books as stories. I was not ready to give up stories. If I didn't actually read *all* the children's books, I read every one I checked out—from the first word to the last. Today the only books I still read that way are mysteries.

It is only in the occasional glimpses of myself cautiously descending those library stairs that I realize that if I am uneasy about what I will learn in the adult library that may well be because I had yet to learn that *I* could write as well as read books. I am on the brink of believing instead that if I could not read them all, I could at least read the right ones. The right books are literature. Most of Shakespeare's plays and sonnets, some of Donne's lyrics, some of Wordsworth's, *The Canterbury Tales, Paradise Lost, Jane Eyre, David Copperfield,* and *The Scarlet Letter* are literature. I was working from a list. They were on it. It was only later that I learned that it's not that simple, that there is also *the literature*, as in the literature of a field or discipline, the right books *and* the right articles—about history, literature, physics, sociology, law, medicine. And it was much later still that I even thought to ask who made the lists, on which women rarely appear and people of color more rarely still, where America is a far-flung replica of an English village, and most of the rest of the world not even that.

The economics of literature is entirely different from that of stories. Frankly, one animal story was as good as the next as far as I was concerned, one biography, one mystery, one romance, one adventure. But the value of stories as measured against literature is very low indeed. Stories are a dime a dozen. Literature is scarce. Almost anyone can tell or write stories (even a child can do it). Not just anyone can write literature (most adults cannot), and not just anyone can read it. Literature is an acquired taste, it seems, and like a taste for martinis and caviar, it is acquired through associating with the right people, whose discernment guarantees a steady demand for a limited supply of literature. I used my adult card to check out *The House of Seven Gables,* which I probably chose on the recommendation of my fifth-grade teacher but which I read—with some difficulty. I read it not because I liked it, but because I wanted to be someone who liked literature, an experience not unlike that of wondering, while taking the first sip of martini or bite of caviar, if other people actually like the taste of turpentine or cat food, and immediately denying the thought.

Looking back, however, I would not want to have missed a single one of the stories dressed up as literature or, for that matter, all that many of those billed as *the* literature. But I do sometimes wish, on the mornings I wake to watch myself descending those stairs, that I understood why, when I realized I could not read all the books in the adult library, I took smug comfort in believing that only some of them were worth reading. What was my stake in the great books, the ones on the recommended lists distributed to honors students at my school? For years I read exclusively from those mimeographed lists, except for an occasional mistake like *Green Mansions* and some occasional lapses like *Gone with the Wind* and *Peyton Place*, and for many years I was comforted by the list, secure in my choices and certain that I was making progress. No sooner had I knocked off a great book than I had it recorded on a three-by-five card. One per book. Vital statistics on the front—author, title, main characters, and plot—a short memorable quote on the back.

My devotion to that card file bears a suspicious resemblance to my dedication to the *barre*, and I realize now that ballet and literature must be early tokens of my longing to replace the working-class fictions of my childhood with a middle-class fiction in which art transcends class. I see in that file, for instance, the evidence of my desire and struggle to acquire the middle-class habit of privileging authorship. That I remember novels I read in adolescence more readily by title than by author is probably evidence that I retained, despite my files, my earlier belief in stories, and possibly even the economic theory in which stories belong to the people who animate them in their reading. In the world of English professors whose ranks I sought to join, however, such mundane matters as the labor of literary production—the work of writing, placing, selecting, editing, printing, marketing, and distributing books—were thought to be distasteful, akin to asking the host how much the caviar cost. Only when I began studying and teaching writing did I finally remember that esthetics can be as effective a hermetic seal against the economic and political conditions of authorship as are industrial parks and affluent suburbs against the economic privation and desperation of the urban and rural poor.

Sometime during the second year of college I quit recording and filing my reading, probably around the time I began reading books that were banned, or that I believed were: *Tropic of Cancer, Lady Chatterly's Lover, Fanny Hill, The Story of O, The Hundred Dollar Misunderstanding*. But until then no one needed to monitor my reading. I policed myself. Worse, I set out to police my family, whose knowledge of and interest in literature I found sadly lacking. I had to write off my father, who read newspapers, automobile repair manuals, and union materials, but who, to my knowledge, never read stories and only rarely told one. I had to write off my older sister as well, since she dismissed nearly everything I did as childish. I managed to impress the importance of literature on my younger sister, since she was accustomed to being bossed around by her older sisters. It was however my mother I literally harassed, for she read several books a week and each one provided me with an opportunity to improve her taste. So caught up was I in the promise of literature that I chided unconscionably the same mother who first took me to the library and walked me there until I was old enough to go alone, who had the good sense not to tell the first-grade teacher I could already read, so she could "teach" me, who read *War and Peace* with me in the eleventh grade, just to keep me company (I only read *Peace*, but she read both), and who never issued any of those dire warnings—about ruining my eyes, turning into a bookworm, or ending up a spinster—that must have kept generations of female and male children alike from reading much at all.

The list that identified some stories as literature also cast its readers as superior to those who, like my mother, preferred mysteries and romances. I suspect I desperately wanted her to read literature because I believed that if she didn't have her own passport to the middle class I would have to leave her behind when I went away—to college. There are times when I see each great book I filed as also recording an inoculation against the imputed ills of the working-class childhood that infected me and that in turn threatened the middle-class children with whom I studied. I do not think people in the 1950s believed poverty was contagious. They had not yet been taught to see poverty as something people bring on themselves and to spurn the poor as people who didn't get and stay with the program. But I probably did represent a threat to middle-class sensibility that can be ascribed to growing up in a working-class home.

We were a family of five, my parents and three girls, in a four-room house, a kitchen, a living room (known as the front room), two bedrooms, and a bathroom. Attached to the back of the house were an uninsulated and unheated enclosed porch (it would have been a summer kitchen if it had been equipped with a stove) and a storeroom (used as a playroom when the weather was warm). In such small quarters, interior space is social by definition, since to be in a room is to be in either the company or the proximity of others. That I knew how to read when I entered school can probably be attributed as much to this social arrangement of space as to any unusual interest or precocity on my part. I would have been there while my mother checked my older sister's homework. My sister may even have taught me to read. But I would not have simply learned to read. I would have learned to read in the social space of the kitchen.

In a middle-class household, a child who insisted on reading in the kitchen during, say, meal preparation would probably be perceived as hostile, and would no doubt either be asked to set the table or be shunted off to another room, possibly even her own room. My mother was usually surrounded by her children. So, while I regularly read in the kitchen in the company of my mother and sisters and was often more attentive to what I was reading than what they were saying or doing, I can recall no one suggesting that the act itself was hostile or that I should read someplace else. It's not just that there was no place to send me. It's that I wasn't held literally responsible for my reading. Some kids sing, some cook, some read. It was a gift, like perfect pitch, not a skill I was honing or my mother nurturing. What was considered wonderful was my ability to read in the midst of conversation, what my mother called my "remarkable power of concentration." It was not cause for wonder, however, when I focused on grievances, for then my "remarkable power of concentration" became my "one-track-mind."

My reading was not cause for wonder or concern at home because my mother believed she could always call me back if she wanted or needed me. But it was cause for concern at school, in fact, according to my mother, a source of considerable consternation for a beloved first-grade teacher who, exhibiting none of my mother's admiration for my unbridled reading, went to extraordinary lengths to break me of the habit. She took particular exception to my practice of "reading ahead," to find out what happened to the children and household pets in the Basal Reader. It seems strange to me now that I could have confused a primer with a story, but I took it very hard when the teacher taped the unread portion of the book closed to prevent me from "reading ahead" without her permission. I never untaped the book or directly challenged her right to regulate my reading. But in a rare act of childhood defiance, I remember promptly "reading ahead" when I happened on a copy of the reader in the children's library.

If my "reading ahead" concerned the teacher enough to justify taping the book closed, my habit of interrupting the other children while they were reading must have driven her to distraction, since I can still feel the heat of my humiliation and recall my terror as I stood alone and in tears in the cloakroom, where I had been sent for talking during reading. That happened only once that I can remember. The door that isolated me from the others may have terrified me more than it would have a child accustomed to closed doors. I was not in a dark or windowless room, but I could not hear what was being said in the classroom with the door closed. By some standards the punishment fit the crime. Yet it ignores the conflict that the middle-class practice of reading alone and in silence, only what is assigned when it is assigned, created in a working-class child whose reading had, until then, been part and parcel of the social fabric of home and whose choice of reading matter had been regulated by the holdings of the children's library and her reach.

I was not taught to read in the first grade, but was instead taught to unlearn how I already read by a well-meaning and dedicated teacher authorized by the state to regulate my reading. My father once complained that he never understood me after I went to school. I always thought he was referring to the speech lessons in the second grade that radically altered my dialect from the Southern Midland dialect spoken at home to the Northern Midland spoken by most of my teachers. But now I wonder whether it was a class rather than regional dialect that stood between us, whether the door that temporarily isolated me from the other children also threatened to closet me permanently from my family. That the ostensible autonomy of middle-class professionals depends on children internalizing the rules that regulate reading (and writing) seems obvious to me. Less obvious, however, is what part reading and writing practices learned at home, and at variance with those learned at school, continue to play in my intellectual life.

There is no denying that I recreate the cloakroom everywhere I live. It is not uncommon, of course, for academics to furnish their homes with books. It is not even uncommon for academics to read several at a time. But the inordinate pleasure I take from littering all available surfaces with books makes it seem unlikely that in my case books are indexing only my academic enthusiasms. It seems more likely to me, now that I've remembered and reflected on the cloakroom, that the books are there to keep me company, that they are tokens of the absent family and friends whose voices have been muted by time and space. If so, it gives me a measure of satisfaction to believe that this lifelong habit simulates reading as I learned it at home, that even as I read the literature that took me so far from home I have been protecting myself from total class annihilation.

As a young girl, I was not just reading about other people, other places, and other lives. I was reading about people, places, and lives utterly unlike mine. Virtually everything in the fiction I read was fantastic: their houses, their families, their neighborhoods, their neighbors, their clothes, their food, their amusements, their feelings, their romances, their friendships, their conversation, their desires, their problems, their prospects. These things were different not just because literature is not life, but because the drama in the books on the recommended list, at least in the nineteenth-century novels I preferred, either happened in middle-class houses—*Emma* and *Middlemarch*—or, so I now realize, in defense of the middle class and their houses—*Great Expectations* and *War and Peace*. I loved most those novels that held literary open house, the ones that toured prime literary real estate. I doted on the rooms reserved for specific uses, parlors, drawing rooms, sitting rooms, libraries, and only incidentally considered the heroines who retired there to hold conversations, closeted from parents and siblings.

I skimmed descriptions of gardens or grounds, I skipped altogether descriptions of cottages inhabited by tenant farmers, and I seem to have either ignored or forgotten descriptions of servants' quarters and kitchens. The uncertain course of romance and courtship, the tedium of manners, the ceaseless rounds of social obligations also went largely unnoticed. But not interior space, nor threats of its loss. The unheard of privilege of privacy made palpable by the rooms middle-class heroines occupied made an immediate and lasting impression on me. I have no idea if many other children from working-class homes also acquired from their reading an appetite for privacy. But I am certain that the literature that fascinated me kindled and shaped a desire for privacy in me so acute that only hearing my mother's voice reminds me that not only I but an entire family paid the price of my replacing the sociality of my working-class home with the books that now keep me company at home.

I sometimes wonder what it must have been like to have witnessed rather than experienced my reading. Unlike the heroines in the novels I was reading, the women in my family, in my neighborhood for that matter, lived in rather than visited the kitchen. My sisters and I would sit at the kitchen table talking, reading, studying, drawing, writing, sewing, taunting one another, tattling, boasting, snapping beans, kneading bags of margarine, cutting cookies, cutting out paper dolls and their clothes while our mother talked to us as she fixed meals, baked, mended, cut patterns, sewed, talked on the phone. It now seems to me that all serious conversations were held in the kitchen.

My mother usually let us sit at the table and listen while she and the neighbor women or female relatives told the stories that made the kitchen that I remember the hub of our familial and social life. There were stories about pregnancy and childbirth, childhood (theirs and their children's), stories recounting the antics of local doctors, politicians, cops, bosses, nuns, priests, and ministers and their children, and stories encoding the exigent dangers of sex—going too far, getting into trouble, having to get married. Teachers were the only authorities who were never challenged in my presence, though sometimes in my hearing. It seemed to me then that everything of real importance happened in the kitchen, the room where the women talked to each other while their female children listened and learned to be women. But I wonder now if the absence of critique meant the mothers believed the classroom to be an even more important room, though they must at least have suspected they could lose their children, their daughters as well as their sons, to teachers and to the middle class.

My father's familial domain was the living room, where most evenings he would read the local paper and union materials or study car repair manuals and report cards, and where he alone napped, in his chair. The children sometimes also came there to read, perhaps because my mother read there in the daytime, but we were not allowed to talk or play in the living room when my father was there. The family began gathering in the living room only after the television arrived, circa 1955. In what now seems a blink of the eye, the television displaced my father, who finally relinquished his fragile hold on the family to a spate of family programs. I loved those families, perhaps because they confirmed my growing suspicion that even fictive middle-class families were better than real working-class ones, but my father detested the prosaic problems of the television families from whom my mother, sisters, and I were learning the middle-class scripts that we rehearsed on him.

Working-class houses are not miniatures of middle-class houses, neither of real ones nor of those created by literature or constructed for television. So in one of those remarkable generalizations to which children are prone, I seem to have concluded that since middle-class mores governed the dramatic action in fiction, nothing of real consequence could happen to anyone who did not reside in a middle-class house. Little wonder then that I also fervently believed that my parents had only to acquire such a house to assume consequence and persisted in making plans for moving the family into it, despite my parents' quite reasonable insistence that I well knew that they had not the money to do so. Like many other working-class children, by the age of ten I knew what things cost, what my father made, and what the money was used for, not to mention the asking price of real estate, along with suitable locations. I wonder now if my terror of working-class inconsequence was not aggravated by two interdependent historical events in the 1950s: the escalating cold war and the end of the post-war recession. The first event radically altered my education, and the second my neighborhood.

By the late 1950s, some of our neighbors had sold or left their rented homes without dining rooms and a bedroom for each child and taken out government-insured low-interest mortgages on the ideal two-story middle-class house, or barring that, the ersatz middle-class tract houses that developers and realtors were selling the unwary. The ideal had a foyer, a free-standing staircase, and hardwood floors throughout, a fireplace in the living room, a formal dining room, a large kitchen with a walk-in pantry on the first floor, three or four bedrooms upstairs, a bathroom up and down, a screened veranda, a full basement and attic, and a detached garage. The house was made of either brick or stone. While the tract houses possessed none of the virtues of the two-story houses I had encountered in my reading and seen advertised on television, save the illusory privacy of bedrooms with doors, that they were known locally as doll houses would have appealed not to my sense of irony, but to my fantasy (apparently shared by the many adults who purchased them) that a new house would reinvent us as a middle-class family. Such houses did not of course even exist in the neighborhood, so those who moved up also moved out.

My family stayed in the neighborhood until after I left for college. But they must have known that I would move out as early as the ninth grade, when the public schools tracked me into college preparatory classes on the basis of my test scores (I forget which tests) and my performance in classes. It seems, though I remember no one saying so at the time, that I was being drafted for the cold war, which precipitated an educational reform, at least in Quincy, Illinois, that cut across class lines with a flourish that only seems imaginable during periods of extreme nationalism. Nationalism even extended to putting one male and one female Negro on the college track. A fair amount of money was lavished on the education of cold war recruits. Classrooms were well furnished and well maintained, the science and language laboratories (where I studied Russian) were well equipped, the teachers were well educated (most had masters' degrees and a few were PhDs), and the student-to-teacher ratio must have been excellent, for I never wanted for attention.

My school day began at 8:00 A.M. and I was rarely back home before 5:00 P.M. There were few electives, and the ones I chose (like journalism) required more, not less, time than required courses. While I continued to study dance until my senior year (when I finally had to admit that diligence is no substitute for talent), I gradually became the school's daughter: National Honor Society, editor of the school newspaper, Student Council, Latin Club, Russian Club, Pep Club, and other societies and clubs that I am grateful to have forgotten. The homework for these cold war classes took from three to five hours most evenings, which I dutifully completed without fail at the kitchen table and checked or completed on the phone. Most of the daily assignments were graded, and the scheduled tests and pop quizzes were buttressed by periodic batteries of standardized achievement and IQ tests. So thoroughly prepared was I for college during my four years of high school that my first two years at the small state university from which I graduated were mostly review, except for writing.

I had not written much besides journalism in high school, and my professors, who did not much admire my mastery of the inverted pyramid, were looking for an essay whose paragraphs elaborated what I now think of as the *generic corrective display thesis*: A good many scholars/critics have concluded X, but X ignores Y, which is essential/critical to fully understanding Z (the structure of a poem or the universe, the precipitating causes of the Civil War, the Enlightenment, progress, overpopulation). A student can use this thesis in any class because it both corrects errors in previous scholarship or criticism and displays the student's knowledge of the literature. It took me nearly a year to (re)invent the thesis and three more years to perfect it. It kept my grades high and it probably kept me from learning as much as I might have about writing, even though it gave me plenty of time to perfect my style. Not to put too fine a point on it, this quintessentially modern thesis assumes that reality, which exists entirely separate from and independent of language, is superficially complicated but ultimately governed by simple, underlying principles, rules, or verities. It is the thesis of choice among pundits, the thesis that rationalizes what passes for balanced/objective/unbiased reporting by the print and electronic media, the thesis on which most legislation is passed and public policy formulated, and the basis of the recent culture wars in the academy. I no longer believe the thesis, but I believed it then, if only because I desperately wanted to believe in middle-class houses, wherein everything seemed to conspire to protect the inhabitants from any of the complications that beset the people in my house and neighborhood.

I probably visited my first middle-class houses the summer my younger sister and I lay in bed listening to the couple next door read *Gone with the Wind* to each other in their bedroom. They are recorded in my memory as reading voices, one male, one female, quietly enunciating just loud enough for us to hear. We wondered if we should tell them that we could hear them, but we never did because we wanted to hear the story. I never spoke of my affection for the couple next door or of anything that happened at home in the houses of my new classmates or at school. By then I was old enough to know better, old enough to realize that any story I told would incriminate my family and indict my neighborhood. For by then we had been visited by the social worker, who I remember as a singularly humorless man in a suit, perched on my father's chair asking my mother questions and writing down her answers. She didn't offer food, which put him in the class of official census takers rather than writers. He didn't smile when she described the décor as early Halloween, and she didn't contradict him when he pointed out there were no bookcases. She didn't tell him that she and her children borrowed books from the library or that the ones we owned were stored under our beds. I had a complete set of Nancy Drew mysteries under my bed, and among us my sisters and I had collected a fair number of the classic girl's books—*Heidi, Little Women, Anne Frank*—along with the adventures of Trixie Belden, Ginny Gordon, and Sue Barton. Although I never asked my mother why she let the social worker think what he would, I must have taken her reticence as a given because I never attempted to explain home to anyone who didn't live there.

Since none of my classmates had gone to my neighborhood elementary school, my parents knew none of their parents or, more precisely, my mother knew none of their mothers. My mother had made it her business to meet and chat with the mothers of my new working-class girlfriends in junior high. But I made no new friends among the other white working-class recruits in my college preparatory classes, and was forbidden, for the usual racist reasons, to do anything more than mention that the Negro girl was also Catholic. All through high school I kept up with working-class girl friends from the neighborhood school. I even coached my best working-class girl friend from junior high on her dance routine for the "Miss Quincy Pageant" the summer I went to college. But I kept the old friends separate from the new ones, for the worlds were by then as distinct to me as the children's library and the adult library, as stories and literature. Like reading, tracking radically displaced me, conferring on me honorary middle-class privileges on the order of those afforded by my early admission to the adult library.

Alone, I entered houses made familiar by my reading. I particularly enjoyed living the fiction that food is served rather than prepared, and floors, windows, dishes, and clothes endlessly clean rather than cleaned endlessly. These were phenomena already known to me from my reading. Also familiar were ambitious mothers who took their daughters shopping in St. Louis or Chicago, where they were fitted for gowns that the local newspaper would describe in lavish detail. Familiar though I may have found these customs, my interest in fictional real estate had obscured the importance of manners, no less important in the twentieth-century middle-class houses where my new girl friends lived than in nineteenth-century novels. The talk was of honors, grade point averages, colleges, sororities, SATs, country clubs, clothes, dances, and dates. In the light of these topics, I could no longer avoid concluding that in this culture, and in the fictional one on which it seemed to rest, the present is a dress rehearsal for a future whose value will ultimately be determined by whether getting into the right sorority at the right school results in marrying the right man.

My own class-based experience of family shielded me from envying any but the material comforts of my middle-class girlfriends. I learned to speak fluent bourgeois in those houses.

And what I learned there contributed to my college grades and probably even my academic career. Fluency has not however made me a native speaker, for when left to my own devices I continue to measure the value of the present in terms of itself rather than the future. The future only interests me when the present becomes intolerable. That I still consider material conditions the *sine qua non* of my intellectual life is doubtless a legacy of my viewing the middle classes with a literary map of their houses in hand rather than a copy of their conduct book committed to memory. That I never fully assimilated the bourgeois belief that rehearsal predicts the future is without a doubt a working-class legacy. This is not to say that I neither plan nor rehearse. But since neither raises any expectations about my literal ability to control events, I am more inclined to view plans and rehearsals as the moments when I am forcibly reminded of my devotion to contingencies—to the possibility that the essay will be better than the plan and the performance a considerable improvement over the rehearsal, acknowledging all the while the essays that came to naught and the performances that fell flat.

It is probably a measure of their extraordinary faith in education that my parents, who regularly challenged the authority of medicine, the church, and the state, never questioned the authority of the schools over their daughters in our hearing, never resisted the tracking of their middle daughter into college preparatory classes, even though they could ill afford either the new courses or the new friends. The courses radically diminished my chances of fully developing or properly valuing the domestic competencies that other working-class girls acquired at home (cooking, baking, cleaning, ironing, sewing, mending), or those that the girls in my family learned during summers spent on our aunt and uncle's farm (truck gardening, canning, preserving, tending livestock). To make matters worse, the middle-class houses seeded unspeakable desires having to do with the pleasures of romance, solitude, and economic independence that would naturally follow from the "college education" vaunted at school and taken for granted by my new friends and their parents.

The educational opportunities that thrilled me contradicted most of what was expected of me at home. Yet my parents accepted the economic privations that accompanied my tracking. I paid for my ballet classes by teaching younger children, and the part-time job I held as an honors student required neither that I work the hours nor that I work as hard as my older sister had.

My going to college meant not just that my parents would contribute to my support beyond the usual age of eighteen, but that
I would not be contributing to theirs in return for room and
board. There is a sense in which my parents reconciled my pro-
longed economic dependence by turning me into the youngest
daughter. They guarded me so carefully that even serious problems and illnesses went unmentioned until I was home on
break. Little wonder then that I was younger at twenty than I
had been at sixteen or that I began to prefer school to home, the
more so since many of my college courses indulged my fantasy
of America as a society where I could reinvent myself as a class-
less, genderless, raceless scholar. I wanted little more during
that time than to be free of the town that had held me in thrall,
where neighborhoods mapped class and race with a ruthless
precision neither acknowledged nor validated by my reading and
where the prospects for women at either my house or the
houses of my friends had begun to look equally uninviting.

At my house gender was defined in terms of money and
work. Among themselves women talked about neither the accu-
mulation of capital nor the consolidation of wealth and privilege
through marriage. Women like my mother saw their work as
steering adolescent girls through the present tense dangers of
dating and pregnancy, rather than the future tense possibilities
of marrying well. Marriage posed financial problems, and its
topics were employment, housing, the care and feeding of children, and in my case the loss of financial independence. These
working-class marriage-narratives did not hold the same promise of untroubled futures that the middle-class ones seemed to
hold for my girl friends. Bearing and raising children are not
nearly as attractive propositions for girls who watch and even
help their mothers do the work. Nor, for that matter, is keeping
house, if the old carpet is not a threadbare heirloom and the
provenance of the second-hand furniture unknown.

Since it was the body of neither a working-class mother nor
a middle-class wife but that of the female dancer that had attracted me from childhood through adolescence, I cannot but
wonder if on realizing that I would not be a dancer, I somehow
imagined that as a professor I could turn myself inside out like
a reversible garment and cloak my female body in what I believed (via courses and grades) to be my genderless and class-
less mind. While traces of this desire remain, it nonetheless
comes as something of a surprise to realize that I am never

more my mother's daughter than when I am writing the essays, papers, lectures, books that organize my academic life. I realize that I must have learned to write from watching my mother sew. What I saw, or now believe I must have seen, was a woman whose pleasure while sewing matched mine while playing. I suppose what I remember is seeing her thoroughly at ease, for the woman who sewed was entirely different from the one who cooked, cleaned, shopped, talked, and cared for her children. That woman was preoccupied, often weary and worried, and awkward in the presence of strangers. The woman who sewed was none of these. This woman would discuss ideas that animated her long before she ever spread out the newspapers she saved for her patterns, bought the fabric, laid out the pieces on the bias, cut the cloth, hand-basted and machine-stitched the darts and seams of a garment.

Sewing relieved the tyranny of money over my mother's life. She made all her children's clothes by copying ready-to-wear clothing, except her seams were more generous and her hems deeper, so they could be let out as we grew. My mother never though of herself as (or allowed anyone to call her) a seamstress. It may have been undue modesty on her part, or she may have preferred her high standing among local amateurs to joining the ranks of anonymous professionals. But I like to think it is because she knew seamstresses do not sew to please themselves. And my mother pleased herself when she sewed. I can remember no time during my childhood when my mother was *not* sewing: our clothes, our doll clothes, our costumes for Halloween and school plays and my dance recitals, not to mention first communion dresses, confirmation dresses, "outfits" for Easter and Christmas, party dresses, and formals. Dresses, skirts, blouses, and trousers hung perfectly, we were given to understand, only when she found and cut the cloth on the bias. The clothes, the doll clothes, and the costumes were all given equal attention, each made as if it were to last forever and to be viewed by an eye as appreciative of detail as my mother's. When I think about this esthetic as a tribute to her children's acuity, I regret even more the careless indifference each of us assumed during adolescence to these tokens of her esteem. She was literally outclassed by the inexpensive ready-to-wear clothing that devalued and finally supplanted "home-made" clothes, and simultaneously the one domestic practice at which my mother thrived.

In the mid-summer, my mother would take each of her girls on a day-long shopping trip that she always referred to as buying our back-to-school clothes. It must have been her little joke because she bought nothing at the department stores and children's shops whose stock inspired her copies. Instead, we were directed to try on the school clothes and party dresses we liked—for size. I never saw her make a sketch or take a note. Yet even now I can see my mother examining garments, turning them inside out to scrutinize the mysteries of design, before bustling off to buy fabric. She required us to look at and feel all fabrics she considered suitable and to compare endless combinations of and variations in texture, hue, and print. Selections of fabrics prefaced even more lengthy discussions of the relative merits of threads, buttons, belts, sashes, laces, piping, decals. These periodic conversations my mother held with each of her girls amidst bolts of cloth exuding the fumes of dye and sizing were supremely pedagogical, for she sought nothing less during these lessons than our full allegiance to the axiology that measures worth in finely wrought distinctions known only to those with intimate knowledge of production. The value of a garment is in its stitchery, which is not solely a measure of competence but also of practice. One slipped stitch spoiled a garment for my mother, and she wanted us to value such details of production. That esthetic was disappearing even as my mother was teaching it to her children, a fact brought home to her as each of us in turn succumbed to the esthetic of fashion on entering adolescence.

None of my mother's children would fully appreciate her esthetic again until we were adults, and my own appreciation has been tempered with varieties of remorse. I lack the skill, the capital, and even the patience to clothe myself with the rigorous attention to detail I learned from my mother. Yet I am never more confident than when I am wearing something I believe she would admire. It is less a particular style of clothing than the certitude that my mother could tell just from the hang of it that I had not forgotten how much depends on the bias. While few garments I own would please my mother, that my best essays are written on the bias would. Even more than what I finally produce, that I do not even attempt to write an essay until I have found a bias would please her, for my practice as a writer is as intricately tied to seeking and following oblique lines that cut across the grain as was my mother's.

A girl can, it seems, learn a great deal about work and its pleasures from watching her mother sew. While I never learned to sew, that I write as my mother sewed probably explains why I take a good deal more obvious pleasure in the intellectual work of being an academic than those of my peers who have difficulty believing writing to be real work. If I enjoy the labor of writing, that can at least in part be explained by my writing as my mother sewed. She made clothes. I make prose. There is a sense in which just as my mother was always sewing, I am always writing. I understood her to be sewing in even her most casual remarks. Once when my son was very young, he asked if we were just talking or if I was also writing. I could have asked my mother that question about her sewing when I was young, and I could now ask my son the same question he once asked me about his writing. A boy, it seems, can also learn something about these pleasures from watching his mother write. He learned to write from his mother, who learned from her mother, and none of us knows when we are talking if we are just talking—or writing—or sewing.

Writing begins for me with something once heard or seen or read that recurs in my mind's eye as a troubling image—myself as a little girl cautiously descending a staircase—which in turn prompts me to seek a narrative explanation for its persistence. My search for a narrative is guided by the bias of the image, in this essay by the inexplicable sorrow the child evoked in me. As I trace lines of inquiry that depend on the bias, I can see there are others besides mine, for there are at least as many biases woven into the fabric of a life as into poplins, wools, and satins. I can see differences in how from one bias I construe the cloakroom as an effort to eradicate traces of working-class sociality from a classroom, and from another I could justify the teacher who sent me there, for I am also a teacher. That I follow my bias does not mean that I cannot see others. It means instead that rather than extol the triumph of the child, I meet my sorrow by sorting the details of her longing to be middle class from those of her struggle against the indiscriminate eradication of the intellectuality of her family at school.

I wish everyone were taught to write on the bias, for finding and following a bias is as critical to writing as sewing. Yet if bias seems even more counterintuitive in writing than in sewing, that is because students are taught that third-person statements are unbiased (objective) and those in the first person are biased (subjective). Little wonder then that by the time they reach college, most students have concluded that to avoid bias they have only to recast their first person claims into the third person. Delete "I believe" from "racism is on the rise in this country" or "racism has virtually disappeared in this country," and the assertion assumes a reality independent of the writer, who is no longer the author but merely the messenger of news or fact. Students learn what they have been taught, and they have been taught that grammatical person governs the objectivity and subjectivity of actual persons. Step on a crack. Break your mother's back. Hop over it. Save her life.

Most students have learned rules that readers rather than writers believe govern prose. They have not been taught what every writer knows, that one writes on the bias or not at all. A bias may be provided by a theory or an experience or an image or an ideology. Without a bias, however, language is only words as cloth is only threads. To write is to find words that explain what can be seen from an angle of vision, the limitations of which determine a wide or narrow bias, but not the lack of one. Far from guaranteeing objectivity, third-person assertions too often record an unexamined routine in which the writers who follow a bias provided by, say, the "objectivity" of journalism or science confound that world view/theory/ideology with reality. The bias that we should rightly disparage is that which feigns objectivity by dressing up its reasons in seemingly unassailable logic and palming off its interest as disinterest—in order to silence arguments from other quarters.

Writing is about following a bias that cuts against the grain because, like sewing, writing recognizes the third dimension of seemingly two-dimensional material. My mother looked at fabric and imagined clothes she could make from it. I look at language and imagine essays I could write. Just as a piece of cloth can be fashioned into any number of garments, the essay I construct from language is not the only one I could have written. The pleasures in playing out possibilities are matched only by the labor taken to complete the one that eventually stands for them all. It seems to me that middle-class culture and schooling gratuitously and foolishly rob children of the pleasures of the physical and intellectual work of learning generally and writing in particular. Most successful students learn to disown their labor (to claim they have not read the assignment or studied for the test). They disdain their own scholastic achievement as luck or intelligence, and grudgingly accept in its stead tokens to be exchanged for symbolic opportunities. Take tests for grades, exchange the grades for credentials, use the credentials to launch a career, measure the career by the number of promotions and the size of the paychecks and the amount of stock. Writing is only incidental in this cycle. It is incidental because the cycle deflates the value of the intellectual work of practices like writing in order to artificially inflate the value of ritual performances (achievement tests, reading scores) that can be calculated and minted as cultural currency.

That the present is hostage to the future in any culture that devalues labor seems to me both obvious and tragic. That this country has historically substituted tokens of literacy for literacy practices and then cloaked its anti-intellectualism in alarming statistics about illiteracy and illiterates makes it all the more important that those of us who have learned to write teach ourselves to remember how and where that happened, what it was we learned, and especially how the lessons learned from an unofficial curriculum protected us from the proscriptions that have ruthlessly dominated the official curriculum from the outset. The problem is not that writing cannot be learned, for many have learned to write, but that writing cannot be taught as a set of rules or conventions that must be acquired prior to and separate from performance. Leaching all evidence of the labor that produces texts teaches students to see literacy as a spectacle. Writing is not a spectator sport. Learning *how to write* follows from *wanting to write*, for the path a child follows on taking a census seems to lead more directly to writing than the detour that sends children first to reading. Writing is seated in desires as complicated as those that give rise to dancing and sewing, where the rules of play are also subject to the contingencies of performance.

Chapter 7

And May He Be Bilingual:
Notes on Writing, Teaching, and Multiculturalism

Judith Ortiz Cofer

Latin women pray
In incense sweet churches
They pray in Spanish
To an Anglo God
With a Jewish heritage.
And this Great White Father
Imperturbable
In his marble pedestal
Looks down upon
His brown daughters
Votive candles shining like lust
In his all seeing eyes
Unmoved
By their persistent prayers.
Yet year after year
Before his image they kneel
Margarita Josefina Maria and Isabel
All fervently hoping
That if not omnipotent
At least He be bilingual.
                              —Judith Ortiz Cofer

In this early poem I express the sense of powerlessness I felt as a non-native speaker of English in the United States. Non-native. Non-participant in the mainstream culture. *Non*, as in no, not, nothing. This little poem is about the non-ness of the non-speakers of the ruling language making a pilgrimage to the only One who can help, hopeful in their faith that someone is listening, yet still suspicious that even He doesn't understand their language. I grew up in the tight little world of the Puerto Rican community in Paterson, New Jersey, and later moved to Augusta, Georgia, where my "native" universe shrunk even further to a tiny group of us who were brought to the Deep South through the military channels our fathers had chosen for our lives, out of economic necessity. I wrote this ironic poem years ago, out of a need to explore the loneliness, the almost hopelessness, I had felt and observed in the other non-native speakers, many my own relatives, who would never master the English language well enough to be able to connect with the native speakers in significant ways as I did.

Having come to age within the boundaries of language exiles, and making only brief forays out into the vast and often frightening landscape called *the mainstream*, it's easy for the newcomer to become ethnocentric. That's what a Little Italy/Korea/Havana, Chinatown, and barrio is, a center of ethnic concerns. After all, it's a natural human response to believe that there is safety only within the walls around the circle of others who look like us, speak like us, behave like us: it is the animal kingdom's basic rule of survival in their part of the jungle or forest—if whatever is coming towards you does not look like you or your kin—either fight or fly.

It is this primal fear of the unfamiliar that I have conquered through education, travel, and my art. I am an English teacher by profession and a writer by vocation. I have written several books of prose and poetry based mainly on my experiences in growing up Latina in the United States. Until a few years ago, when multiculturalism became part of the American political agenda, no one seemed to notice my work; suddenly I find myself a Puerto Rican/American (Latina)/Woman writer. Not only am I supposed to simply share my particular vision of American life, but I am also supposed to be a role model for a new generation of Latino students who expect me to teach them how to get a piece of the proverbial English language pie. I actually enjoy both of these public roles, in moderation. I love teaching literature. Not my own work, but the work of my literary ancestors in English and American literature—my field, that is, the main source of my models as a writer. I also like going into my classrooms at the University of Georgia where my English classes at this point are still mainly composed of white American students, with a sprinkling of African American and Asian, and only occasionally a Latino, and sharing my bicultural, bilingual views with them. It is a fresh audience. I am not always speaking to converts.

I teach American literature as an outsider in love with the Word—whatever language it is written in. They, at least some of them, come to understand that my main criterion when I teach is excellence and that I will talk to them about so-called minority writers whom I admire in the same terms as I will the old standards they know they are supposed to honor and study. I show them why they should admire them, not blindly, but with a critical eye. I speak English with my Spanish accent to these native speakers. I tell them about my passion for the genius of humankind, demonstrated through literature: the power of language to effect, to enrich, or to diminish and destroy lives; its potential to empower someone like me, someone like them. The fact that English is my second language does not seem to matter beyond the first few lectures, when the students sometimes look askance at one another, perhaps wondering whether they had walked into the wrong classroom and at any moment this obviously "Spanish" professor will ask them to start conjugating regular and irregular verbs. They can't possibly know this about me: in my classes, everyone is safe from Spanish grammar recitation; since almost all of my formal education is in English, I avoid all possible risk of falling into a discussion of the uses of the conditional or of the merits of the subjunctive tense in the Spanish language: Hey, I just *do* Spanish, I don't explain it.

Likewise, when I *do* use my Spanish and allude to my Puerto Rican heritage, it comes from deep inside me where my imagination and memory reside, and I do it through my writing. My poetry, my stories, and my essays concern themselves with the coalescing of languages and cultures into a vision that has meaning first of all for me; then, if I am served well by my craft and the transformation occurs, it will also have meaning for others as art.

My life as a child and teenager was one of constant dislocation. My father was in the U.S. Navy, and we moved back to Puerto Rico during his long tours of duty abroad. On the island, my brother and I attended a Catholic school run by American nuns. Then it was back to Paterson, New Jersey, to try to catch up, and sometimes we did, academically, but socially it was a different story altogether. We were the perennial new kids on the block. Yet when I write about these gypsy days, I construct a continuity that allows me to see my life as equal to any other, with its share of chaos, with its own system of order. This is what I have learned from writing as a minority person in America that I can teach my students: Literature is the human search for meaning. It is as simple and as profound as that. And we are all, if we are thinking people, involved in the process. It is both a privilege and a burden.

Although as a child I often felt resentful of my rootlessness, deprived of a stable home, lasting friendships, the security of one house, one country, I now realize that these same circumstances taught me some skills that I use today to adapt in a constantly changing world; a place where you can remain in one spot for years and still wake up every day to strangeness wrought by technology and politics. We can stand still and find ourselves in a different nation created overnight by decisions we did not participate in making. I submit that we are all becoming more like the immigrant and can learn from her experiences as a stranger in a strange land. I know I am a survivor in language. I learned early that possessing the secret of words was to be my passport into mainstream life. Notice I did not say "assimilation" into mainstream life. This is a word that has come to mean the acceptance of loss of native culture. Although I know for a fact that to survive everyone "assimilates" what they need out of many different cultures, especially in America, I prefer to use the term "adapt" instead. Just as I acquired the skills to adapt to American life, I have now come to terms with a high-tech world. It is not that different. I learned English to communicate, but now I know computer language. I have been greedy in my grasping and hoarding of words. I own enough stock in English to feel secure in almost any situation where my language skills have to serve me; and I have claimed my rich Puerto Rican culture to give scope and depth to my personal search for meaning.

As I travel around this country I am constantly surprised by the diversity of its peoples and cultures. It is like a huge, colorful puzzle. And the beauty is in its complexity. Yet there are some things that transcend the obvious differences: great literature, great ideas, and great idealists, for example. I find Don Quixote plays almost universal; after all, who among us does not have an Impossible Dream? Shakespeare's wisdom is planetary in its appeal; Gandhi's and King's message is basic to the survival of our civilization, and most people know it; and other voices that are like a human racial memory speak in a language that can almost always be translated into meaning.

And genius doesn't come in only one package: The Bard happened to be a white gentleman from England, but what about our timid Emily Dickinson? Would we call on her in our class, that mousy little girl in the back of the room squinting at the chalkboard and blushing at everything? We almost lost her art to neglect. Thank God poetry is stronger than time and prejudices.

This is where my idealism as a teacher kicks in: I ask myself, who is to say that at this very moment there isn't a Native American teenager gazing dreamily at the desert outside her window as she works on today's assignment: seeing the universe in a grain of sand? preparing herself to share her unique vision with the world. It may all depend on the next words she hears, which may come out of my mouth, or yours. And what about the African American boy in a rural high school in Georgia who showed me he could rhyme for as long as I let him talk. His teachers had not been able to get him to respond to literature. Now they listened in respectful silence while he composed an ode to his girl and his car extemporaneously, in a form so tight and so right (contagious too) that when we discuss the exalted Alexander Pope's oeuvre, we call it heroic couplets. But he was intimidated by the manner in which Mr. Pope and his worthy comrades in the canon had been presented to him and his classmates, as gods from Mt. Olympus, inimitable and incomprehensible to mere mortals like himself. He was in turn surprised to see, when it was finally brought to his attention, that Alexander Pope and he shared a good ear.

What I'm trying to say is that the phenomenon we call culture in a society is organic, not manufactured. It grows where we plant it. Culture is our garden, and we may neglect it, trample on it, or we may choose to cultivate it. In America we are dealing with varieties we have imported, grafted, cross-pollinated. I can only hope the experts who say that the land is replenished in this way are right. It is the ongoing American experiment, and it has to take root in the classroom first. If it doesn't succeed, then we will be back to praying and hoping that at least He be bilingual.

Works Cited

Cofer, Judith Ortiz. 1995. "Latin Women Pray." *Reaching for the Main-land and Selected New Poems.* Tempe, Arizona: Bilingual Press.

Chapter 8

The Point at Which Past
and Future Meet

Lynne Crockett

New Mexico 1956–1960

I was born in New Mexico, and I can still feel the heat of the sun on my back. I remember in our yard the ground was hard and cracked, forming squares, triangles, and other geometric forms, and I would spend my time patiently trying to lift one of these shapes from the earth, intact, so I could eat it. The cracks went deep into the dirt, and my little fingers couldn't fit down far enough to get a decent grip. The earth would crumble away at the edges so the sharpness of the form would deteriorate, and pieces would come up in piles of dry dust, not whole chunks. I never succeeded in pulling up a piece of earth.

Our backyard in Albuquerque was flat, then there was a wall, and then more flatness until the mountains loomed up many miles away. I always thought that the wall was out of place, separating flatness from more flatness. The land was a lot like the sky—large and open and never ending. One feels small in New Mexico, a feeling that is somehow calming. I could look up to the nighttime sky at the stars and the immensity and would want to cry, not from fear but longing or something else, a realization of so much more.

Between Santa Fe and Los Alamos where I was born is a rock formation shaped like a camel and named, appropriately, Camel Rock. Every time we drove by Camel Rock my mother would tell me to say hello to the camel. When we left New Mexico to come to

New York, Mum said: "Say good-bye to the camel. This is the last time you will see him!"

A few summers ago, more than thirty years later, we drove out west to New Mexico, and on the road from Santa Fe to Los Alamos I again greeted the camel. He is not deteriorated, nor is he desecrated by graffiti. In fact, he looks exactly the way I remember him. As we came upon him, I shouted: "Look, look, the camel, the camel!" And then I cried. I cried for the old camel and for my parents, young and hopeful and in love. I cried for myself, beautiful and unscarred with love and hope supporting me. I cried for all we had hoped for and all we had lost. And I cried for all that is and all that I know and feel that fills me with daily longing.

* * *

New York State 1960–

Both of my parents read every night. I am excluded because I cannot read. I sit behind the blue chair by the bookcase and take out the biggest book I can find. I can read. I can read. Years later we laugh to find that *The Rise and Fall of the Third Reich* has crayon marks all over the opening pages.

When I start kindergarten I am plummeted into a social hierarchy of boys and girls that I never knew existed. It is expected that each girl will be paired off with a boy to whom she will be loyal: we playact. My boyfriend kisses me in the coat room. It seems very strange to me; I don't know that I like him or want to kiss him. I don't want to say no because I am not sure of what the social effect will be; I do not know the rules. Every day my kindergarten teacher plays World War II songs on the piano and teaches us the words. All of the boys want to fight and go to war. All of the girls . . . I don't know what we want.

John Glenn orbits the earth. We spend days hanging solar systems in front of the class and identifying the planets. The thought of the unknown expanses in outer space intrigues me; I want to see these different planets, and I imagine the nothingness of space. How can there be nothing? No oxygen, no molecules—nothing. "Nothing" is so abstract that I love it; I am hooked. I am the smartest kid in the class and the fastest runner. I want to be an astronaut when I grow up. Ha Ha Ha Ha. You can't be an astronaut: You're a GIRL.

Class is interrupted because the President has been shot. We are lined up into the buses and sent home. There are no joyful cries due to our newly released status: there is no solidity in life: we are floating without gravity. I walk into the house and Mum asks why I am home. I tell her the President has been shot. She says, he has? I hope that if she doesn't know it isn't true. She turns on the TV, and the President dies.

I am always afraid. I have horrible nightmares in which the planet is ending in a fiery war. I have nightmares in which I am alone in an echoing chamber. I have nightmares in which my mother is coming to kill me. I cannot be alone because I am filled with horror. I dress with my parents in the living room. I take my brother downstairs with me, to the bedroom with me, to the kitchen with me. I come to sleep in my parents' bed at night. No one has patience with me and I am afraid.

When school starts in the fall, I bring my reading book home and read it all the way through. I feel like a starving person seated before a chocolate cake; it is the best possible treat to have a book with different lives and textures and worlds before me. I am the best reader in the class and am always chosen to read out loud and act in the holiday plays. Dean is a boy in my class. When we read stories in class, Dean has a hard time forming the words. I feel sorry for him but admire his lack of embarrassment. My best friend is Carol: I love her. Carol and I visit each other on weekends and know each other's families and pets. One day as we line up to go to lunch, I grab Carol and kiss her. The kids make faces and squirm because I am a lesbian (whatever that is). Dean pushes me on the floor and spits on me. I am bewildered. Carol never speaks to me again.

The most exciting time in school is when we can order books. I get the list of possibilities and try to decide which one I want the most. All of them. I read all of the time. My mother complains because I read at the dinner table. I really don't care whether I eat or not. Reality exists between the covers of the book; it certainly isn't to be found in school. I decide at eleven that I will be a writer when I grow up.

* * *

September 1995

I am in my family's vacation home in the Adirondacks, looking out of the window at the lake. It is late afternoon, and the light is changing, with darkness shading the lower part of my view and a strange, opaque brightness lighting the upper, skyward part. The mountain across the lake is illuminated in color, with its bright leaves contrasted against the dark hemlocks and pines, and the lake beneath the mountain is a shimmery black strip, calm like glass. I too feel calm, as though I do not matter, as though I am just an observer of lake and life: I am the point at which past and future meet.

I remember when we first came to our land in the Adirondacks in the early 1960s. We travelled across the lake in a large, mahogany Chris Craft, which shot through the water at a high speed. I sat in the stern of the boat, the swift wind numbing my face, my dragging hand bouncing off of the cold, clear, glasslike wave that rose by its side. I became a part of the lake and the mountains; nothing mattered but the physical sensation of sun and wind and water. The boat slowed, and glided into a cove of tangled, overgrown trees and rocks and logs, and we scrambled onto the shore through the underbrush. While the grownups talked, Tom and I played, splashed in the water, and caught tiny brown toads that I collected in a cellophane cigarette wrapper given to me by my mother. The earth was black and alive and spongy, thick with undergrowth; the air smelled clean and fertile, a combination of new growth and rotten wood. Before we left, my mother made sure that I released the toads.

* * *

The sun is down a little more, and the lake now appears to be in stripes of contrast, blue darkness and purpley-pink lightness. The lake has its own colors, moods, and changing tempers; I could watch it constantly. I feel very emotionally in tune with everything right now; I can even think of the past without flinching.

When I was twelve years old and going into the seventh grade we moved to a nearby town, one that was small, old, and pretty, into an old house right in the village.

My bedroom is very big and there is a bathroom right next to it. When I look out of my bedroom window at night, the street looks like a well-lighted stage with the overhanging trees forming an archlike ceiling. I watch the cars drive past and imagine that when the house was new someone in my room looked out upon the horses and buggies. I wish we lived in the time of horses and buggies. I wonder if anyone has ever died in my bedroom. I imagine there are spirits of the past occupants co-existing with me; I try to feel their thoughts. I wonder if they will influence me while I live here, if they will form me differently than I would have been formed had we stayed in the relatively new house that we just left.

School starts and I am excited. In our old town, new students were eagerly questioned and befriended when they came to school. Here, no one talks to me. One boy makes fun of something I say. In math class I get a zero because we were in the Adirondacks when the teacher gave a test. I cry; I have never gotten a zero before. The teacher sneers. A student laughs at me for crying. In music class no one sings. I befriend two girls who are also new to the school.

As time passes, I try to be different than I am, less booklike, in order to be less lonely: I act the role of a teenaged girl. I have a boyfriend who drives me to school every day in his rusty old car. On the way, we smoke pot. He swerves all over the road and laughs; I am a little worried but not too much. When we get to school, I want my friends to know I am high. My classes don't matter that much to me, except English class because I like English. I don't think much about there being a future, and I forget the past as well; the immediate present is all that concerns me. At lunch time we go into the woods behind the school, and sometimes we smoke more pot or cigarettes. It seems like fun, but I am aware of a void within me that isn't filled by the socialization of high school; in fact, I feel emptier and in need of more and more stimulation. I hate myself most of the time: I am anxious and know I am ugly and too serious. I hate being serious and try to talk less like a book; I try to be more like other people, normal people. I hate being so weird.

I have dreams in which I am filled with worms writhing inside me and eating me. I am afraid that people will discover that inside I am wormy. The worms come out of my belly; I am exposed. I wake up feeling more anxious than ever. The Vietnam War is at its peak, and I have continuations of my end-of-the-world dreams. I am upset that the Vietnamese people are being killed and their country destroyed while the news seems only interested in how Americans are being affected. I am upset that I think at all; why can't I be a bubbly cheerleader? Why can't I be fun?

I argue with my friends about everything. They are very narrow-minded and it infuriates me. One day I am talking about politics with some of my male classmates while their girlfriends are talking about someone's wedding. One of the men tells me to shut up and go talk with the "girls"; I am furious because he is less intelligent than I am but he is born a man and is thus privileged; he doesn't have to listen to me because I am a woman, and his rejection of my opinion is perfectly acceptable to everyone there. I am powerless. Though I know my peers are wrong, I feel odd and rejected. My self-disgust spills over into my family—I am irritable and deeply unhappy—and their patience is wearing thin. My parents no longer seem to like me, and my brother and I have less and less in common. I really wish I would die.

I have dreams in which I walk down a street of old houses and enter different ones; each house has a personality of its own. The street upon which I search is much like the street upon which I live, and the houses are all old and similar in structure to each other and to my real house. I enter a two-story white colonial with old, green shutters; it is tall and uptight-looking. It emanates hostility: I feel exposed as I walk around the rooms. Inside it is dark and cramped, and I am not allowed access into its small, musty recesses. I leave and enter a house further down the block, much like the one I just left. This one isn't dangerous or welcoming; it is just a building. Continuing down the street, I come to another house chosen at random, also a two-story colonial. This one, however, is warm and loving and accepting. As I walk through the rooms, I feel that they are embracing me, sheltering me. I awake from the dream relaxed, without my normal anxiety.

I like to sleep and read better than almost anything else. I read in bed, and my dreams are more vividly real and interesting than my waking life. I start to keep a journal, though I do not think of it as such. I want to remember all of my dreams; I feel that knowing them will help me, somehow, to know myself. The notebook is right next to my bed, and I write the dreams down as soon as I awaken. Soon I carry the notebook with me wherever I go, and I jot down other impressions and thoughts that occur to me. I worry when I cannot find it, and I am comforted as soon as the pen begins moving across the page.

* * *

Why is it so painful to think of the past? The sun is much lower now, and I look at the deck, which is in my immediate line of vision. It is cracked and splitting with age; I remember when we built it in 1975; I was nineteen years old. Am I aged like the deck? I imagine my insides cracked and splitting like the cedar planks, with rotten places and holes. Will I wake up tomorrow with my face seamed and wrinkled, aged by the sun and the wind? I feel younger now than I did at nineteen; how could I possibly be this old?

I read Doris Lessing's *Children of Violence* series when I was nineteen or twenty. I identified with Martha Quest, and when reading about her, I felt less alone.

Martha hangs out with stupid people and drinks too much, then marries an uninteresting man and has a child with him. During this phase she seems to have lost her self; she is fat and shapeless and life is lived in a daze, as though from a distance. After her divorce, she becomes a communist and works with intellectuals who argue constantly about socialism and the problems facing Africa. Their discussions and actions seem important, but contain more self-importance than social value. She finally leaves Africa, and her child, and goes to England to begin a new life by herself. Martha seems like someone I could be. I had thought that women got married and had babies and just existed; I had no clear idea of what they did or of what my role would be. It was very vague to me as was everything in the future.

After high school my father suggested that I go to a community college; I had no job and no plans, so I went. Amazingly, I discovered that I actually liked school. In college I was treated like an adult; the teachers expected that I would do the work, and none of them sneered at me or belittled me if I didn't.

My political science professor has lunch with me, and we discuss my interests and my future. She is disappointed to discover that I am majoring in secretarial studies; she expects more from me. This is my major because I have no goals in life and must earn a living somehow. But I love English, so I change my major to literature. From barely passing high school, I am on the Dean's list during my first semester at college, and I am meeting people who have visions of the future that I can live with.

* * *

The lake is pink now as the sun goes down. I am coming out of the trance and wonder how I ever got to where I am now. I think that without having my home in the Adirondacks it would be more difficult to recall the past; this place has my blood in it. How do people like my parents move forward all of the time without having a place to which they can return? Maybe I am more primitive than most modern, mobile people; I want a life and a career that reflect my values, and I want a place that knows me and that allows me to visit with my past and to imagine my future.

I went to several colleges, changing majors from English to more practical subjects, trying to find a balance between my love of literature and writing and the world of money and "real" jobs. My brother graduated from college with a degree in Engineering and got a job. I worked as a secretary on a college campus and took literature classes for pleasure and for sanity. After finally receiving my degree in English, I was hired as an administrator in the Telecommunications department on campus; again, a swing away from my passion, language, toward the more technical and practical world with which I was so familiar, one that I thought would be more acceptable.

The first vacation I had after getting my job in Telecommunications was in the Adirondacks. My boss gave me the fax machine to bring on vacation, and I was supposed to work on something—I can't remember what—and fax the copies to him. I was seething inside; how could I relax? Trying to feel self-important, I told people that I had to work, but I felt sick. My boss called me two days before my vacation was over, and for the time remaining I was rigid in my chair, drinking too much wine and dreading my return to work.

* * *

The sun is now down, and I need to feed the dog and myself. I open the door, look into the night, and take a deep breath of air. I have always been sensitive to my surroundings and can be made happy or uncomfortable simply because of where I am. I remember one afternoon when my ex-boss and I were walking around campus looking at manholes for running fiber optic cable. He was talking about all sorts of technical things, and I was dreamy, feeling the warm sun on my back and smelling the grass and wondering whether the partially obscured bird in the tree was a nuthatch or a chickadee. My inability to focus on technical issues and to take my job as seriously as I took my classes finally forced me to leave Telecommunications and to pursue my passions: literature and writing.

When teaching writing, I use with my students the same techniques that worked for me as an adolescent: a great deal of personal writing and exploration. Many people still think of the personal as not being appropriate in the classroom. Yet a crucial part of young adulthood is the process of learning about oneself, and learning about oneself is an important element in learning how to think critically. How can one learn to think for oneself if one does not know oneself?

In a writing class, the students' personal interests can be brought into the class by discussing—and writing about—experiences from their own lives that may then be related to external issues such as reading assignments or current events. In one of my classes, the students began with a freewrite and discussion about a specific decision they each had to make, explaining what factors in their lives influenced their particular decisions. This led into a class discussion about Sarah Orne Jewett's short story, "A White Heron." The students discussed Sylvia's decision to allow the bird to remain free, thus forfeiting the money offered by the young man, and explained why, given Sylvia's circumstances, they agreed or disagreed with her choice. Since the majority of my students were from the New York City area, they found it very difficult to understand, or to even care about, a nineteenth-century girl living in rural Maine; most of them thought she was stupid to give up the money for a bird. After having approached the story from a personal angle, they were better able to understand Sylvia's decision; and although they didn't necessarily agree with her, they could understand why she chose to keep the location of the bird's nest a secret. We ended the discussion by talking about the ways in which our individual actions and choices affect others, circling back to the personal issues that interested the students while showing them that, like Sylvia, they were responsible for more than their own interests.

The small, personal assignment can expand outward, encompassing many related—and often unforeseen—issues, leading the students and the teacher to learn more about themselves, each other, and their world. Deena Metzger writes of the world within us as being

> . . . vast, endless, and complex. It is the world of worlds. It is infinite. To enter it is to come to know something of it and to learn of the boundlessness of the self. To go within, therefore, is never a diminishment. To stay adamantly without is always a limitation,

for the self, the inner world, the imagination, all open out into everything that has ever existed or can ever or may ever exist. (Metzger 1992, 228)

By excluding the students' inner worlds from the classroom, we are excluding the boundlessness of learning; we are limiting ourselves to a world without depth or discovery.

Teaching allows me to forget that I am a body weighted down by cares and earthly concerns; class passes by so quickly that I forget all sense of "real" time. Writing, in this sense, is very much like teaching: in both we lose time and the self. Though it seems paradoxical, by gaining an understanding of one's self, one is then free to move away from it, to become free of the burden of self-consciousness. The self is necessary to elude at times. It becomes big and fat and important when given center stage for too long and needs to be subdued in order to understand its true place in history and in life—outside of time and space, a particle in the crowd, unimportant in itself yet important as it fits into and influences the whole.

I had a dream before the semester began that it was the beginning of school, and I was teaching. It was my first class, and I was nervous. Then the class started, everyone got involved in a discussion, and we moved forward as a group, our individual thoughts growing as others fed into them. I felt light in my dream: I was free of the old burdens that had once made me writhe with anxiety: I was laughing and animated and totally at ease.

* * *

The dog eats and I stare out into the blackness of night. The lake and mountains are invisible to me, but I know they are there and have been there and will be there. The night is clear and cold: the stars are sharp in the dark sky, like points of ice. I am where I want to be, the point at which past and future meet.

Works Cited

Metzger, Deena. 1992. "Writing for Your Life." In *Landmark Essays on Writing Process* 1994. Edited by Sondra Perl. Davis, Ca: Hermagoras Press, 227–229.

Chapter 9

Teaching and Writing "As If [My] Life Depended On It"

Ann Victoria Dean

Writing is as necessary to me as breathing. I believe something written for the first time has a freshness which is inimitable, of value to the writer and the reader, resembling life itself; it cannot be recaptured, yet it can be captured. I write "as if [my] life depended on it: to write across the chalkboard, putting up there in public words [I] have dredged, sieved up from dreams, from behind screen memories, out of silence—words [I] have dreaded and needed in order to know [I] exist" (Rich 1993, 33). I have learned that I *must* write to know myself and to know myself is to claim self/authority/authorization, which is the wellspring of my teaching.

All writing is autobiographical, reflecting self-interest, interpretation, and narrative—narrative defined as "a primary act of the mind" (Hardy 1987, 1), the "principle by which people organize their experience in, knowledge about, and transactions with the social world" (Bruner 1990, 35). Narrative is at the heart of all of my writing, including the writing I do in the academic field of education. Writing, infused with narrative understanding, fends off proliferous cant that belies fresh, original thinking, and erases ambiguity and the possibility of insight. I believe we need to return educational practice to the world and to do this it is crucial that we encourage "women to [offer] their own experience as wisdom, [recognize] how each individual perception is vital [and validate] the importance of telling the truth, each of us writing out of the unique vision our lives have given us" (Allison 1994, 75).

There is a vital connection between writing, thinking, and teaching. Meigs (1991) argues that when we write clearly we clarify our thinking, for writing even one sentence forces you to think, and in the strangest way, enables you to know *what* you think. This leads to a deeper awareness of the self. What, if anything, can I learn about my teaching self as autobiographee? Will I become a better teacher? A better person? Or are these categories inseparable, as Sylvia Ashton-Warner (1967) suggests. The stories I choose to tell support the inner structure of my identity and color my evolving view of the world; and it is through examining their themes and patterns that I can discover new truths about myself and my place in the culture in which I live. Performing the "autobiographical act," as Bruss (1976) calls it, allows me to engage in an interpretation of life that invests the past and the "self" with coherence and meaning that may not have been evident before the act of writing itself.

Fabricating a Woman's Life

As a woman, each time I sit down to write I must struggle to find my autobiographical voice. That I know I am going to be read as a woman affects what I write, as Miller (1986) points out. The self-representational possibilities of autobiography differ widely for men and for women because the ideology of gender drives the way people read and interpret writing. This means that when I attempt to write freely from my own perspective—of my personal experiences, of my thoughts and questions—the specter of my reader always looms on the horizon of my mind.

Most men who write autobiography write their life histories chronologically; the reader follows the development of his thinking, the unfolding "epic" events of his public life, and the important contributions he has made to culture.

Writing autobiography is quite different for women, who are perceived differently and positioned differently in the dominant culture. Sidonie Smith (1987) identifies the problematic relationship women have with writing autobiography. Because a woman has no *autobiographical self* in the same sense a man does, no "public story" to tell, she "looks from within and without through another pair of eyes, if often dimmed by the dark glasses of language's convention and in her creative gesture, a woman speaks to her culture from the margins. . ." (Smith, 1987, 176).

Smith defines the conflict experienced by women, who in writing autobiography must come face-to-face with the problematic figure of *male selfhood*:

> Acutely sensitive to her reader's expectations and to her own often conflicting desires, she negotiates a sometimes elegant, cramped balance of anticipated reader expectations and responsive authorial maneuvers. Particularly in the dramatic passages of her text, where she speaks directly to her reader about the process of constructing her life story, she reveals the degree of her self-consciousness about herself writing in an androcentric genre. Always, then, she is absorbed in a dialogue with her reader, and to justify her decision to write about herself in a genre that is man's. (Smith 1987, 50)

I experienced this conflict of marginality head on, when I began to write the central chapter of my doctoral thesis, "Teachers Writing about Themselves." My advisor, chuckling as he read the first draft, told me he thought my life text had assumed "epic proportions without epic events." Unabashedly, he suggested that I include further details about "the men in my life," especially the young Black priest I had met while teaching in the West Indies and later married. Thus, I set out to depict how my "female story" had become deeply entwined with the "male story" of this popular island figure, Fr. Bonaventure. I told the story from the perspective of a young woman who had fallen in love with a very powerful man in a time when there was no real public life available to women like me.

I described how I began to live through the priest's seductive, male narrative—to participate vicariously in his public career by supporting him intellectually and to participate in his private life by making love with him. But my attempt to represent our relationship from a female perspective, from *my* perspective, was thwarted by my editor-advisor, who engaged me in a power struggle over who would control the telling of my story. Comments such as "omit all pages clipped here" appeared, as he censored text that revealed my desire to represent myself as playing a part in the priest's public life. The following "clipped" passage is an example:

> Seduced by the delights of the male voice and the male narrative, I found his [the priest's] stories of the search for truth and

justice and the need for revolution irresistible. There were no
women's stories that could compete with this exciting male
world where possibilities for developing intellect, exercising
power and actively participating in social change existed. As a
woman I was excluded from this world and left to imagine myself
as having human agency in the public sphere. I listened with
longing to the persuasive, prophetic rhetoric of his speeches:
"There is *a need* to curb corruption; there is *a need* to eliminate
injustice, oppression and racism; there is *a need* to extend the
'square deal' to all true nationals through all the islands . . ."

I was, however, encouraged by my advisor to describe the
supportive, "behind-the-scenes" part I played in the priest's life,
and, thus, I was positioned in the culturally acceptable, caring-
for-the-other, status-quo female role. As it was really Fr. Bonaventure's "story" that interested my advisor-reader, I could insert
myself into the text only with craft and cunning: For example:

> I had been reading books by major contributors to the formula-
> tion of the American Black ideology of the nineteen sixties—
> Fanon, Cleaver, Malcolm X, Baldwin and Wright—to name a few,
> when Fr. Bonaventure asked *me* to help him write an important
> speech on "Black Power/Black Consciousness." I did this will-
> ingly because I perceived helping him in this way a 'natural' ex-
> tension of our relationship.
>
> The speech, delivered in the heat of political upheaval, well
> before Bahamian independence, was one of the first public cri-
> tiques of the hegemony of British cultural values and practices
> in the colony. In it *we* raised questions such as how long would
> there be blind allegiance to a white governor from Britain? And
> more importantly, how long would an education system that
> served the needs of the white elite be seen as the only way to ed-
> ucate a Bahamian?
>
> I enjoyed working behind the scenes in this way; I felt a fusion
> of our minds. I loved listening to him speak in public. He was a
> born speaker . . . He was a born leader. . . And he was born
> *male*.

Because I wanted to speak from a *female* self, to present a
woman's body, bravely and fully, I tried to "write my body" as
Cixous (1991) advises, but my editor-advisor continued to chop
and rearrange. I became less and less visible in my text. My love
life, as I describe it below, captures that painful disembodiment.

Bonaventure and I first became lovers in a furnished flat in a small, colonial-style building named "Snug Haven." I had sublet the seedy-looking apartment from a "Brit," a female journalist who wrote for *The Tribune*, Nassau's daily newspaper. After a tragic love affair, she went back to London.

An important part of recollection for me is "setting the scene" properly. I have to get the colours right—the deep, Prussian blue of a particular bowl, the exact tone of faded chintz slipcovers . . . The living room of Snug Haven starts to appear—it amuses me now that my most vivid memory of the momentous occasion of my first lovemaking is of the place and not the act.

Self-representation was further complicated by my elevated social position as a "white" woman in a relationship with a "black" man, but race went unexamined in my autobiography. My advisor thought to talk of race divisive.

When I revisit my autobiography, I am not surprised to find a fabric woven of self-denial and cultural powerlessness. I write from a place so marginal that I become an "invisible woman" in my own life story. Is my trivialized self-representation merely a ruse or an inescapable result of being a female autobiographee writing under the piercing reader's gaze of the all-male doctoral committee? Was it the icy atmosphere of surveillance that caused me to doubt myself and to hide behind masks that covered my authentic *self*?

Surviving the intense self-doubt the culture promotes in women often requires women to hide behind such "cover stories." An example taken from literature is found in Michael Cunningham's novel, *A Home at the End of the World*. Clare is a character who insulates herself from truths she cannot acknowledge: truths about herself as a woman, about her relationships with the people in her life, and about her subjective position in the culture in which she lives. Her behavior is interpreted by Clare's male friend Jonathan, who observes:

> [Clare] could exaggerate so artfully she herself sometimes lost track of the line between hyperbole and the undramatic truth. She was not self-serving. If anything, she chose to portray herself in an unflattering light, usually figuring in her own stories as a guileless, slightly ridiculous character, doomed to comeuppance like Lucy Ricardo . . . She would always sacrifice veracity for color—her lies were lies of proportion, not content. She reported

on her life in a clownish, surreal world that was convincing to her
and yet existed at a deep remove from her inner realm . . . . (Cunningham 1991, 178)

I portrayed myself through a similar split consciousness/
bifocality; for as I wrote I simultaneously viewed my text through
my own eyes and the eyes of an imagined reader, in this case a
misogynist academic who was not concerned with female "inner
realms."

There is an oft-quoted passage found in Virginia Woolf's *A
Room of One's Own* in which she describes "The Angel of the
House," a female phantom who resides in Woolf's consciousness
and behaves as a censor to guide her pen and especially to
check her anger. The angel tells Virginia she must never deal
freely and openly with the truth about her passions, nor tell the
truth about her experiences; instead, she must "charm," "con-
ciliate," and "to put it bluntly, tell lies" (Woolf 1929, 286). Woolf,
in self-defense, kills the angel; had she not, the angel would
have killed her by "plucking the heart out" of her writing. In
order not to offend my reader, I had to keep my *self* in check
while writing about my life, and in the process I strangled my
own self/representation.

Here is another sample from my autobiography, *Teacher
Under My Skin*, in which I laboriously chronicle my school years
in the traditional style of the male model of autobiography. The
linear text is also meant to hint at the mind-dulling effect of
year after year of mass education.

In grade five, Miss Huber, our teacher, gave me the class mural
to take home; it was a room-length scene of our village—vivid
pastels on brown paper. It hung in our basement until I went
away to college. I was ten years old when she told me I'd be a famous artist or writer when I grew up.

In grade six, my class moved into the newly constructed Village Green School. Three weeks after the school opened, Miss
Lily, our sixty-year-old veteran teacher, kicked lazy Larry in the
backside and he fell on the floor. Some people said he deserved
it but I never believed that. Miss Lily reminded me of a scrawny,
old barnyard hen. Patches of leathery, hen-leg-skin hung from
her elbows, a Plymouth Rock. She retired at the end of the year.

After school each day, my best friend Gail and I walked home
together. We'd cut across the expanse of green in front of the

school, jump the brook, and make our way down Sabbath Day Path, passing the "Colored" Baptist Church to stop at the wall in front of the small, local hospital. When we heard the high-pitched whine of a siren, we'd scramble up the steep drive in chase of the flashing tail lights of an ambulance on its way to the Emergency door. Fascinated, we'd speculate on a bleeding body inside.

One of the kids in grade six died two days before Christmas. Marshall Stigletts rode his bicycle down West Hill Street without holding on to the handle bars and ended his life under a sand truck. I was mad at Marshall because he had let me down badly the week before. The kids had drawn names to decide who would receive presents and Marshall had drawn my name. I was terrified he'd forget to buy a present and force me to face the class, empty-handed. Marshall's gift, a huge bundle of torn, dirty comics rolled in a piece of red paper was *worse* than no gift at all. I was more curious than shocked at his death—young Stigletts, whose bony knees had gripped the center bar of his bicycle, whose bare hands had taunted the traffic—what time of day did it happen? what was he thinking about as he plunged down that icy, unsanded, hill? what was I doing at that exact moment? I felt a vague sense of guilt as I threw away his tattered gift.

I experienced the female writer's particular kind of gendered torment as I tried to write; when I found myself thinking of a "woman" reading my autobiography, I began to construct my story as a woman's story, revealing little bits of plot here and there, introducing people haphazardly and turning back occasionally to retrieve others or to embellish an event, capturing memory, as memories came to me, in no particular order. But when I thought of a "man" reading my text, I constructed a man's story; suddenly stepping briskly on a straight path, forward march, as above. It made me furious to have to worry about the way I represented myself. I felt caught in a trap. I could please no one, least of all myself.

Can a woman ever be taken seriously by readers in a culture that promotes women's repression and self-censorship, two "forces that bury the real subjects in women's writing and complicate the task of truth-telling" (Braham 1995, 55)? I continue to search for ways to trust the validity of my own experience through writing, writing that has been so important to me since childhood, writing that has the potential to deliver me to my *self*.

Eakin (1985) argues that knowledge of the self is inseparable from the practice of language; I believe women must be allowed to write uncensored if they are to know themselves and to
create worlds in which they can live. Anais Nin (1985) describes
a woman's need to write in this way: "I could not live in any of
the worlds offered to me—the world of my parents, the world of
war, the world of politics. I had to create a world of my own, like
a climate, a country, an atmosphere in which I could breathe,
reign, and recreate myself when destroyed by living" (Nin 1985,
24). This process requires that we "travel back," to revisit old
sites/sights so that we will be free to ask the questions we have
been forced to repress, questions that may point us toward new
truths. Poet Dionne Brand (1994) captures the process, "we
were born thinking of traveling back. It is our singular occupa-
tion, we think of nothing else . . . We are continually uncomfortable where we are. We do not sleep easily, not without dreaming
of traveling back. This must be the code written on the lining of
[the] brain, go back, go back, like a fever" (Brand 1994, 58–59).
I feel the pull to travel back, to revisit old scenes and settings, to
recreate myself and the world through living memories.

Living Memories

Memories come unbidden, in sudden autobiographical flash-
backs. At once, it is 1952 and I am a young schoolgirl. It is winter, half-past-four, the cold light fading outside the Cape Cod-style
house. I step into the warm kitchen and catch the smell of lamb
stew, predictable and familiar. My mother and I sit at the kitchen
table, and I ask her to tell a story. I want to feel close to my
mother, and she wants to share memories of her childhood in
Britain, which are integral to her sense of self, an immigrant in a
new country. Her stories become my stories.

At school I am learning to write. I write my first *real* story. It
is my mother's biography.

The Donkey and My Mother

When my mother was about six she went to the beach. At the
beach they had donkey rides. My mother went on one. As they
were going along the donkey stopped. He saw a banana peel. He
stretched his long neck down to get it. Then all of a sudden my
mother slipped down his neck. Now she won't go on a horse or a
donkey. (Ann, Grade 5, Miss Huber's Class)

My mother changes the tone and the small details of her story to suit her purpose; sometimes she injects joy into the tale, and it becomes a typically English "going-to-the-seaside-tale." At other tellings, her story ends in fear and self-deprecation: "Father was very put-out with me for falling off the animal. Jack [her brother] and Josephine [her sister] could ride well. I didn't get back on the donkey. I was so frightened . . . such a stupid girl!" I catch my breath when my mother's quivering voice reveals her sense of failure brought about by her father's impatience with her. I am young, and I love her; how can I not absorb her limited sense of self deeply within myself?

After reading my story, "The Donkey and My Mother," my mother tells stories about other writers in the family. "Remember, you are a descendent of the poet William Cowper. You have writing in your blood," she says with pride. Then she tells a story about another writer, her sister Jo, the educated one. In the telling, I sense ambivalence about her female sibling, for although there is status in having a sister who is formally educated, my mother depicts Josephine as the "bad girl"—the girl who leaves home, does what she wants, and lives the life of an artist until she dies, a pauper. My mother depicts herself as the "good girl"—the girl who is loyal to her father until his death; it is her sister who shames him with her unconventionality. Never stated, but acted out through our complex mother/daughter relationship is the question, which will you be, the bad girl or the good girl?

My mother saves my donkey story and all of my "art work" in a large cardboard box, which I find after she dies. I glance quickly at the huge, round, penciled child-script of the story, and I am plunged again into "living memory." Such autobiographical experience of personal remembrance enables me to bridge the gap between the past and the present so that they become dialectically intertwined; a way is provided for me to trace my lifelong interest in writing and teaching (and in pursuing a life of the mind). By examining the personal cultural artifacts of my youth, journals, letters, photographs, and observations jotted down on slips of paper, I begin to make connections that help me make sense of my life. I remember my young writing self as I read through the stories I submitted for publication to magazines such as *American Girl* and *Seventeen*. The handwritten glosses that cover each poorly typed text— "Sent Out to Seventeen, 1959—Good Luck!"—position me as my own empathic reader.

Retrieving Fragments of Self from the Past

In undergraduate school I wrote many letters and kept journals. Here are two samples:

1963 Letter

Dear Professor:
The past two years have been completely sterile. I want to write. I believe in writing for itself. I read Camus' *Notebooks* last week and I felt lost and heavy and drained. I stayed in bed for two days, staring at nothing or sleeping. I feel painfully close to Emily Dickinson. Will I become a recluse? I am pulled apart by existence.

My moods change rapidly; I am aware of my heartbeat, my blood pumping, my skin; I feel overwhelmed (Whitman-like; the oversoul idea?). I also feel bitter and critical of the other students in your seminar. Tom's pompous attitude. David's arrogance. You asked us to define the true artist. Howard comes close to my idea of an artist because he searches for truth in his writing. I feel disgusted with the others (the artists as neurotics). Your class is a *crushing* experience.

When I am with you—riding on the subway, walking in the yellow woods—I slip into frozen helplessness; so self-conscious I hear only my own voice—little grunts between ragged breaths—my feelings dart back and forth inside me like fireflies.

Ann

1964 Journal

Falling in love is an explosion, life's start-up; something you can live on.

A.

Writing such letters and private jottings helped me negotiate the inhospitable world of undergraduate school. By creating a personal world constructed around meaningful relationships with other students and faculty members, I escaped the betrayal of an academic environment that claims objectivity as the highest human endeavor. Certainly the "student-teacher relationship" I had with my professor was not objective, nor free from desire. I knew I could never really learn anything from someone I did not love, nor benefit from a "body" of knowledge that did not stir my emotions as well as my rationality. It has always been that way for me.

I was in love with my professor; and, in retrospect, I believe that I also was in love with his wife, a concert soprano and voice instructor. At least I was in love with their lives as artists. Memories of their apartment on the Upper West Side return: I see a grand piano jammed into the room at the front overlooking the street; a galley kitchen leads to two tiny, back rooms; he writes in one and she gives private lessons in the other. I see the narrow, New York-apartment-style-bathroom with the cat's litter box under the sink and a wooden drying frame extending from the wall, listing badly under the weight of nylons and underwear; folded cloth diapers are piled on the back of the toilet. Things *happened* in that apartment; the minute I stepped through the door I felt myself come alive.

I hear his wife giving a voice lesson at the baby grand, her vibrant voice and the tinkle of keys as her student tries to imitate her "Ba, Ba, Ba," and "Da, Da, Da, Da," as they work their way up the scales. Her nine-year-old daughter plays with the baby on the floor in the living room, and spaghetti sauce simmers in an aluminum pot on the stove in the kitchen. My professor greets me and then dashes to the corner store for a loaf of Italian bread, while I sit on the couch taking it all in.

What did I seek from the relationship with my professor and his wife? I wanted a model for my life—I wanted to travel as they did—Puerto Rico, India, Indonesia—to study, compose, write, teach; to live in a great city surrounded by other artists, to acquire grants from foundations that support the arts—to spend six months at the MacDowell Colony; above all, I wanted to *feel* passionately about everything and be able to communicate that feeling to others through language.

This longing for the creative life of the artist stretched in front of me, carrying me through thirty years of international job-hopping and geographic relocations. I have lived and taught in schools in the Bahamas and in different provinces of Canada. More recently, I have returned to the United States, where teaching and writing, defined and practiced as an art, continue to sustain me, offering a vision of the way I want to be in the world that is fundamental to my identity.

Writing/Riding Out the Terror of Your New/Old Self

Now, as I move through middle age, a sense of loss threatens to wash over me. I feel coolly distanced from the stories of my past, and from the familiar. Life possibilities seem fewer and more narrowly defined. I feel displaced/replaced by a new and an old self. What will I write? What "stories" will there be left to tell?

> I could make a dozen stories of what he said, of what she said—
> I can see a dozen pictures. But what are stories? Toys I twist,
> bubbles I blow, one ring passing through another. And some-
> times I begin to doubt if there are stories. What is my story?
> (Woolf 1959, 275)

Suddenly it is year fifty of my life. I am desperate to write something meaningful, yet I feel I have barely begun. I cannot find the words I need. Virginia Woolf captures this urgent need I feel for new language:

> My book, stuffed with phrases, has dropped to the floor. It lies
> under the table to be swept away by the charwoman when she
> comes at dawn looking for scraps of paper, old tram tickets, and
> here and there a note screwed into a ball and left with the litter
> to be swept up. What is the phrase for the moon? And the
> phrase for love? By what name are we to call death? I do not
> know. I need a little language such as lovers use, words of one
> syllable such as children speak when they come into the room
> and find their mother sewing and pick up some scrap of bright
> wool, a feather, or a shred of chintz. I need a howl; a cry . . . .
> (Woolf 1959, 381)

I begin new articles and books about autobiography and education; I write and rewrite, and I try to patch together the piles of papers that are strewn around my home office. There seems nothing else to my life but this eternity of writing, which I do when I am not teaching. A pattern develops: teaching and writing, writing and teaching; it is the singular rhythm of my life.

> Another day; another Friday; another twentieth of March, Janu-
> ary or September. Another general awakening. The stars draw
> back and are extinguished. The bars deepened themselves be-
> tween the waves. The film of mist thickens on the fields. A red-
> ness hangs by the bedroom window. A bird chirps. Cottagers

light their early candles. Yes, this is the eternal renewal, the in-
cessant rise and fall and rise again . . . . (Woolf 1959, 382–383)

It is near the end of the spring semester at the university
where I teach. Writing autobiographically has made me a more
courageous and self-accepting person (Brookes, 1992) and as
self-acceptance begets acceptance of others, I have deepened my
relationship with students in my graduate courses in autobiography and education. We have been engaged together in the
risky business of personal reflection, and this experience of the
most intimate form of writing/teaching I have ever done has altered my expectations of students and myself radically. I need
no longer present myself as an "expert" who delivers a curriculum and evaluates students' products. I have learned, by helping students explore their lives through writing and at the same
time by writing about my own life, that the only legitimate place
from which to teach is from a deep sense of *self-authority*. (Self
not defined as fixed and unchanging, but situated within a web
of human relationships in a cultural/historical context.)

A student describes her experience of the course and of the
meaning of reflection in her teaching life: "Sometimes the course
was painful, but I learned how to reflect on my own life. I feel it
is very important to be reflective in order to become a better
teacher. You need to know about yourself and why you react in
certain ways. You need to know yourself in order to share yourself with your students . . ." Another student points out the vital
role played by the teacher-participant and gives testimony to
the potential of autobiography in the lives of teachers: "Your autobiographical writing became a framework, a new model—it
was honest—the instructor as participant opened the discussion, created a trusting space where no one was asked to do
something the instructor was not comfortable with herself . . . I
got a sense, through autobiographical analysis, of teachers as
persons in the process of becoming."

And in me too the wave rises. It swells; it arches its back. I am
aware once more of a new desire, something rising beneath me
like the proud horse whose rider first spurs and then pulls him
back. What enemy do we now perceive advancing against us,
you whom I ride now, as we stand pawing this stretch of pave-
ment? It is death. Death is the enemy. It is death against whom
I ride with my spear couched and my hair flying back like a

young man's . . . I strike spurs into my horse. Against you I will
fling myself, unvanquished and unyielding, O death!
The waves broke on the shore. (Woolf 1959, 383)

I write and rewrite the "stories" of my life; life's repeating
patterns well up in steep banks; I am tossed about in their boil-
ing swells and pulled under by the force of the pounding surf of
autobiographical memory; seconds later, I shoot back to the
surface, gasping, alive. I write and teach "as if [my] life depended on it" (Rich 1993, 33).

Works Cited

Allison, Dorothy. 1994. "To Tell the Truth." *Ms.* (July/August): 72–75.
Ashton-Warner, Sylvia. 1967. *Myself.* New York: Simon and Schuster.
Braham, Jeanne. 1995. *Crucial Conversations.* New York: Teachers Col-
lege Press.
Brand, Dionne. 1994. *Bread Out of Stone.* Toronto: Coach House Press.
Brookes, Anne-Louise. 1992. *Feminist Pedagogy, An Autobiographical
Approach.* Halifax: Fernwood Books.
Bruner, Jerome. 1990. *Acts of Meaning.* Cambridge: Harvard University
Press.
Bruss, Elizabeth. 1976. *Autobiographical Acts: The Changing Situation
of a Literary Genre.* Baltimore: Johns Hopkins University Press.
Cixous, Hélène. 1991. *Coming to Writing and Other Essays.* Edited by
Deborah Jenson. Cambridge: Harvard University Press.
Cunningham, Michael. 1991. *A Home at the End of the World.* New
York: Knopf.
Dean, Ann Victoria. 1992. "Teachers Writing About Themselves." Diss.
Dalhousie University.
Eakin, Paul John. 1985. *Fictions in Autobiography: Studies in the Art of
Self-Invention.* Princeton: Princeton University Press.
Hardy, Barbara. 1987. *The Collected Essays of Barbara Hardy.* Two
vols. Sussex: Harvester Press.
Meigs, Mary. 1991. *In the Company of Strangers.* Vancouver: Talonbooks.
Miller, Nancy, K., ed. 1986. *The Poetics of Gender.* New York: Columbia
University Press.
Nin, Anais. 1985. *The White Blackbird.* Santa Barbara: Capra Press.
Rich, Adrienne. 1993. *What is Found There, Notebooks on Poetry and
Politics.* New York: W. W. Norton.
Smith, Sidonie. 1987. *A Poetics of Women's Autobiography.* Blooming-
ton: Indiana University Press.
Woolf, Virginia. 1959. *Jacob's Room and The Waves.* New York: Har-
court, Brace and World, Inc.

Chapter 10

From Silence to Words: Writing As Struggle

Min-zhan Lu

Imagine that you enter a parlor. You come late. When you arrive, others have long preceded you, and they are engaged in a heated discussion. . . . You listen for a while, until you decide that you have caught the tenor of the argument; then you put in your oar. Someone answers; you answer him; another comes to your defense; another aligns himself against you, to either the embarrassment or gratification of your opponent, depending upon the quality of your ally's assistance. However, the discussion is interminable. The hour grows late, you must depart. And you do depart, with the discussion still vigorously in progress.

—Kenneth Burke, *The Philosophy of Literary Form*

Men are not built in silence, but in word, in work, in action-reflection.

—Paulo Freire, *Pedagogy of the Oppressed*

My mother withdrew into silence two months before she died. A few nights before she fell silent, she told me she regretted the way she had raised me and my sisters. I knew she was referring to the way we had been brought up in the midst of two conflicting worlds—the world of home, dominated by the ideology of the Western humanistic tradition, and the world of a society dominated by Mao Tse-tung's Marxism. My mother had devoted her life to our education, an education she knew had made us suffer political persecution during the Cultural Revolution. I wanted to find a way to convince her that, in spite of the persecution, I had benefited from the education she had worked so hard to give me. But I was silent. My understanding of my education was so dominated by memories of confusion and frustration that I was unable to reflect on what I could have gained from it.

This paper is my attempt to fill up that silence with words, words I didn't have then, words that I have since come to by reflecting on my earlier experience as a student in China and on my recent experience as a composition teacher in the United States. For in spite of the frustration and confusion I experienced growing up caught between two conflicting worlds, the conflict ultimately helped me to grow as a reader and writer. Constantly having to switch back and forth between the discourse of home and that of school made me sensitive and self-conscious about the struggle I experienced every time I tried to read, write, or think in either discourse. Eventually, it led me to search for constructive uses for such struggle.

From early childhood, I had identified the differences between home and the outside world by the different languages I used in each. My parents had wanted my sisters and me to get the best education they could conceive of—Cambridge. They had hired a live-in tutor, a Scot, to make us bilingual. I learned to speak English with my parents, my tutor, and my sisters. I was allowed to speak Shanghai dialect only with the servants. When I was four (the year after the Communist Revolution of 1949), my parents sent me to a local private school where I learned to speak, read, and write in a new language—Standard Chinese, the official written language of New China.

In those days I moved from home to school, from English to Standard Chinese to Shanghai dialect, with no apparent friction. I spoke each language with those who spoke the language. All seemed quite "natural"—servants spoke only Shanghai dialect because they were servants; teachers spoke Standard Chinese because they were teachers; languages had different words because they were different languages. I thought of English as my family language, comparable to the many strange dialects I didn't speak but had often heard some of my classmates speak with their families. While I was happy to have a special family language, until second grade I didn't feel that my family language was any different than some of my classmates' family dialects.

My second grade homeroom teacher was a young graduate from a missionary school. When she found out I spoke English, she began to practice her English on me. One day she used English when asking me to run an errand for her. As I turned to close the door behind me, I noticed the puzzled faces of my classmates. I had the same sensation I had often experienced when some stranger in a crowd would turn on hearing me speak English. I was more intensely pleased on this occasion, however, because suddenly I felt that my family language had been singled out from the family languages of my classmates. Since we were not allowed to speak any dialect other than Standard Chinese in the classroom, having my teacher speak English to me in class made English an official language of the classroom. I began to take pride in my ability to speak it.

This incident confirmed in my mind what my parents had always told me about the importance of English to one's life. Time and again they had told me of how my paternal grandfather, who was well versed in classic Chinese, kept losing good-paying jobs because he couldn't speak English. My grandmother reminisced constantly about how she had slaved and saved to send my father to a first-rate missionary school. And we were made to understand that it was my father's fluent English that had opened the door to his success. Even though my family had always stressed the importance of English for my future, I used to complain bitterly about the extra English lessons we had to take after school. It was only after my homeroom teacher had "sanctified" English that I began to connect English with my education. I became a much more eager student in my tutorials.

What I learned from my tutorials seemed to enhance and reinforce what I was learning in my classroom. In those days each word had one meaning. One day I would be making a sentence at school: "The national flag of China is red." The next day I would recite at home, "My love is like a red, red rose." There seemed to be an agreement between the Chinese "red" and the English "red," and both corresponded to the patch of color printed next to the word. "Love" was my love for my mother at

home and my love for my "motherland" at school; both "loves"
meant how I felt about my mother. Having two loads of homework forced me to develop a quick memory for words and a sen-
sitivity to form and style. What I learned in one language carried
over to the other. I made sentences such as, "I saw a red, red
rose among the green leaves," with both the English lyric and
the classic Chinese lyric—red flower among green leaves—running through my mind, and I was praised by both teacher and
tutor for being a good student.

Although my elementary school took place during the fifties,
I was almost oblivious to the great political and social changes
happening around me. Years later, I read in my history and political philosophy textbooks that the fifties were a time when "China
was making a transition from a semi-feudal, semi-capitalist, and
semi-colonial country into a socialist country," a period in which
"the Proletarians were breaking into the educational territory
dominated by Bourgeois Intellectuals." While people all over the
country were being officially classified into Proletarians, Petty-
bourgeois, National-bourgeois, Poor-peasants, and Intellectuals,
and were trying to adjust to their new social identities, my parents were allowed to continue the upper middle-class life they
had established before the 1949 Revolution because of my father's affiliation with British firms. I had always felt that my family was different from the families of my classmates, but I didn't
perceive society's view of my family until the summer vacation
before I entered high school.

First, my aunt was caught by her colleagues talking to her
husband over the phone in English. Because of it, she was criticized and almost labeled a Rightist. (This was the year of the
Anti-Rightist movement, a movement in which the Intellectuals
became the target of the "socialist class-struggle.") I had heard
others telling my mother that she was foolish to teach us English when Russian had replaced English as the "official" foreign
language. I had also learned at school that the American and
British Imperialists were the arch-enemies of New China. Yet I
had made no connection between the arch-enemies and the
English our family spoke. What happened to my aunt forced the
connection on me. I began to see my parents' choice of a family
language as an anti-Revolutionary act and was alarmed that I
had participated in such an act. From then on, I took care not
to use English outside of the home and to conceal my knowledge of English from my new classmates.

Certain words began to play important roles in my new life at the junior high. On the first day of school, we were handed forms to fill out with our parents' class, job, and income. Being one of the few people not employed by the government, my father had never been officially classified. Since he was a medical doctor, he told me to put him down as an Intellectual. My homeroom teacher called me into the office a couple of days afterwards and told me that my father couldn't be an Intellectual if his income far exceeded that of a Capitalist. He also told me that since my father worked for Foreign Imperialists, my father should be classified as an Imperialist Lackey. The teacher looked nonplussed when I told him that my father couldn't be an Imperialist Lackey because he was a medical doctor. But I could tell from the way he took notes on my form that my father's job had put me in an unfavorable position in his eyes.

The Standard Chinese term "class" was not a new word for me. Since first grade, I had been taught sentences such as, "The Working class are the masters of New China." I had always known that it was good to be a worker, but until then, I had never felt threatened for not being one. That fall, "class" began to take on a new meaning for me. I noticed a group of Working-class students and teachers at school. I was made to understand that because of my class background, I was excluded from that group.

Another word that became important was "consciousness." One of the slogans posted in the school building read, "Turn our students into future Proletarians with socialist consciousness and education!" For several weeks we studied this slogan in our political philosophy course, a subject I had never had in elementary school. I still remember the definition of "socialist consciousness" that we were repeatedly tested on through the years: "Socialist consciousness is a person's political soul. It is the consciousness of the Proletarians represented by Marxist Mao Tse-tung thought. It takes expression in one's action, language, and lifestyle. It is the task of every Chinese student to grow up into a Proletarian with a socialist consciousness so that he can serve the people and the motherland." To make the abstract concept accessible to us, our teacher pointed out that the immediate task for students from Working-class families was to strengthen their socialist consciousnesses. For those of us who were from other class backgrounds, the task was to turn ourselves into Workers with socialist consciousnesses. The teacher never explained exactly how we were supposed to "turn" into Workers. Instead, we were given samples of the ritualistic annual plans we had to write at the beginning of each term. In these plans, we performed "self-criticism" on our consciousnesses and made vows to turn ourselves into Workers with socialist consciousnesses. The teacher's division between those who did and those who didn't have a socialist consciousness led me to reify the notion of "consciousness" into a thing one possesses. I equated this intangible "thing" with a concrete way of dressing, speaking, and writing. For instance, I never doubted that my political philosophy teacher had a socialist consciousness because she was from a steelworker's family (she announced this the first day of class) and was a Party member who wore grey cadre suits and talked like a philosophy textbook. I noticed other things about her. She had beautiful eyes and spoke Standard Chinese with such a pure accent that I thought she should be a film star. But I was embarrassed that I had noticed things that ought not to have been associated with her. I blamed my observation on my Bourgeois consciousness.

At the same time, the way reading and writing were taught through memorization and imitation also encouraged me to reduce concepts and ideas to simple definitions. In literature and political philosophy classes, we were taught a large number of quotations from Marx, Lenin, and Mao Tse-tung. Each concept that appeared in these quotations came with a definition. We were required to memorize the definitions of the words along with the quotations. Every time I memorized a definition, I felt I had learned a word: "The national red flag symbolizes the blood shed by Revolutionary ancestors for our socialist cause"; "New China rises like a red sun over the eastern horizon." As I memorized these sentences, I reduced their metaphors to dictionary meanings: "red" meant "Revolution" and "red sun" meant "New China" in the "language" of the Working class. I learned mechanically but eagerly. I soon became quite fluent in this new language.

As school began to define me as a political subject, my parents tried to build up my resistance to the "communist poisoning" by exposing me to the "great books"—novels by Charles Dickens, Nathaniel Hawthorne, Emily Bronte, Jane Austen, and writers from around the turn of the century. My parents implied that these writers represented how I, their child, should read and write. My parents replaced the word "Bourgeois" with the word "cultured." They reminded me that I was in school only to learn math and science. I needed to pass the other courses to stay in school, but I was not to let the "Red doctrines" corrupt my mind. Gone were the days when I could innocently write, "I saw the red, red rose among the green leaves," collapsing, as I did, English and Chinese cultural traditions. "Red" came to mean Revolution at school, "the Commies" at home, and adultery in *The Scarlet Letter*. Since I took these symbols and metaphors as meanings natural to people of the same class, I abandoned my earlier definitions of English and Standard Chinese as the language of home and the language of school. I now defined English as the language of the Bourgeois and Standard Chinese as the language of the Working class. I thought of the language of the Working class as someone else's language and the language of the Bourgeois as my language. But I also believed that, although the language of the Bourgeois was my real language, I could and would adopt the language of the Working class when I was at school. I began to put on and take off my Working class language in the same way I put on and took off my school clothes to avoid being criticized for wearing Bourgeois clothes.

In my literature classes, I learned the Working-class formula for reading. Each work in the textbook had a short "Author's Biography": "X X X, born in 19— in the province of X X, is from a Worker's family. He joined the Revolution in 19—. He is a Revolutionary realist with a passionate love for the Party and Chinese Revolution. His work expresses the thoughts and emotions of the masses and sings praise to the prosperous socialist construction on all fronts of China." The teacher used the "Author's Biography" as a yardstick to measure the texts. We were taught to locate details in the texts that illustrated these summaries, such as words that expressed Workers' thoughts and emotions or events that illustrated the Workers' lives.

I learned a formula for Working-class writing in the composition classes. We were given sample essays and told to imitate them. The theme was always about how the collective taught the individual a lesson. I would write papers about labor-learning experiences or school-cleaning days, depending on the occasion of the collective activity closest to the assignment. To make each paper look different, I dressed it up with details about the date, the weather, the environment, or the appearance of the Master-worker who had taught me "the lesson." But as I became more and more fluent in the generic voice of the Working-class Student, I also became more and more self-conscious about the language we used at home.

For instance, in senior high we began to have English classes ("to study English for the Revolution," as the slogan on the cover of the textbook said), and I was given my first Chinese-English dictionary. There I discovered the English version of the term "class-struggle." (The Chinese characters for a school "class" and for a social "class" are different.) I had often used the English word "class" at home in sentences such as, "So and so has class," but I had not connected this sense of "class" with "class-struggle." Once the connection was made, I heard a second layer of meaning every time someone at home said a person had "class." The expression began to mean the person had the style and sophistication characteristic of the Bourgeoisie. The word lost its innocence. I was uneasy about hearing that second layer of meaning because I was sure my parents did not hear the word that way. I felt that therefore I should not be hearing it that way either. Hearing the second layer of meaning made me wonder if I was losing my English.

My suspicion deepened when I noticed myself unconsciously merging and switching between the "reading" of home and the "reading" of school. Once I had to write a report on *The Revolutionary Family*, a book about an illiterate woman's awakening and growth as a Revolutionary through the deaths of her husband and all her children for the cause of the Revolution. In one scene the woman deliberated over whether or not she should encourage her youngest son to join the Revolution. Her memory of her husband's death made her afraid to encourage her son. Yet she also remembered her earlier married life and the first time her husband tried to explain the meaning of the Revolution to her. These memories made her feel she should encourage her son to continue the cause his father had begun.

I was moved by this scene. "Moved" was a word my mother and sisters used a lot when we discussed books. Our favorite moments in novels were moments of what I would now call internal conflict, moments which we said "moved" us. I remember that we were "moved" by Jane Eyre when she was torn between her sense of ethics, which compelled her to leave the man she loved, and her impulse to stay with the only man who had ever loved her. We were also moved by Agnes in *David Copperfield* because of the way she restrained her love for David so that he could live happily with the woman he loved. My standard method of doing a book report was to model it on the review by the Publishing Bureau and to dress it up with detailed quotations from the book. The review of *The Revolutionary Family* emphasized the woman's Revolutionary spirit. I decided to use the scene that had moved me to illustrate this point. I wrote the report the night before it was due. When I had finished, I realized I couldn't possibly hand it in. Instead of illustrating her Revolutionary spirit, I had dwelled on her internal conflict, which could be seen as a moment of weak sentimentality that I should never have emphasized in a Revolutionary heroine. I wrote another report, taking care to illustrate the grandeur of her Revolutionary spirit by expanding on a quotation in which she decided that if the life of her son could change the lives of millions of sons, she should not begrudge his life for the cause of Revolution. I handed in my second version but kept the first in my desk.

I never showed it to anyone. I could never show it to people outside my family, because it had deviated so much from the reading enacted by the jacket review. Neither could I show it to my mother or sisters, because I was ashamed to have been so moved by such a "Revolutionary" book. My parents would have been shocked to learn that I could like such a book in the same way they liked Dickens. Writing this book report increased my fear that I was losing the command over both the "language of home" and the "language of school" that I had worked so hard to gain. I tried to remind myself that, if I could still tell when my reading or writing sounded incorrect, then I had retained my command over both languages. Yet I could no longer be confident of my command over either language because I had discovered that when I was not careful—or even when I was—my reading and writing often surprised me with its impurity. To prevent such impurity, I became very suspicious of my thoughts when I read or wrote. I was always asking myself why I was using this word, how I was using it, always afraid that I wasn't reading or writing correctly. What confused and frustrated me most was that I could not figure out why I was no longer able to read or write correctly without such painful deliberation.

I continued to read only because reading allowed me to keep my thoughts and confusion private. I hoped that somehow, if I watched myself carefully, I would figure out from the way I read whether I had really mastered the "languages." But writing became a dreadful chore. When I tried to keep a diary, I was so afraid that the voice of school might slip in that I could only list my daily activities. When I wrote for school, I worried that my Bourgeois sensibilities would betray me.

The more suspicious I became about the way I read and wrote, the more guilty I felt for losing the spontaneity with which I had learned to "use" these "languages." Writing the book report made me feel that my reading and writing in the "language" of either home or school could not be free of the interference of the other. But I was unable to acknowledge, grasp, or grapple with what I was experiencing, for both my parents and my teachers had suggested that, if I were a good student, such interference would and should not take place. I assumed that once I had "acquired" a discourse, I could simply switch it on and off every time I read and wrote as I would some electronic tool. Furthermore, I expected my readings and writings to come out in their correct forms whenever I switched the proper discourse on. I still regarded the discourse of home as natural and the discourse of school alien, but I never had doubted before that I could acquire both and switch them on and off according to the occasion.

When my experience in writing conflicted with what I thought should happen when I used each discourse, I rejected my experience because it contradicted what my parents and teachers had taught me. I shied away from writing to avoid what I assumed I should not experience. But trying to avoid what should not happen did not keep it from recurring whenever I had to write. Eventually my confusion and frustration over these recurring experiences compelled me to search for an explanation: how and why had I failed to learn what my parents and teachers had worked so hard to teach me?

I now think of the internal scene for my reading and writing about *The Revolutionary Family* as a heated discussion between myself, the voices of home, and those of school. The review on the back of the book, the sample student papers I came across in my composition classes, my philosophy teacher—these I heard as voices of one group. My parents and my home readings were the voices of an opposing group. But the conversations between those opposing voices in the internal scene of my writing was not as polite and respectful as the parlor scene Kenneth Burke has portrayed (see epigraph). Rather, these voices struggled to dominate the discussion, constantly incorporating, dismissing, or suppressing the arguments of each other, like the battles between the hegemonic and counter-hegemonic forces described in Raymond Williams' *Marxism and Literature* (108–14).

When I read *The Revolutionary Family* and wrote the first version of my report, I began with a quotation from the review. The voices of both home and school answered, clamoring to be heard. I tried to listen to one group and turn a deaf ear to the other. Both persisted. I negotiated my way through these conflicting voices, now agreeing with one, now agreeing with the other. I formed a reading out of my interaction with both. Yet I was afraid to have done so because both home and school had implied that I should speak in unison with only one of these groups and stand away from the discussion rather than participate in it.

My teachers and parents had persistently called my attention to the intensity of the discussion taking place on the external social scene. The story of my grandfather's failure and my father's success had from my early childhood made me aware of the conflict between Western and traditional Chinese cultures. My political education at school added another dimension to the conflict: the war of Marxist-Maoism against them both. Yet when my parents and teachers called my attention to the conflict, they stressed the anxiety of having to live through China's transformation from a semi-feudal, semi-capitalist, and semi-colonial society to a socialist one. Acquiring the discourse of the dominant group was, to them, a means of seeking alliance with that group and thus of surviving the whirlpool of cultural currents around them. As a result, they modeled their pedagogical practices on this utilitarian view of language. Being the eager student, I adopted this view of language as a tool for survival. It came to dominate my understanding of the discussion on the social and historical scene and to restrict my ability to participate in that discussion.

To begin with, the metaphor of language as a tool for survival led me to be passive in my use of discourse, to be a bystander in the discussion. In Burke's "parlor," everyone is involved in the discussion. As it goes on through history, what we call "communal discourses"—arguments specific to particular political, social, economic, ethnic, sexual, and family groups—form, re-form and transform. To use a discourse in such a scene is to participate in the argument and to contribute to the formation of the discourse. But when I was growing up, I could not take on the burden of such an active role in the discussion. For both home and school presented the existent conventions of the discourse each taught me as absolute laws for my action. They turned verbal action into a tool, a set of conventions produced and shaped prior to and outside of my own verbal acts. Because I saw language as a tool, I separated the process of producing the tool from the process of using it. The tool was made by someone else and was then acquired and used by me. How the others made it before I acquired it determined and guaranteed what it produced when I used it. I imagined that the more experienced and powerful members of the community were the ones responsible for making the tool. They were the ones who participated in the discussion and fought with opponents. When I used what they made, their labor and accomplishments would ensure the quality of my reading and writing. By using it, I could survive the heated discussion. When my immediate experience in writing the book report suggested that knowing the conventions of school did not guarantee the form and content of my report, when it suggested that I had to write the report with the work and responsibility I had assigned to those who wrote book reviews in the Publishing Bureau, I thought I had lost the tool I had earlier acquired.

Another reason I could not take up an active role in the argument was that my parents and teachers contrived to provide a scene free of conflict for practicing my various languages. It was as if their experience had made them aware of the conflict between their discourse and other discourses and of the struggle involved in reproducing the conventions of any discourse on a scene where more than one discourse exists. They seemed convinced that such conflict and struggle would overwhelm someone still learning the discourse. Home and school each contrived a purified space where only one discourse was spoken and heard. In their choice of textbooks, in the way they spoke, and in the way they required me to speak, each jealously silenced any voice that threatened to break the unison of the scene. The homogeneity of home and of school implied that only one discourse could and should be relevant in each place. It led me to believe I should leave behind, turn a deaf ear to, or forget the discourse of the other when I crossed the boundary dividing them. I expected myself to set down one discourse whenever I took up another just as I would take off or put on a particular set of clothes for school or home.

Despite my parents' and teachers' attempts to keep home and school discrete, the internal conflict between the two discourses continued whenever I read or wrote. Although I tried to suppress the voice of one discourse in the name of the other, having to speak aloud in the voice I had just silenced each time I crossed the boundary kept both voices active in my mind. Every "I think . . ." from the voice of home or school brought forth a "However . . ." or a "But . . ." from the voice of the opponents. To identify with the voice of home or school, I had to negotiate through the conflicting voices of both by restating, taking back, qualifying my thoughts. I was unconsciously doing so when I did my book report. But I could not use the interaction comfortably and constructively. Both my parents and my teachers had implied that my job was to prevent that interaction from happening. My sense of having failed to accomplish what they had taught silenced me.

To use the interaction between the discourses of home and school constructively, I would have to have seen reading or writing as a process in which I worked my way towards a stance through a dialectical process of identification and division. To identify with an ally, I would have to have grasped the distance between where he or she stood and where I was positioning myself. In taking a stance against an opponent, I would have to have grasped where my stance identified with the stance of my allies. Teetering along the "wavering line of pressure and counter-pressure" from both allies and opponents, I might have worked my way towards a stance of my own (Burke, *A Rhetoric of Motives* 23). Moreover, I would have to have understood that the voices in my mind, like the participants in the parlor scene, were in constant flux. As I came into contact with new and different groups of people or read different books, voices entered and left. Each time I read or wrote, the stance I negotiated out of these voices would always be at some distance from the stances I worked out in my previous and my later readings or writings.

I could not conceive such a form of action for myself because I saw reading and writing as an expression of an established stance. In delineating the conventions of a discourse, my parents and teachers had synthesized the stance they saw as typical for a representative member of the community. Burke calls this the stance of a "god" or the "prototype"; Williams calls it the "official" or "possible" stance of the community. Through the metaphor of the survival tool, my parents and teachers had led me to assume I could automatically reproduce the official stance of the discourse I used. Therefore, when I did my book report on *The Revolutionary Family*, I expected my knowledge of the official stance set by the book review to ensure the actual stance of my report. As it happened, I began by trying to take the official stance of the review. Other voices interrupted. I answered back. In the process, I worked out a stance approximate but not identical to the official stance I began with. Yet the experience of having to labor to realize my knowledge of the official stance or to prevent myself from wandering away from it frustrated and confused me. For even though I had been actually reading and writing in a Burkean scene, I was afraid to participate actively in the discussion. I assumed it was my role to survive by staying out of it.

Not long ago, my daughter told me that it bothered her to hear her friend "talk wrong." Having come to the United States from China with little English, my daughter has become sensitive to the way English, as spoken by her teachers, operates. As a result, she has amazed her teachers with her success in picking up the language and in adapting to life at school. Her concern to speak the English taught in the classroom "correctly" makes her uncomfortable when she hears people using "ain't" or double negatives, which her teacher considers "improper." I see in her the me that had eagerly learned and used the discourse of the Working class at school. Yet while I was torn between the two conflicting worlds of school and home, she moves with seeming ease from the conversations she hears over the dinner table to her teacher's words in the classroom. My husband and I are proud of the good work she does at school. We are glad she is spared the kinds of conflict between home and school I experienced at her age. Yet as we watch her becoming more and more fluent in the language of the classroom, we wonder if, by enabling her to "survive" school, her very fluency will silence her when the scene of her reading and writing expands beyond that of the composition classroom.

For when I listen to my daughter, to students, and to some composition teachers talking about the teaching and learning of writing, I am often alarmed by the degree to which the metaphor of a survival tool dominates their understanding of language as it once dominated my own. I am especially concerned with the way some composition classes focus on turning the classroom into a monological scene for the students' reading and writing. Most of our students live in a world similar to my daughter's, somewhere between the purified world of the classroom and the complex world of my adolescence. When composition classes encourage these students to ignore those voices that seem irrelevant to the purified world of the classroom, most students are often able to do so without much struggle. Some of them are so adept at doing it that the whole process has for them become automatic.

However, beyond the classroom and beyond the limited range of these students' immediate lives lies a much more complex and dynamic social and historical scene. To help these students become actors in such a scene, perhaps we need to call their attention to voices that may seem irrelevant to the discourse we teach rather than encourage them to shut them out. For example, we might intentionally complicate the classroom scene by bringing into it discourses that stand at varying distances from the one we teach. We might encourage students to explore ways of practicing the conventions of the discourse they are learning by negotiating through these conflicting voices. We could also encourage them to see themselves as responsible for forming or transforming as well as preserving the discourse they are learning.

As I think about what we might do to complicate the external and internal scenes of our students' writing, I hear my parents and teachers saying: "Not now. Keep them from the wrangle of the marketplace until they have acquired the discourse and are skilled at using it." And I answer: "Don't teach them to 'survive' the whirlpool of crosscurrents by avoiding it. Use the classroom to moderate the currents. Moderate the currents, but teach them from the beginning to struggle." When I think of the ways in which the teaching of reading and writing as classroom activities can frustrate the development of students, I am almost grateful for the overwhelming complexity of the circumstances in which I grew up. For it was this complexity that kept me from losing sight of the effort and choice involved in reading or writing with and through a discourse.

Works Cited

Burke, Kenneth. 1967. *The Philosophy of Literary Form: Studies in Symbolic Action.* 2nd ed. Baton Rouge: Louisiana State University Press.
———. 1967. *A Rhetoric of Motives.* Berkeley: University of California Press.

Freire, Paulo. 1970. *Pedagogy of the Oppressed.* Trans. M. B. Ramos.
     New York: Continuum.
Williams, Raymond. 1977. *Marxism and Literature.* New York: Oxford
     University Press.

Chapter 11

Mothers/Daughters/Writing/Teaching

Elaine P. Maimon and
Gillian B. Maimon

Mother, father, and daughter, weary from a cross-country car trip from our home in Philadelphia to Georgia O'Keefe's New Mexico, felt revived as we walked into "Nicholas Potter, Booksellers," in Santa Fe. "I love the smell of bookstores," I said to my twenty-five-year-old daughter, Gillian. "So do I," she exhaled. This olfactory bond between mother and daughter gave perceptible form to our project of autobiographical co-authorship.

Gillian—Gill, pronounced "Jill," but spelled with a "G" with respect to the British origin of the name—departed on our mid-August automobile odyssey, partially on the legendary Route 66, after an exhausting June and July of graduate courses in education at the University of Pennsylvania. She had filled the four years since her graduation from Brown with many explorations: Production coordinator for a magazine; playwright for "Old Aunt Bea," produced off-off Broadway by the National Improvisational Theater; associate producer for a local television news and information program; traveler to Delphi and climber of Mount Parnassus to consult the oracle at the Temple of Apollo; press assistant to Mario Cuomo during the doomed 1994 campaign; bicyclist around the Ring of Kerry in Ireland; temporary secretary at the New York Academy of Sciences.

Perhaps, it was the Delphic oracle, but somewhere along this four-year journey she had found her vocation—teaching, but teaching defined inclusively, the physical schoolroom and the virtual classroom of the media age: radio, television, and computer technology. She had decided to connect her seemingly disparate experiences to become a teacher for the twenty-first century, first acquiring a foundation in classroom practice and then drawing on her background in the media and in politics to create new and exciting contexts for teaching.

The Penn program began with an intensive summer of education courses to be followed by more courses and a year of student teaching in the Philadelphia public schools. We decided to co-author this chapter for *Women/Writing/Teaching* at this special moment when Gill was on the threshold of her teaching career and I was reflecting on twenty-five years as a writer, teacher, and mother. The automobile trip out West gave us extended opportunities to collect and compare stories of ourselves as mothers and daughters, readers and writers, teachers and students.

The aroma of the Santa Fe bookstore was my madeleine. I remembered another bookstore, from my childhood. In Philadelphia, where I grew up, Leary's Bookstore was a famous place for books, some rare, all well-read and, one hopes, well-employed in past lives. Those scents in Nicholas Potter, Booksellers, of other times, other experiences, and other thoughts brought me back to Leary's. I could hear my mother telling me once again that when Gimbel's department store expanded, Leary's would not move, and giant Gimbel's had to build around little Leary's. Such, she said, was the power of books. When Leary's was finally torn down in the 1970s, the owners found an original copy of the Declaration of Independence, acknowledging what I had known twenty-five years earlier—that Leary's held undiscovered treasures.

At the age of four or five, before I entered school and learned to read for real, I had my own special ritual at Leary's. While my mother, Gertrude, browsed, I would quite importantly approach a salesclerk and ask to see a book by Alfred Lord Tennyson. The astonished clerk would find the book for me and watch as I scanned the table of contents for the one word that I could read: "Elaine," my name, and also the name of one of the "Idylls of the King," which I would later study as an English major and graduate student. But then, as I breathed in the aroma of the treasured book, I heard my mother, misquoting, as I later learned (and did not care): "Elaine, the beautiful, Elaine, the fair."

What was important was that I was named (and deemed beautiful) in a book. My mother, deprived of a college education, nonetheless bequeathed to me her love of books. From that ritual at Leary's, I became a reader/writer/teacher.

More than two decades later.

"PMLA Bibliography" pipes the two-year-old baby girl's voice as she pats the volume on the living room table. Gill, fascinated by the sound of this strange grouping of syllables, repeats these words that identify her as a child growing up in an academic household. Her grandmother, Gertrude, for whom she is named, died eight years before her birth. But her grandmother's love of books lives on in her. Gillian, so British in its origin, was still the closest we could come in modern English to Gittel, the Yiddish name by which her grandmother Gertrude was called in the family. My daughter's name synthesizes my professional and family history: dedication to a language spoken by the Anglo-Saxons, tempered by the Normans, made luminous by Chaucer, Shakespeare, and Jane Austen, combined with a family history of late nineteenth-century immigration to America, escaping the pogroms of Lithuania.

We almost named her "Gatsby," since I was doing research on my Ph.D. dissertation on Scott Fitzgerald throughout my pregnancy. One summer day, when my husband and I were vacationing on a Cape Cod beach, we thought that naming our daughter Gatsby would ensure that in her twenties she would be as sophisticated as Zelda, but then we remembered what happened to poor Zelda in her thirties. We also worried how "Gatsby" would ever survive junior high.

Gillian's gestation and birth actually proved helpful to the efficient completion of my dissertation. Unlike many of my graduate student colleagues, I had strong motivation *not* to procrastinate on the research phase of the dissertation. In fact, on December 15, 1969, my due date, I sat in the Princeton University Library, completing my last scheduled piece of research on the Fitzgerald papers. As I pored over the unpublished letters on the right side of the table, I had open on the left side a map of Princeton with the hospital circled. My Philadelphia ob/gyn had told me to continue with my research, since I would have plenty of time when labor pains began to return by train to Philadelphia. Anyone who has ever lurched through the ride from Princeton to Princeton Junction will understand my alternative plan to go directly to the Princeton hospital and phone my husband from there.

Gillian Blanche, born five days later on December 20, 1969, was named for her two grandmothers, my mother Gertrude (Gittel) and my husband's mother, Blanche, who had died a month before Gill's birth. Gill's connection with the family's past was destined to be indirect, through great aunts and uncles. Her connection with the professional life of academics predominated. When my graduate school classmates in the English Department at the University of Pennsylvania returned to the Van Pelt Library after the January 1970 winter break, I stayed home with my newborn baby. No long coffee breaks, gossipy lunches, or TGIF's at Smokey Joe's for me. Instead, I systematically reviewed the months of research notes that I had accumulated during my pregnancy and wrote my dissertation, chapter by chapter, during my baby daughter's naps. At the age of one month, she slept through the night, awoke cheerfully for breakfast, and then took a three- to four-hour morning nap. I was lucky.

The winter of 1970 was cold and icy in Philadelphia. I remember that our front door actually froze shut, so that we had to go in and out through the back door. I hibernated that winter, warding off acute cabin fever by giving concentrated attention to my two babies: Gill and "The Biographical Myth of F. Scott Fitzgerald." As a consequence, I completed my Ph.D. by the end of 1970—thanks to Gill.

Gill's household offered the privileges and liabilities of a two-academic-career family. In 1972, my husband, Mort, completed his dissertation in education and co-authored a book entitled, *Stories of the Inner City.* For most of Gill's childhood, he served as English Department Chair at Philadelphia High School for Girls, a public high school for academically talented young women. In a tight job market for hiring college professors, I was fortunate to hold academic positions from Gill's first birthday onward, first at Haverford College, then Beaver College, Brown University, Queens College, and now Arizona State University West. In December 1972, while I was one of only two female professors on full-time appointment at Haverford College (but that is a chapter for another book), Gill's brother Alan was born. (I have always believed that giving birth to each of my children in December proves that my biorhythms are uncannily in tune with the academic calendar.) While the children were small, my career was necessarily confined to the Philadelphia metropolitan area. When Gill was a senior in high school, I began commuting to Philadelphia on weekends, first from Providence and now from Queens.

When I began teaching at Beaver College, part-time from 1973 to 1975, full-time until 1986, I developed a strong professional interest in composition and rhetoric, initiating what David

Russell calls, "the most influential of the early private, liberal arts WAC (writing-across-the curriculum) programs" (Russell 1991, 284). Gill grew up in a house, where three books on writing-across-the curriculum were being co-authored, where visiting rhetoricians and poets would come to be entertained after Wednesday evening lectures, where faculty seminars would continue informally after hours, and where cross-disciplinary cluster courses were planned and debated. Whereas my mother loved books but was not a reading/writing professional, Gill had the blessing and the curse of growing up in a household where at two years old she found it natural to chant "PMLA Bibliography."

* * *

It is no accident that families who write spawn writers. I was not born with a silver pen in my fist, but I was raised to have a voice. One of my earliest memories is of a book my father used to read to me at bedtime called *Harry the Dirty Dog*. Harry was a great favorite of mine, and I remember him now with fond emotion of such strength that one would think he had actually been my pet. Harry's adventures were not limited to a single book. My father would frequently create new Harry stories on demand, and he encouraged me to come up with my own. We would often talk about Harry during the day as if he were a mutual acquaintance. This ritual of extending the story of Harry helped me to locate a place for myself in the book. My voice was well-developed long before I entered school.

There is a story that my first-grade teacher, Mrs. Day, once told to my mother that Mom has often repeated. Many years after I had completed first grade, the two women met at a school conference. When my mother identified herself, Mrs. Day told her how memorable I was because of the way I had learned to read. As the story goes, reading came to me as a revelation one day during story time. Mrs. Day structured story time so that each student in the class would periodically have a chance to "tell" a book to the rest of the class. I say "tell" rather than "read" because, while some members of the class had grasped the concept of sounding out words, others of us would recite a book we had memorized or create a story based on illustrations when our turn came. I began telling my book, as always, using one of the latter methods. However, somewhere in the middle of the story, it became clear to Mrs. Day that I had started to make words of the letters. When she took me aside to ask about this great change, I replied with astonishment, "I don't know what happened, but all of a sudden I could read!"

The Curious Case of the Instant Reader is a popular piece of family lore, yet it is not a history; it is a legend. While Mrs. Day may have witnessed the moment when something clicked, and letters became words for me, I had been a reader long before that day. School was the place where I finally put the letters together, but books and words began to mean something in my home.

That I don't remember this first-grade adventure taking place is itself as telling as what actually happened. My own memory of these events is irrelevant, for I am the subject, not the narrator, of this story. My parents have composed me in flesh, in thought, and on paper. It knocked the wind out of me at first to read my mother's portion of this chapter. I read about myself, but it is a version of me that is not mine. Perhaps it is a merciful thing that writers raise writers. At least I have been equipped with proclivities and skills to aid in responding to writing that is about me but is not me.

Where in my mother's telling of me can I begin to reclaim my story? Mount Parnassus seems a good place to start. While my mother attaches great consequence to my consultation with the Delphic oracle, I must admit that I took my turn in front of the ruins primarily to affirm for her the significance that she had attached to our Greek vacation. I acted in order to fit within a frame of meaning constructed by her. Many times, my words have been shaped to say what I thought she wanted to hear. When I was seven or eight, I wrote a poem called, "What is Writing?," which hung for years on the door of my mother's office. There was no better place that it could have been displayed because I wrote the piece to speak to her.

> What is writing?
> It's sometimes frightening.
> You have to do it.
> Then a teacher looks through it.
> If it's not neat,
> You have to repeat.
> Mine is usually great,
> Because I use Papermate.
>
> What is writing?
> It's sometimes exciting
> About dragons and soldiers

And rocks and boulders,
But mine's usually funny,
Because I write about Pooh and honey.

I remember being so proud of that poem when I wrote it, and I smile to look at it now after so many years. But I am struck to see that I was writing about writing rather than simply writing. This second-grade metacomposition seems to be written from me, but not by me. It is my little girl vision of the writing process, complete with reference to writing across genres and writing in drafts. I was raised to have a voice, but sometimes I wanted to hear myself speak in my mother's.

These days, most of the writing that I do goes into a journal I am keeping to record my observations of the remedial first-grade classroom in which I will be student teaching. While this special first grade was set up to serve the needs of a group of young children all deemed "at risk" by their kindergarten teachers, I can imagine more nurturing cell blocks. Much of what I see in this room serves to remind me how blessed I have been in my upbringing. While I've struggled, at times, to find my voice, I've always been encouraged to speak. Too often, I must bear witness while these students are silenced. It is tempting to cast my cooperating teacher, Barbara (not her real name), as villain, but I am afraid it is not nearly so simple. I see clearly how her actions are designed to meet the mandates of a principal, whose own expectations of children are low. If, as I fear, in this school at least, she is but a cog in a system of mediocrity, mine are not the only students "at risk."

One of the first things Barbara did with the class after introducing herself to them was to hold up cards with students' names on them to see if they could identify their names in print. At one point, she held up a card with the name "Robert" on it. When nobody claimed it, she asked each of the boys his name in order to determine which was Robert. It turned out that the mystery Robert was a boy who called himself "Bobby." He explained that he was confused when he saw the card because he thought that his name began with a "B," not an "R." While I found this an amusing misunderstanding, Barbara became angry. She sternly admonished, "Your name is not Bobby; it is Robert." I find it upsetting that Barbara believed it her place to rename this boy. In her mind, the way that a child's name appears on the school rolls is the name that he must become. But it seems to me that

Barbara is tampering with this boy's identity. How can Bobby find a place for himself in this classroom when he is no longer called by a name he recognizes as his own?

Unfortunately, this was not the only time that Barbara saw fit to rename a student. When reading the roll book yesterday, we saw that three of the seven boys in the class are named "Timothy." At the time we learned of this strange and inconvenient coincidence, Barbara commented, "We'll just call one 'Timothy,' one 'Timmy,' and one 'Tim.' " I laughed, thinking that she was joking, but today it became clear that she was quite serious about this plan of action. She went as far as to tell each Timothy which name would be his. As I was packing up bookbags at the end of the day, I happened to notice that one of the Timothys had the name 'TJ' written on his lunch box. I told Barbara about my discovery and she conceded that this nickname would as effectively differentiate this Timothy as the one that she had chosen for him. I wonder what the other Timothys' real names are.

That teachers see fit to rename children is not so much an act of re-definition as it is de-definition. That is, a child may find when he enters school that he is less than who he thought he was. He has only just established an identity before he becomes one of a collection that he must be whittled to fit. I fought often to defend my name. Teachers and classmates found "Gillian" a mouthful. Sometimes I was called "Gilligan," or "Gill" with a hard "G." While these mispronunciations were accidental, more than one teacher deliberately attempted change by suggesting that I abandon my "G" for a "J." My mother writes of the care that was taken in naming me. They took great care as well to preserve my name in the days I was made to wish it away.

Because my parents are both teachers, they have always felt comfortable in the company of other educators. They had great respect for my teachers but would not hesitate to question any classroom policy that didn't seem right. Students in Barbara's classroom are not so fortunate. I have seen parents accept, without question, decisions that I found very troubling. During the third week of school, Barbara decided that some of our students needed to be transferred into other classrooms. While some were found fit for traditional first-grade rooms, others were designated to be sent back to kindergarten. One of this group was Bobby, the same boy who did not recognize the name Robert on the first day of school.

Bobby tends to fidget and have trouble focusing, but his academic performance seems to me on par with the others in the class. In preparation for a meeting with his mother this afternoon, Barbara asked me to give him a worksheet to do, so that she would have documentation that his work was not good. I sat down with him, explained the task once, and (as Barbara asked me) gave him no help in completing the work. It turned out that he got everything right. When I gave Barbara the sheet, she yelled at me, "You gave him too much help!" Barbara decided that she would re-test him herself. Somehow, the boy performed terribly this time.

This incident has moved me to think a lot about testing in general and what a difference it makes to a student to see how well the person giving the test expects him to perform. I realize now that the "extra help" that I gave Bobby was communicating to him (and not even in so many words) my belief that he could do the work. Bobby's mother was very reluctant to sign the transfer form. I sat in the room during the meeting wanting to scream, "Don't do it! Don't do it!" But, of course, as a powerless student teacher, I said nothing. Finally, after Barbara went on and on about how he was simply not intellectually ready for first grade and how cruel it would be to keep him there, Bobby's mother signed the form. I'm very sad about this.

As uncomfortable as I was with Bobby's exile from our room, I was even less happy with a new threat that Barbara adopted following the transfer.

More than once, when a child was disruptive, Barbara would say, "If you don't behave, I will send you back to kindergarten. I've already sent two back and I can send you, too." This bothers me for a couple of reasons. First, there is no reason that she should be stigmatizing Bobby and Ariana, who the students know are now in kindergarten. Second, I would hate to think that their misbehavior was truly the reason that they were sent back.

Barbara effectively put a dunce cap on the two children (we have since transferred two more) she sent to kindergarten by intimating that they were cast out because they had been found lacking. When classrooms and schoolwork are portrayed as forms of punishment, children come to fear school. When I see students in Barbara's classroom shiver at the mention of "kindergarten," I imagine a legacy of academic alienation set into motion.

If not for my parents, I, too, might have come to fear things meant to set me free. I remember, during one particularly insubordinate period of my adolescence, spending many nights handcopying articles out of the newspaper as punishment for some science class infraction. When my mother learned that my science teacher was using writing as a form of punishment, she went on the warpath. She incited me to set aside my tedious assignment and compose, instead, an essay about why writing is not an appropriate penalty. While I certainly believed in the argument I was leveling, I do not remember righteous indignation as the salient emotion of the moment. Rather, I recall the thrill of thumbing my nose at a teacher with my mother's endorsement.

Only in retrospect do I realize that our shared rebellion shielded me, in ways that Barbara's students are not, from accepting as truths the hidden, twisted whims of teachers who make schools vengeful places. Mom did not change the reality of my science class existence, for I was still periodically punished with writing assignments, but she did change my vision of my reality because she helped me take a stand and realize that teachers are not always right to force from us what they do.

It pains me to realize how many children go through school without people who will be their advocates. Despite the occasional trials of growing up in a family of writers, I never lacked for support of my voice and vision. The more time I spend observing Barbara's classroom, the stronger my commitment is to teach, for I am compelled to protect this new generation of writers and readers. To allow these students' voices to be heard, I must further develop my own voice. My journal records my process of learning to speak up.

> Today I feel a small sense of achievement. After an upsetting episode in the classroom, I was actually able to let Barbara know that I was uncomfortable with a choice she made. It all began during journal time. Barbara instructed the students to draw a circle on a page of their notebook and to use a crayon to color their favorite color inside the circle. The two of us then went around the room to write a sentence about their favorite color for each student to copy. Stephen chose red, so I wrote, "My favorite color is red." Nicole chose pink, so I wrote, "My favorite color is pink."
>
> When I got to Melissa, I saw that she had colored inside the circle in many colors. I said to her, "Mrs. Y. would like us to

write a sentence about your favorite color. Which one of these is your favorite?" She replied, "They're all my favorite. My favorite color is rainbow!" I loved this answer and happily wrote down, "My favorite color is rainbow." Ten minutes later when Barbara walked by to check everyone's work, she spotted what Melissa had done and flipped out. "This is wrong! Rainbow is not a color!" Melissa seemed shocked and embarrassed and I felt terrible for encouraging her to record an answer that proved so displeasing to the teacher. How confusing it must have been for her to have one adult compliment her work and the other negate it.

At the end of the day, I casually brought up the "rainbow" incident with Barbara. I said, "I'm sorry that I misunderstood your journal instructions this morning. I am curious, though, to know why Melissa's entry was unacceptable." Barbara told me, "These kids have got to learn how to follow the rules. Rainbow is not a color." I replied that I could understand how rules were important for many activities in a classroom, but that journal writing seemed to be a forum for open expression. Barbara told me that children must master the rules before they are permitted to be creative. I responded that I thought that there was always time to learn rules, but that once creativity was quashed, it was gone forever. Barbara vehemently disagreed. She said that if I knew anything about child development, I would know that I was wrong. I know that I am not wrong.

I will teach for the same reason that I write, for I have grown up believing in the sovereignty of a child's voice.

* * *

The students in my introductory writing seminar at Queens College (BALA 100) have commented on drafts of this chapter. They responded strongly to Gill's section on the perils of the "remedial" first-grade classroom by conjuring up their own memories as readers and writers. One student, who is herself the mother of a first grader, felt better armed by the essay to protect her daughter's educational identity.

One goal in sharing a draft of my own work-in-progress was to encourage my students to see me as someone who valued their criticism (as I hoped they would value my suggestions and those of their peers about their own writing). I also wanted to model for them the process of listening carefully to criticism but then finally asserting ownership, that is, the authority of an author, by making judgments about what and how to revise. Most important, I wanted my students to see all of us—students, teacher, daughter—as members of a community of writers. Besides—and there is no doubt on this point—my students' comments have made this a better essay.

The class discussion moved away from the idea of a writing community to the theme of taking ownership of one's own education—what Gill calls "the sovereignty of a child's voice." Such sovereignty is difficult to achieve in the first grade but essential at every level, even those beyond childhood, including college. Several students in my seminar described elementary, secondary, and college classrooms in which their identities as readers and writers had been discouraged. I thought of Bobby, who was robbed of self-definition by a teacher's insistence that his name was Robert. How lucky I was to hear my mother's voice making my name into a poem and then finding that poem in a book.

Like Bobby, I also had a nickname, actually my middle name, Bonnie, that stuck from babyhood because my mother thought "Elaine" was too sophisticated and special for everyday, household use. I was called Bonnie in the family and in the neighborhood, but I always knew that my real name was Elaine (the beautiful, the fair) and that we were saving that name for a very special place. We were saving it for school.

Today, I am Elaine—to my husband, to my colleagues and friends, to the world. The only people who still call me Bonnie are those who knew me before I was five years old, kindergarten age. Gill's portion of this essay has inspired reflection on many points in my development as a reader, writer, and teacher. Robert (Bobby) felt confusion over his two names. My two names helped me understand, as well as a five-year-old could, that school was an important place where I would use my grown-up name, although I could still be Bonnie at home. Soon, I would be a big school person—a reader, a writer, maybe even a teacher. I could read my name and become my name.

As I write, I am seeing my experiences as a reader and writer through my adult eyes and, because of this co-authored essay, through Gill's eyes, too. I see three generations of storytellers, weaving tales to create meaning for ourselves but, as mothers and daughters, often catching each other in our own narrative web.

After the first pangs of saying good-bye to my mother at the schoolroom door, I brought reading-readiness and enthusiasm for learning to Longstreth Elementary School in Southwest

Philadelphia. Several of my classmates came from families that also belonged to the neighborhood synagogue, Beth Am Israel. I saw many of these children after school twice a week and then again on Sunday morning at the Hebrew School, where we had early training in a non-Indo-European language and in world history.

Our parents held jobs that would be considered working class or lower-middle-class—newspaper vendor, postal clerk, restaurant worker, secretary. As Eastern European immigrants or the children of immigrants themselves, growing up in Depression America, most of them had not had the opportunity to attend college, but they assumed that their children would. "I'm going to college and then getting married," I would answer mantra-like when I was asked what I wanted to do when I grew up.

When I was not quite nine years old, my father died. My brother, much older, was married and out of the house, and my sister, two years older than he, would soon follow. Working as a secretary, my mother spent most of her leisure hours with me. We went to the movies and took long walks to the library, each returning with as many books as we could carry. I particularly recall my mother reading her way through the novels of Theodore Dreiser. I remember seeing the movie version of *An American Tragedy*, with Elizabeth Taylor and Montgomery Clift.

And we went to the theater. In the Fifties and the Sixties, Philadelphia was still a try-out town for Broadway, and we saw everything: *No Time for Sergeants*, *Teahouse of the August Moon*, *The Diary of Anne Frank*, usually from the last row in the second balcony, where each seat cost $1.80, as I recall. (Could that really be so?) At six, I had seen my first Broadway production, *South Pacific*, long after Mary Martin and Enzio Pinza had left the cast.

Plays, movies, books (often read aloud)—all were connected in my mind as occasions for literary performance. I strongly identified with the characters in all of the genres. Like Gill, for whom Harry the Dirty Dog became as real as a pet of her own because she was a part of the story, I felt a part of every literary occasion, whether on the screen, in the theater, or between the covers of a book.

When I was five, our family acquired a television set, black and white, with a ten and a half-inch screen. The small screen, like the movie screen, became another vehicle for interactive identification and performance. Many educators give television a bad rap, making it synonymous with passivity. My fascination with television never interfered with my life as a reader and writer. In fact, it helped. I remember a third-grade ritual at recess: reenacting the previous episode of "I Remember Mama," the television drama adapted from *Mama's Bank Account*, starring Peggy Wood as Mama, the Norwegian immigrant who lived on Steiner Street in San Francisco. I was always Katrin, the narrator, the writer.

In 1952, our ten and a half-inch screen transported me to the coronation of Queen Elizabeth II. I watched, transfixed by the pomp and circumstance, seeing Camelot, Elaine, and all the "Idylls of the King" come alive in my living room. I participated in the event by making a coronation scrapbook. Elizabeth II connected me with Elizabeth I, Shakespeare, and the full pageantry of English literature. I probably became an English major in front of the television set. All of these childhood experiences prepared me to love stories, to listen to them, to write them, and to share them with others. My favorite color was rainbow.

Enveloped in a soft-cushioned brown chair, I read through all the books by Louisa May Alcott: *Little Women*; *Little Men*; *Jo's Boys* (yes, I identified with Jo, the writer); *Eight Cousins*; *Rose in Bloom*; and *Jack and Jill*. By the third grade, I wanted to read grown-up books. Edna Ferber was one of my mother's favorites, so I read *Giant*, not exactly third-grade fare, but the movie (with Rock Hudson, Elizabeth Taylor, and James Dean) later helped me understand the prose. My next grown-up book was *Gone With the Wind* (the movie helped here, too), then on through more Edna Ferber, *So Big* (my mother's favorite) and *Show Boat* (yes, I saw the film with Joe E. Brown as Cap'n Andy). Books came alive in my mind as visual performances because I associated books with the living stories I saw on film, on the stage, and on television. These performances carried over into my dreams. I remember a particularly vivid nocturnal reenactment of scenes from *Gone With the Wind*, confused in a surreal way with scenes from *Show Boat*. Sometimes, I would dream I was in a movie theater and the dream-within-a-dream would appear on the screen.

Since reading and watching engaged me actively, I thought that it was natural to create my own texts. Writing, performance, and approval were closely connected in my mind. Almost from the time I could form the letters, I wrote plays and stories, but mostly plays because these could be performed. The youth group at the synagogue provided opportunities to write alternative song lyrics commemorating or spoofing local events. From the time I was ten years old, I heard my versions of these songs performed and applauded.

In public school I eagerly sought creative approaches to assignments. In the ninth grade, for a class project, I organized a dramatic version of "The Trial of Percy Bysshe Shelley," with Poetry personified as the only witness for the defense (as Shelley had once defended her!).

In high school, academics were not a problem, but gym class was the site of recurring humiliation. We never learned sports or played games in this large urban high school gym. We had "apparatus"—climbing ropes and swinging from rings—and we marched. I hated every minute of this military regimentation. In eighth grade, even though I had come in early every morning to practice the "climbing position" in gym, the teacher, nonetheless, gave me a grade of "D," keeping me off the honor roll, even though I had As in every other subject. Thus, I experienced first-hand what Gill calls "the twisted whim" of a teacher who made school "a vengeful place."

In tenth grade, several of my friends and I heard that you could get out of the regimen of regular gym by feigning poor posture and thereby securing a spot in remedial gym. (Remediation by choice—or by subterfuge—is quite different from the situation of Gill's unfortunate students in remedial first grade.) My greatest success as a high school playwright occurred in the setting of remedial gym. Mr. Gentile, the remedial gym instructor, soon realized that he was supervising a number of academically talented girls. He suggested that we produce an assembly program to raise the image of remedial gym, so that those who really did have posture problems would not be embarrassed to join. Thus was born "Selma Slouch," the character in my play who made remedial gym cool at John Bartram High School and who confirmed my identity as a writer.

"The sovereignty of a child's voice"—yes, I had a wide realm. During my senior year in high school, I looked over my mother's shoulder as she filled out financial information on the aid forms for my college applications. I looked at the figure for her annual salary. "Mother, that number can't be right," I said. But it was. "My God, Mother, we're poor! Why didn't you ever tell me?"

Yes, as sovereign over a vast realm of reading and writing, I was rich indeed, even without monetary advantages. Mother was ill when she was filling out those financial aid forms. I recited my speech as high school valedictorian so often that all the nurses at Presbyterian Hospital knew it by heart. Mother was too weak to attend my graduation, and two weeks later she died.

The University of Pennsylvania made it possible for me to pursue my academic career thereby providing scholarships for full tuition and room and board. In shock from the loss of my mother, I moved through my undergraduate years in something of a daze, although the habits of academic achievement were so ingrained that I was able to retreat into my studies, earn junior-year election to Phi Beta Kappa, and win a fellowship for the Ph. D. program in the Penn English Department. Even shell-shocked, I joined Penn Players to perform in Giraudoux's "The Enchanted." Performance was a part of my life. The memory of my mother's voice sustained me: "Elaine, the beautiful, Elaine the fair. . . ."

Writing, teaching, mothering—in their ways, all are forms of performance—creating an alternative reality for the approval of other people. Writing this essay with Gill has made me understand that daughters (Gill and I both, as examples) must learn to cherish and resist the fictions that our mothers create for us and about us. Gill has inherited a love of language, but she successfully resists becoming a character in my story. As storyteller and subject of her own narrative, she fictionalizes me without the help of the Delphic oracle.

From the moment she named me Elaine, my mother made me a character in her story. Now she is a character in mine. As I read and write these sentences, she is with me in the room. We are three generations of mothers and daughters writing and reading together, weaving an intricate web, sharing the authorship of our lives.

This is a story of mothers and daughters, so fathers, husbands, and sons have been relegated to the background. Gillian, who is named for Gittel, becomes a teacher and writer in a way that does not complete the circle but forms a double helix, affirming life and the telling of stories.

Works Cited

Russell, David R. 1991. *Writing in the Academic Disciplines, 1870–1990, A Curricular History*. Carbondale and Edwardsville: Southern Illinois University Press.

Chapter 12

Between the Drafts

Nancy Sommers

I cannot think of my childhood without hearing voices, deep, heavily accented, instructive German voices.

I hear the voice of my father reading to me from *Struvelpater*, the German children's tale about a messy boy who refuses to cut his hair or his fingernails. Struvelpater's hair grows so long that birds nest in it, and his fingernails grow so long that his hands become useless. He fares better, though, than the other characters in the book who don't listen to their parents. Augustus, for instance, refuses to eat his soup for four days and becomes as thin as a thread; on the fifth day he is dead. Fidgety Philip tilts his dinner chair like a rocking horse until his chair falls backward; the hot food falls on top of him and suffocates him under the weight of the tablecloth. The story that frightened me most tells of Conrad, who couldn't stop sucking his thumb and whose mother warned him that a great, long, red-legged scissor-man would—and, yes, did—snip both his thumbs off.

As a child, I hated these horrid stories with their clear moral lessons exhorting me to listen to my parents: do the right thing, they said; obey authority, or else catastrophic things—dissipation, suffocation, loss of thumbs—will follow. As a child, I never wondered why my parents, who had escaped Nazi Germany in 1939, were so deferential to authority, so beholden to sanctioned sources of power. I guess it never occurred to them to reflect or to make any connections between generations of German children reading *Struvelpater*, being instructed from early childhood to honor and defer to the parental authority of the state, and the Nazis' easy rise to power.

I hear the voice of my grandmother instructing me that when I invite people to dinner, I should always cook two chickens even if only one is needed. Nothing more humiliating, she would say, than having your guests leave your dinner table hungry.

When I hear my mother's voice, it is usually reading to me from some kind of guidebook showing me how different *they*, the Americans, are from us, the German Jews of Terre Haute. My parents never left home without their passports; we had roots somewhere else. When we traveled westward every summer from our home in Indiana, our bible, the AAA tour guide gave us the officially sanctioned version of America. We attempted to "see" America from the windows of our 1958 two-tone green Oldsmobile. We were literally the tourists from Terre Haute described by Walker Percy in "The Loss of the Creature," people who could never experience the Grand Canyon because it had already been formulated for us by picture-postcards, tourist folders, guidebooks, and the words GRAND CANYON. Percy suggests that tourists never see the progressive movement of depths, patterns, colors, and shadows of the Grand Canyon, but rather measure their satisfaction by the degree to which the canyon conforms to the expectations in their minds. My mother's AAA guidebook directed us, told us what to see, how to see it, and how long it should take us to see it. We never stopped anywhere serendipitously, never lingered, never attempted to know a place.

As I look now at the black-and-white photographs of our trips, seeing myself in ponytail and pedal pushers, I am struck by how many of the photos are taken against the car or, at least, with the car close enough to be included in the photograph. I am not sure we really saw the Grand Canyon or the Painted Desert or the Petrified Forest, except from the security of a parking lot. We were traveling on a self-imposed visa that kept us close to our parked car; we lacked the freedom of our own authority and stuck close to each other and to the guidebook itself.

My parents' belief that there was a right and a wrong way to do everything extended to the way they taught us German. Wanting us to learn the correct way, not trusting their own native voices, they bought us language-learning records with the officially sanctioned voice of an expert language teacher; never mind that they themselves spoke fluent German.

It is 1959; I am eight years old. We sit in the olive-drab living room, the drapes closed so the neighbors won't see in. What those neighbors would have seen strikes me now as a scene out of a "Saturday Night Live" Coneheads skit. The children and their parental unit sit in stiff, good-for-your-posture chairs that my brother and I call "the electric chairs." The chairs are at odd angles so we all face the fireplace; we don't look at each other. I guess my parents never considered pulling the chairs around, facing each other, so we could just talk in German. My father had invested in the best 1959 technology he could find; he was proud of the time and money he had spent so that we could be instructed in the right way. I still see him there in that room removing the record from its purple package placing it on the hi-fi.

—Guten Tag.
—Wie geht es Dir?
—Wie geht es Werner/Helmut/Dieter?
—Werner ist heute krank.
—Oh, dass tut mir Leid.
—Gute Besserung.

We are disconnected voices worrying over the health of Werner, Dieter, and Helmut, foreign characters, mere names, who have no place in our own family. We go on and on with that dialogue until my brother passes gas or commits some other unspeakable offense, something that sets my father's German sensibility on edge, and he finally says, "We will continue another time." He releases us back into another life, where we speak English, forgetting for yet another week about the health of Werner, Helmut, or Dieter.

When I was in college, I thought I had the issue of authority all settled in my mind. My favorite T-shirt, the one I took the greatest pleasure in wearing, was one with the bold words QUESTION AUTHORITY inscribed across my chest. It seemed that easy. As we said then, either you were part of the problem or you were part of the solution; either you deferred to authority or you resisted it by questioning. Twenty years later, it doesn't seem that simple. I am beginning to get a better sense of my legacy, beginning to see just how complicated and how far-reaching is this business of authority. It extends into my life and touches my students' lives, reminding me again and again of the delicate relation between language and authority.

In 1989, thirty years after my German lessons at home, I'm having dinner with my daughters in an Italian restaurant. The waiter is flirting with eight-year-old Rachel, telling her she has the most beautiful name, that she is *una ragazza bellissima*. Intoxicated with this affectionate attention, she turns to me passionately and says, "Oh, Momma, Momma, can't we learn Italian?" I, too, for the moment am caught up in the brio of my daughter's passion. I say, "Yes, yes, we must learn Italian." We rush to our favorite bookstore where we find Italian language-learning tapes packaged in thirty-, sixty-, or ninety-day lessons; in our modesty, we buy the promise of fluent Italian in thirty lessons. Driving home together, we put the tape in our car tape player and begin lesson number one.

—Buon giorno.
—Come stai?
—Come stai Monica?

As we wend our way home, our Italian lessons quickly move beyond preliminaries. We stop worrying over the health of Monica, and suddenly we are in the midst of a dialogue about Signor Fellini who lives at 21 Broadway Street. We cannot follow the dialogue. Rachel, in great despair, betrayed by the promise of being a beautiful girl with a beautiful name speaking Italian in thirty lessons, begins to scream at me: "This isn't the way to learn a language. This isn't language at all. These are just words and sentences; this isn't about us; we don't live at 21 Broadway Street."

And I am back home in Indiana, hearing the disembodied voices of my family learn a language out of the context of life.

In 1987, I gave a talk at the Conference on College Composition and Communication entitled "New Directions for Researching Revision." At the time, I liked the talk very much, because it gave me an opportunity to illustrate how revision, once a subject as interesting to our profession as an autopsy, had received new body and soul, almost celebrity status, in our time. Yet as interesting as revision had become, it seemed to me that our pedagogies and research methods were resting on some shaky, unquestioned assumptions. I had begun to see how students often sabotage their own best interests when they revise, searching for errors and assuming, like the eighteenth-century theory of words parodied in *Gulliver's Travels*, that words are a load of things to be carried around and exchanged. It seemed to me that, despite all those multiple drafts and all the peer workshops we were encouraging, we had left unexamined the most important fact of all: revision does not always guarantee improvement; successive drafts do not always lead to a clearer vision. You can't just change the words around and get the ideas right.

Here I am four years later, looking back on that now-abandoned talk, thinking of myself as a student writer and seeing that successive drafts have not led me to a clearer vision. I have been under the influence of a voice other than my own.

I live by the lyrical dream of change, of being made anew, always believing that a new vision is possible. I have been gripped, probably obsessed, with the subject of revision since graduate school. I have spent hundreds of hours studying manuscripts, looking for clues in the drafts of professional and student writers, looking for the figure in the carpet. The pleasures of this kind of literary detective work, this literary voyeurism, are the peeps behind the scenes, the glimpses of the process revealed in all its nakedness, of what Edgar Allan Poe called "the elaborate and vacillating crudities of thought, the true purposes seized only at the last moment, the cautious selections and rejections, the painful erasures."

My decision to study revision was not an innocent choice. It is deeply satisfying to believe that we are not locked into our original statements, that we might start and stop, erase, use the delete key in life, and be saved from the roughness of our early drafts. Words can be retracted; souls can be reincarnated. Such beliefs have informed my study of revision, and yet, in my own writing, I have always treated revision as an academic subject, not a personal one. Every time I have written about revision, I have set out to argue a thesis, present my research, accumulate my footnotes. By treating revision as an academic subject, by suggesting that I could learn something only by studying the drafts of other experienced writers, I kept myself clean and distant from any kind of scrutiny. No Struvelpater was I; no birds could nest in my hair; I kept my thumbs intact. I have been the bloodless academic, creating taxonomies, building a hierarchy from student writers to experienced writers, and never asking myself how I was being displaced from my own work. I never asked, "What does my absence *signify?*"

In that unrevised talk from CCCC, I had let Wayne Booth replace my father. Here are my words:

> Revision presents a unique opportunity to study what writers know. By studying writers' revisions, we can learn how writers locate themselves within a discourse tradition by developing a persona—a fictionalized self. Creating a persona involves placing the self in a textual community, seeing oneself within a discourse, and positing a self that shares or antagonizes the beliefs that a community of readers share. As Wayne Booth has written, "Every speaker makes a self with every word uttered. Even the most sincere statement implies a self that is at best a radical selection from many possible roles. No one comes on in exactly the same way with parents, teachers, classmates, lovers, and IRS inspectors."

What strikes me now, in this paragraph from my own talk, is that fictionalized self I invented, that anemic researcher who set herself apart from her most passionate convictions. I am a distant, imponderable, impersonal voice—inaccessible, humorless, and disguised like the packaged voice of Signor Fellini, giving lessons as if absolutely nothing depends on my work. I speak in an inherited academic voice; it isn't mine.

I simply wasn't there for my own talk. Just as my father hid behind his language-learning records and my mother behind her guidebooks, I disguised myself behind the authority of "the researcher," attempting to bring in the weighty authority of Wayne Booth to justify my own statements, never gazing inward, never trusting my own authority as a writer.

Looking back on that talk, I know how deeply I was under the influence of a way of seeing: Foucault's "Discourse on Language," Barthes's *S/Z*, Scholes's *Textual Power*, and Bartholomae's "Inventing the University" had become my tourist guides. I was so much under their influence and so detached from my own voice that I remember standing in a supermarket parking lot holding two heavy bags of groceries, talking with a colleague who was telling me about his teaching. Without any reference, except to locate my own authority somewhere else, I felt compelled to suggest to him that he read Foucault. My daughter Alexandra, waiting impatiently for me, eating chocolate while pounding on the hood of the car with her new black patent-leather party shoes, spoke with her own authority. She reminded me that I, too, had bumped on cars, eaten Hershey Bars, worn party shoes without straps, never read Foucault, and knew, nevertheless, what to say on most occasions.

One of my colleagues put a telling cartoon on the wall of our photocopy room. It reads "Breakfast Theory: A morning methodology." The cartoon describes two new cereals: Foucault Flakes and Post-Modern Toasties. The slogan for Foucault Flakes reads: "It's French, so it must be good for you. A breakfast commodity so complex that you need a theoretical apparatus to digest it. You don't want to eat it; you'll just want to read it. Breakfast as text." And Post-Modern Toasties: "More than just a cereal, it's a commentary on the nature of cereal-ness, cereal-ism, and the theory of cerealtivity. Free decoding ring inside."

I had swallowed the whole flake, undigested, as my morning methodology, but, alas, I never found the decoding ring. I was lost in the box. Or, to use the metaphor of revision, I was stuck in a way of seeing: reproducing the thoughts of others, using them as my guides, letting the poststructuralist vocabulary give authority to my text.

Successive drafts of my own talk did not lead to a clearer vision because it simply was not my vision. Like so many of my students, I was reproducing acceptable truths, imitating the gestures and rituals of the academy, lacking confidence in my own ideas and trust in my own language. I had surrendered my authority to someone else, to those other authorial voices.

Three years later, I am still wondering: Where does revision come from? Or, as I think about it now, what happens between the drafts? Something has to happen or else we are stuck doing mop-and-broom work, the janitorial work of polishing, cleaning, and fixing what is and always has been. What happens between drafts seems to be one of the great secrets of our profession.

Between drafts, I take lots of showers, hot showers, talking to myself as I watch the water play against the gestures of my hands. In the shower, I get lost in the steam. There I stand without my badges of authority. I begin an imagined conversation with my colleague, the one whom I told in the parking lot of the grocery store, "Oh, but you must read Foucault." I revise our conversation. This time I listen.

I understand why he showed so much disdain when I began to pay homage to Foucault. He had his own sources aplenty that nourished him. Yet he hadn't felt the need to speak through his sources or interject their names into our conversation. His teaching stories and experiences are his own; they give him the authority to speak.

As I get lost in the steam, I listen to his stories, and I begin to tell him mine. I tell him about my father not trusting his native voice to teach me German, about my mother not trusting her own eyes and reading to us from guidebooks, about my own claustrophobia in not being able to revise a talk about revision, about being drowned out by a chorus of authorial voices. And I surprise myself. Yes, I say, these stories of mine provide powerful evidence; they belong to me; I can use them to say what I must about revision.

I begin at last to have a conversation with all the voices I embody, and I wonder why so many issues are posed as either-or propositions. Either I stop sucking my thumb *or* the great red-legged scissor-man will cut it off. Either I cook two chickens *or* my guests will go away hungry. Either I accept authority *or* I question it. Either I have babies, in service to the species, *or* I write books, in service to the academy. Either I be personal *or* I be academic.

These either-or ways of seeing exclude life and real revision by pushing us to safe positions, to what is known. They are safe positions that exclude each other and allow for no ambiguity or uncertainty. Only when I suspend myself between *either* and *or* can I move away from conventional boundaries and begin to see shapes and shadows and contours—ambiguity, uncertainty, discontinuity, moments when the seams of life just don't want to hold; days when I wake up to find, once again, that I don't have enough bread for the children's sandwiches or that there are no shoelaces for their gym shoes. My life is full of uncertainty; negotiating that uncertainty day to day gives me authority.

Maybe this is a woman's journey, maybe not, maybe it is just my own; but the journey between home and work, between being personal and being authoritative, between the drafts of my life, is a journey of learning how to be both personal and authoritative, both scholarly and reflective. It is a journey that leads me to embrace the experiences of my life and gives me the insight to transform these experiences into evidence. I begin to see discontinuous moments as sources of strength and knowledge. When my writing and my life actually come together, the safe positions of either-or will no longer pacify me, no longer contain me and hem me in.

Foucault still makes sense to me because his is an anti-authoritarian voice. It is a voice that speaks to me about a struggle I know: the necessary and inevitable struggle all writers face in finding a voice within and against the voices of institution and inclination, between conventions and desire, between limits and choices.

In that unrevised talk, I had actually misused my sources. What they were saying to me, if I had listened, was pretty simple; don't follow us, don't reproduce what we have produced, don't live life from secondary sources like us, don't disappear. I hear Bob Scholes's and David Bartholomae's voices telling me to answer them, to speak back to them, to use them and make them anew. They say, in a word, revise me. The language lesson starts to make sense, finally: by confronting these authorial voices, I find the power to understand and gain access to my own ideas. Against all the voices I embody—the voices heard, read, whispered to me from offstage—I must bring a voice of my own. I must enter the dialogue on my own authority, knowing that, though other voices have enabled mine, I can no longer subordinate mine to theirs.

The voices I embody encourage me to show up as a writer and to bring the courage of my own authority into my classroom. I have also learned about the dangers of submission from observing the struggles of my own students. When they write about their lives, they write with confidence. As soon as they begin to turn their attention toward outside sources, they too lose confidence, defer to the voice of the academy, and write in the voice of EVERYSTUDENT to an audience they think of as EVERYTEACHER. They disguise themselves in the weighty, imponderable voice of acquired authority: "In today's society . . ."; "Since the beginning of civilization mankind has . . ."; or, as one student wrote about authority itself, "In attempting to investigate the origins of authority of the group, we must first decide exactly what we mean by authority."

In my workshops with teachers, the issue of authority, or deciding exactly what we mean by authority, always seems to be at the center of many heated conversations. Some colleagues are convinced that our writing programs should be about teaching academic writing. They see such programs as the Welcome Wagon of the academy, the Holiday Inn where students lodge as they take holy orders. Some colleagues fear that if we don't control what students learn, don't teach them to write as scholars

write, we aren't doing our job and some great red-legged scissor-
man will cut off our thumbs. It is another either-or proposition:
either we teach students to write academic essays, or we teach
them to write personal essays—and then who knows what might
happen? The world might become uncontrollable: students
might start writing about their grandmother's death in an essay
for a sociology course. Or even worse, something more uncontrollable, they might just write essays and publish them in professional journals, claiming the authority to tell stories about
their families and their colleagues. The uncontrollable world of
ambiguity and uncertainty opens up, my colleagues imagine, as
soon as the academic embraces the personal.

But, of course, our students are not empty vessels waiting
to be filled with authorial intent. Given the opportunity to speak
their own authority as writers, given a turn in the conversation,
students can claim their stories as primary source material and
transform their experiences into evidence. They might, if given
enough encouragement, be empowered not to serve the academy and accommodate it, not to write in the persona of EVERY-
STUDENT, but rather to write essays that will change the academy.
When we create opportunities for something to happen between
the drafts, when we create writing exercises that allow students
to work with sources of their own that can complicate and enrich their primary sources, they will find new ways to write
scholarly essays that are exploratory, thoughtful, and reflective.

I want my students to know what writers know—to know
something no researchers could ever find out, no matter how
many times they pin my students to the table, no matter how
many protocols they tape. I want my students to know how to
bring their life and their writing together.

Sometimes when I cook a chicken and my children scuffle
over the one wishbone, I wish I had listened to my grandmother
and cooked two. Usually, the child who gets the short end of the
wishbone dissolves into tears of frustration and failure. Interject-
ing my own authority as the earth mother from central casting, I
try to make their lives better by asking: On whose authority is it
that the short end can't get her wish? Why can't both of you, the
long and the short ends, get your wishes?

My children, on cue, as if they too were brought in from
central casting, roll their eyes as children are supposed to when
their mothers attempt to impose a way of seeing. They won't let

me control the situation by interpreting it for them. My interpretation serves my needs, temporarily, for sibling compromise
and resolution. They don't buy my story because they know
something about the sheer thrill of the pull; they are not going
to let *me* deny *them*. They will have to revise my self-serving
story about compromise, just as they will have to revise the
other stories I tell them. Between the drafts, as they get outside
my authority, they too will have to question and begin to see for
themselves their own complicated legacy, their own trail of
authority.

It is in the thrill of the pull between someone else's authority and our own, between submission and independence, that
we must discover how to define ourselves. In the uncertainty of
that struggle, we have a chance to find the voice of our own authority. Finding it, we can speak convincingly . . . at long last.

Part III

Visions of Embodied Teaching

Chapter 13

Freedom, Form, Function:
Varieties of Academic Discourse

Lillian Bridwell-Bowles

Let me begin my address by invoking three voices other than my own: First, Langston Hughes, whom I discovered in desperation during my first year of teaching:

> Hold fast to dreams
> For if dreams die,
> Life is a broken-winged bird that cannot fly.

And then Adrienne Rich, whom I discovered in more recent years: "We might hypothetically possess ourselves of every recognized technological resource on the North American continent, but as long as our language is inadequate, our vision remains formless, our thinking and feeling are still running in the old cycles, our process may be 'revolutionary,' but [it will not be] transformative" (247–48).

And finally, Hélène Cixous: "I do not want to tell a story to someone's memory" (qtd. in Conley 1).

In my opinion, the most significant issue facing our profession as we move into the twenty-first century is embodied in these quotations: That our language and our writing should be adequate enough to make our dreams, our visions, our stories, our thinking, and our actions not just revolutionary but transformative. When Rich chooses transformative processes over revolutionary ones, she strikes a chord with me and with many others of my generation. Like Langston Huges, we were youthful dreamers, but our visions of revolution have given way to practical questions about how we can change our own institutions, our own departments, and our own classrooms. And finally, I have invoked Hélène Cixous, who challenges me to try to think in new ways even when I cannot. I want to bring the passions and the dreams of transformation to our classrooms.

In the 1990s, it is not always easy to invite our students to participate in transformation, to write with passion about subjects that are complex, politically charged, politically correct, or even politically incorrect. To do so invites labels such as "tenured radical" and accusations that politics is corrupting higher education, to paraphrase Roger Kimball. To do so invites media attention to our textbooks, as was the case just last week on the Rush Limbaugh Show.[1] To do so invites departmental discord and strife, as past events at the University of Texas have taught us.

And yet, we must continue to make our classrooms vital places where students learn not only the various conventions of academic writing, but also the power of communication to change things, to transform. Academic discourse must help us and our students create community in a world that often seems torn apart by difference. As my title suggests, I want to know how the various forms and functions of academic writing have anything to do with educating ourselves for our whole lives, and by this I mean all of our multiple identities and our multiple dreams for ourselves. To be successful, we need to teach students conventional forms and better analytical skills, but also we need to encourage them to dream, to think in new cycles and to have visions for the future that are hopeful.

Some details from my personal history explain why I care about these issues. One of the things I have learned about rhetoric from feminist theory, especially bell hooks, is how very important it is to position oneself clearly with one's listeners or readers, especially when the subject is complicated.[2] My experience in this profession will resonate with some of you, particularly those who were in school during the late sixties or early seventies. Others will have had entirely different experiences, and you will agree or disagree with me for your own reasons, but I also hope that we have common professional ground.

I was born in 1947, and promptly nicknamed "Lilly," which was extremely appropriate, given the nature of my middle class, lily-white surroundings in central Florida. Our neighborhood was typical of many built by those seeking to forget what they had experienced during the Great Depression and World War II. Our home was my father's "castle" and my mother was the superwoman who ran it and orchestrated the lives of the children she considered "gifted." Our world was fairly homogenized, as many were in the 1950s. I recall hearing murmurs in the neighborhood when a Cuban doctor bought a house during the first wave of Cuban immigration before Castro's revolution. He was very "light-skinned," they said, and welcome, of course, but no one invited him or his family to dinner. I had to travel to North Carolina to my grandparents' homes to actually meet any people of color whose names and histories were accessible to me. There, as a small child, I saw my father's hand remain at his side when a friend from his childhood extended his hand in friendship, a hand that happened to be black. This act, which is indelibly recorded in my memory, made no sense to me, coming as I did from that lily-white world where white hands clasped in greeting all the time.

Perhaps, then, you can imagine my surprise when I read Zora Neale Hurston's *Their Eyes Were Watching God* and learned of another world I had never seen even though it was only a few miles down the road. I am still educating myself about that world down the road. Melissa Fay Greene's *Praying for Sheetrock*, which describes the lives of black and white families in a county intersected by Highway 17, is literally about the road we took every summer on our way back to North Carolina. My world in Florida is gone now, bulldozed and rebuilt as a fantasy world where athletes go when they win medals and diamond rings. It is no longer lily-white, but the people there still attempt to hold on to other kinds of fantasies.

I am a dreamer from that world, but until I went away to college, my dreams were, for the most part, ordinary. As Adrienne Rich suggests, my vision was formless and my thinking ran in the old cycles. The only hint of something else was that my high school counselor complained that I had an exaggerated sense of my personal rights when I refused to take the home economics course required for graduation from a Florida high school. I didn't even know the word "sexist" then; I just knew that I couldn't allow my dreams to be limited to cutting out dress patterns and going on tours of mobile home parks where we were supposed to learn how to finance a home with a kitchen like Betty Crocker's.

The writing that I did in high school was mainly summarization. The only essays that I recall at all were a halting attempt to describe the architecture of Frank Lloyd Wright, largely plagiarized by stringing together quotes from several books, and a term paper on becoming a psychologist, complete with notecards and an outline written at the last minute. Writing at that time was not a source of discovery or a way of knowing for me. I learned patterns of paragraph development and parts of speech, but I did not learn to write. I did not feel the power of the written word to change anything.

In 1965, I went off the college in yet another lily-white world, though it is now, I am told, a more colorful place. That institution began a radical transformation during the years I was there, as others did across the country, but my courses still reflected old patterns. Nearly all of the important writing that I produced was extracurricular, not a part of my "formal" education, which is one of the reasons why Anne Gere's address last year was so meaningful to me. My final exams were interrupted by the deaths of Bobby Kennedy and Martin Luther King. My real literacy education was about what was happening in the streets. [There] . . . for example, is a poem that I found outside the classroom, a poem that I have carried in my heart for twenty-six years. . . .

That is Countee Cullen's "Epitaph For A Poet." It might have been the first piece of writing by an African American that I had ever read, for the anthologies of literature in my high school and even in the "southern literature" class that I took at Florida State University in 1970 were still lily-white. I could hardly believe that it could have been written by an African American. I could also not imagine that this African-American man was more educated than my father. Nothing in my childhood world nor in my segregated education had prepared me for this poem. It came to me from an alternative source, from the person who was the most influential teacher I had throughout late adolescence and early adulthood. This was Joan Baez, whose album, *Baptism: A Journey Through Our Time*, introduced me to poetry that mattered and politics that I was supposed to participate in. These things inspired me to write on my own, outside of school.

On the *Baptism* album, Baez read and sang other poems,
anti-war poems like Wilfred Owen's parable about Abram and
Isaac. . . . This was the first time that my old Sunday school
lessons had any connection with the world in which I lived. And
Norman Rosten's "Guernica," about the little children slain in
Guernica, little children just like those in Sarajevo, Palestine,
Somalia, or Haiti today. . . .

And Walt Whitman's "I Saw The Vision Of Armies":

> I saw battle-corpses, myriads of them,
> And the white skeletons of young men—I saw them;
> I saw the debris and debris of all dead soldiers;
> But I saw they were not as was thought;
> They themselves were fully at rest—they suffer'd not;
> The living remain'd and suffer'd—the mother suffer'd,
> And the wife and the child, and the musing comrade suffer'd,
> And the armies that remained suffer'd.

These, my most important literacy lessons, were poems I found
on a folksinger's record, outside the classroom, away from the
places where literature was supposed to be affecting my life. So
I left my lily-white world and began to learn about gaps, especially the gaps in my supposedly privileged education. I joined in
marches and went off to teach high school English in a predom-
inantly African American community where the average income
per family in the county was $3,000. I began to try to figure out
how I would teach these students to read and write, why and
how they might or might not want to learn to talk like me. I
learned a lot from them about the literatures and cultures of
people who did not talk like me. Then and since, writing has
also helped me to understand many issues in my personal and
professional worlds. It has helped me feel a sense of personal
power in my work for social change, and it has helped me with
my own personal transformations.

But the main insight I have about my own literacy history
is that none of the important or meaningful writing I have ever
produced happened as a result of a writing assignment given in
a classroom. None of it. And I had some good teachers. And,
unlike many of our students, I was one of the ones for whom
education supposedly worked, considering that I have a plaque
with the word "Valedictorian" on it. In the ninth grade, Warrene
H. Fugitt gave me A's for my book reports, all of which I have

forgotten, but she also wrote on the board one day a line from Robert Browning that I wrote down in a private journal she never saw: "Ah, but a man's reach should exceed his grasp, Or what's a heaven for?" In college, I produced more "A" papers in a class taught by James McCrimmon, whose textbook in its multiple editions is legendary, but they were exercises in form, practice-writing that would prepare me for something else, later. So much of my education seemed to be about "later."

Foss, Foss and Trapp, writing about Foucault, observe that he "saw his experience in the French educational system as a continual postponement of the promised secret knowledge. In primary school, he was told that the most important things would be revealed in the lycée. At the lycée he was told he would have to wait until his final year, only to be told at that point that the knowledge he wanted was to be found in the study of philosophy, which would be revealed at the university level" (210). The rest of his life was a search for knowledge, an archeological dig to find the secrets and structures of the knowledge he so desperately sought.

Though I hardly compare the range of my intellect to Foucault's, I can identify with parts of his quest. Like Foucault, I and many others of my generation needed alternative sources, alternative visions to learn to think in new ways, to find visions and dreams that didn't run in the same patterns. What I dream about today is that we might *more often* make our classrooms places that connect with the world outside, the here and now; places that show students the power of writing to transform— writing that is not always about later, about jobs and careers, but writing that is about themselves as people, as individuals and as citizens of various communities.

I feel a strong sense of community with colleagues in CCCC who have tried to make education and the teaching of writing "relevant" as we used to say in the 60s and 70s, but finding that sense of solidarity is more complicated than it used to be. Relevant for what? From whose perspective? Our old revolutionary rhetorics are not working. The influence of identity politics has made us cautious, fearful that we would or would not be perceived as "politically correct," depending upon our politics. Within our own profession, we now have significant differences that make it difficult for us to communicate with each other, let alone decide on curriculum, textbooks, or pedagogies. I know first-hand from the politics of my own institution that many people have a vision for education very different from mine.

In fact, it may be because we as a profession have already been transformed in so many ways so quickly that we have a whole new set of problems. As a profession, we are conflicted about the roles we and other faculty members should play in literacy development. If we read Bizzell and Herzberg's *Rhetorical Tradition* from cover to cover, as I just did this quarter in a rhetorical history seminar, we read about rhetoric's fall from grace in western curricula. At the turn of this century, as English departments in higher education established the study of literature and literary criticism as their primary interests, rhetoric and composition became merely a "service" that these departments provided. The conflicted goals of English and composition were summarized in Maxine Hairston's CCCC chair's address in 1985 when she urged us to separate ourselves from departments that put us "at the bottom of the social and political scale" (275). During the 1970s, and especially after Hairston's rallying cry, we sent the message that we were an emerging (now middle-aged) field with a body of professional research and theory that could account for literacy development and generate methods for turning a generation of students into more literate readers and writers. We claimed we had found ways to restore rhetoric to its central and rightful place in the curriculum. Our institutions have, in many cases, believed us and have set up expensive programs, writing centers, and computer labs where our students are supposedly being remediated, educated and trained for professional writing once they leave us.

More recently, despite Hairston's suspicion about the motive for doing so, we have centered our profession by aligning it with some of the most exciting, formerly "marginal," theoretical developments within the academy: feminist theory, multicultural and postcolonial theory, poststructuralism, and the new rhetorics with their connections to contemporary critical theory. We have learned from the black feminist theorist bell hooks about the interplay between margins and centers. In our roles as rhetoricians, we have found new alliances with those on our campuses who would see writing as a crucial site for intellectual, political, and social debate. We have even found some ways to reunite with those who had seen us as mere technicians as we talk about composition in the broader context of literacy, where reading is not separated from writing. As Hairston put it, prophetically then, "by freeing ourselves . . . And by leaving the house in which we grew up, we may finally create the strong connection between literature and composition that most of us feel is good and natural" (282).

We have accomplished a great deal, but there are problems with our success in professionalizing and theorizing our way back into the academy. Our professional solidarity may mask fundamental disagreements about pedagogical practices. In some places, our rhetorical power to convince administrators has outstripped our ability to deliver students with writing skills acceptable to institutional monitors or to employers beyond the groves of academe. We have not always reconciled our theoretical interests in the philosophical issues of language with the goals that our students and our institutions have for us. Critical theory may be helping us as academics, but is it helping our students? Has all of our transformation been more for us than for our students? Despite the efforts of many CCCC committees, including the leaders of various assessment committees and the drafters of the Wyoming resolution, we have no universally accepted professional standards or standards for writing upon which we all agree. We have not reconciled the issues of politics and power that complicate our ability to have students write about topics such as racism, cultural misogyny, class differences, abortion, nationalistic chauvinism, and homophobia.

There are, of course, broader social and historical reasons why we have not made more progress in these areas. Our profession is more complicated now than it was earlier in the country's history, or even in the 1940s when CCCC was founded. There was a time when rhetorical education was simpler, and principles and standards were easier to write. This education was predicated on a limited number of professions, a limited number of students, a limited range of types of students, and relative uniformity about the materials and goals of institutions of higher learning. It was simpler because the notion that all people should be allowed access to literacy and to academic literacy in particular did not exist. As Henry Louis Gates, Jr., reminds us in his recent book *Loose Canons*, it was illegal in eighteenth century South Carolina for African Americans to be taught to read and write.

> Be it enacted that all and every person and persons whatsoever,
> Who shall hereafter teach,
> Or cause any slave or slaves to be taught to write,
> Or shall use or employ any slave as a scribe in any manner of

Writing whatsoever, hereafter taught to write;
Every such person or persons shall, for every offense, forfeit the
sum of one hundred pounds current money (59).

Today my university at least proclaims that we do not discriminate on the basis of race, ethnicity, religion, creed, gender, sexual orientation, physical ability, or nationality. We have made
tremendous progress in naming discriminatory practices, but
we have not yet eliminated them in our classroom practices.

Rhetorical education was also simpler because, among those
hired to teach in higher educational institutions, you could
assume that there was a fairly homogeneous world view. The
complexities of language theory were largely limited to two conditions: "Truth" was obvious, waiting to be conveyed by good writing or speaking, or it was probable, waiting to be discovered by
the patterns of thinking embodied in rhetorical training. Before
the printing press, before the "information explosion" in the
twentieth century, "gathering the available means of persuasion,"
as Aristotle taught us, was intellectually demanding, but not
without boundaries. But now, the old familiar canons have given
way to Gates' loose canons; we have lost our parameters in this
postmodern world. Finally, "we" were all supposedly more alike
than we are today. When I first walked into the faculty club on
my campus thirteen years ago, I recall not seeing another woman
or a person of color in a very large room that held over 150 people. Today, as we celebrate the diversity within our profession,
we discover that we cannot always talk about a common "we."

However "we" define ourselves as we move into the twenty-
first century, we no longer have, and most of us do not want,
these limitations. We are preparing students for professions
and lifestyles we can hardly imagine in our wildest dreams. We
are teaching more of them than ever before. Our students come
from many cultures, and they range in age from early teens to
retirement age. We teach them in community colleges, in four-
year liberal arts colleges, in research universities, and in alternative programs. No wonder, then, that at the annual meeting
of CCCC, we should have to consider our goals for the teaching
of writing and communication. For a long time, we have looked
for and found common ground, common theories, common
pedagogies. As we move toward a new millennium, we, along
with our society and the planet, also have to come to grips with
difference—among ourselves, among our students, among our

institutions, among our nations as we see ourselves as global citizens.

A recent essay in *The Atlantic* entitled "Jihad vs. McWorld" suggests just one kind of tension we live with. Benjamin Barber repeats a common contemporary theme: the dialectical tension between identity politics and the struggle to build a world where we all see things through the same lens, eat the same hamburgers, wear the same brands of athletic shoes, and watch the same movies. As practitioners in the world of composition studies, some of us are confused by the rhetorical problems presented by difference vs. homogenization. This tension affects not only our view of the world, but also our language and our written texts.

If we are blessed, or cursed, with the ability to accommodate what feminist linguist Dale Spender has called a "multidimensional reality," we find ourselves changing perspectives often, really trying to see what "difference" means. Sometimes we see ourselves with a clear identity in a well-defined world. Sometimes we see ourselves as a complex of identities in a complex society. My list of identities includes, but is not limited to: baby-boomer, "white" (but with several Native American ancestors), middle-class, woman, academic with access to international conversations, middle-aged tennis player who might have been great had she started young, life partner to Rick Bowles, mother, stepmother, expatriate southerner, Presbyterian, out-of-fashion liberal, and teacher. Multiple identities, multiple languages, multiple rhetorics.

With regard to the way language works in my multiple worlds, sometimes I think truth is clear and that rhetoric and language should be transparent media for discovering and transmitting it. I remember thinking, for instance, when I sat on a jury: Did this suspect abuse this child? Yes or No? At such times, I require familiar expository forms, clear and lucid speaking and writing. At other times, the very concept of truth is so cloudy that I can hardly get my bearings or believe in a single truth. For example, what is the "real" situation in El Salvador? Whose perspective, whose version of reality, whose documents, whose language can we believe? How could we possible write about a place like El Salvador? As Joan Didion did? With her own experience of terror? But then, if we include too much of ourselves in our writing, we might find ourselves being discounted, as Didion was in a review that described *Salvador* as

"The Perils Of Joan." Or like some reporters with the lens of "objectivity" and investigative journalism?[3] Or how do we write about Bosnia-Herzogovina? Or Haiti? From what vantage point should a U.S. citizen try to describe clearly the multiple perspectives that lead to violence in eastern Europe? Or in the Israeli-occupied Palestinian territories? Or, closer to home, in Los Angeles, or New York, or in my own St. Paul? How can we possibly say all we need to say about the AIDS epidemic in simple expository essays? What else might count as evidence? Journals, fiction, film, photographs, graffiti, posters? Is it better to accept the words of Randy Shilts, author of *And the Band Played On*, before he acknowledged that he had AIDS, or do we believe more of what he wrote and said afterward? How are his words altered by his death? Does his reputation in the gay community matter as we weigh his words? What could possibly be written in a 5,000 word essay on abortion that would change anyone's mind? On complex matters such as these, we need a wide variety of forms of writing, produced from multiple perspectives, alongside a variety of other media. If form follows function, and the functions of most written language are multiple, then we need to investigate new forms.

So what does it mean to write or to learn to write from multiple perspectives? From a personal perspective, my life has been directly touched by racism, by war, by AIDS, and by the feminist movement. As I have been touched, I have changed and my language and my rhetoric have changed. Because we are in the profession we are in, many of us self-consciously reflect on these changes. This may be the one great contribution we have to make to our students, to model for them our self-reflexive analysis of our own discourse practices. Our students sometimes have difficulty imagining how radically their own language might need to change until they see how the English language has already had to change in the twentieth century. They wonder why we still talk about sexist language, but they don't wonder any more when they read textbooks written twenty-five years ago. They wonder why we stress the importance of naming particular groups in careful ways, but they don't wonder any more when they read about racial strife in newspapers written in the 1930s. They also wonder whether they should trust us when we invite them to write in a variety of forms, some of them even labeled "experimental." They also wonder, sometimes, why we don't just give them the formulas and the rules and be done with it. Although some teachers and textbooks do offer students cookbooks, most of us know that the characteristics of writing in particular fields are cloudier and harder to pin down than the recipes acknowledge. The best I can do is to model for students my own process of trying to connect myself with academic writing. They have learned, just as I did, that "self" and "first person" do not belong in academic writing, so we have much in common.

If we accept multiple perspectives, an ever-changing relationship to the concepts of "truth," rapidly changing language, and complex discourse communities as inevitable characteristics of living and writing in a post-modern world, I believe we have to encourage many different kinds of writing, and not just a variety of styles of academic discourse, but experimental writing as well. In the fall of 1992, I published an essay in *CCC* on "discourse and diversity." I included a number of samples of students' writings produced in response to my invitation to attempt something "experimental." Like many of you, I often encourage students to write in ways that are unfamiliar: problem-solution essays with more than one "right" answer, parodies of academic writing, experiments with textual space, position papers from personas different from their own, and so on. Even though all of the samples came from upper division students and from graduate student seminars, some people who read the essay thought that I was writing a radical manifesto for first-year composition, that I wanted to throw out convention and encourage students to ignore standard forms. One such respondent told me that there was no time for "alternate discourse" in the undergraduate curriculum and that I should focus on rational thought and clear exposition, rather than feminist theories of language and subjectivity. Such responses represented my worst fear: that people would see "rational" discourse as separate from the kinds of experiments I encourage, rational writing as opposed to feminist writing. A growing number of award-winning books from members of our own profession are mixing or blending different types of discourse. One of my favorites is Keith Gilyard's *Voices of the Self: A Study of Sociolinguistic Competence,* in which he juxtaposes his own personal experience of language difference with the most conventional of linguistic analyses. Many of us don't think we should separate our thinking into categories and enforce strict dichotomies, but there are many who do.

But finding our common pedagogical ground is far more complicated than simple either-or thinking about types of discourse. To assume that we can have a common language of expository rationality in opposition to what I advocated is to deny a long catalogue of differences that exist within modern (or "postmodern") postsecondary institutions. Likewise, to assume that we agree that writing in our classrooms should always be about cultural transformation is to ignore a range of differences among us. For example, there are the professional differences. Some of us are tenured, some are employed full-time but have no tenure, some are part-time, and some are students. The obvious differences in our status make us more or less willing to talk about difference. The part-time, untenured lecturer may be less likely to challenge a current-traditional paradigm than someone whose job and future are secure. But security doesn't always lead to experimentation either; often it is a ticket to complacency. Then, there are the academic aims of our institutions. Those in the most prestigious liberal arts colleges, for example, can sometimes avoid the immediate pressure to train students for jobs. While this might enable them to avoid or at least to defer the instrumental argument for conventional skills, some of the strongest proponents of "liberal arts" curricula argue loudest for conformity. The liberal arts provide, in Allan Bloom's cynical analysis, the space between an "intellectual wasteland," and the "dreary professional training" that awaits students after a baccalaureate degree (336). According to Bloom and others who share his views, the liberal arts work best when they promote a "unified view of nature and man's place in it" (347) by focusing on canonical books and rational, belletristic essays. Those who teach at public universities or in two-year colleges with a strong career orientation, with terminal degrees in majors such as law enforcement and dental hygiene, have little of this kind of luxury. Their job is to get students from point *a* to point *b* as quickly and as economically as possible. Nonprofessional reading and experimental writing are likely to be less attractive, even though their students, many of them from working-class backgrounds, may be the ones who would benefit most from interrogating the discourse practices of those in powerful positions.

A former member of the faculty at my university, Wlad Godzich, goes even further when he says that "it would not be an exaggeration to state that the effect of the new writing programs [by these he means those that have courses in writing for various fields such as business, technology, and law], given their orientation, is not to solve a 'crisis of literacy' but to promote a new culture of illiteracy, in which the student is trained to use language for the reception and conveyance of information in only one sphere of human activity: that of his or her future field of employment" (29). Godzich argues that programs in advanced, specialized composition, in league with the market forces that drive vocationalism, promote linguistic practices that fragment culture, rather than build common understanding. While he would not endorse my experimental program, he does imply that students should have instruction in "the general problematic of codes and codification in language" (29).

Within writing programs across the United States, however, there is more diversity than Godzich suggests. In many writing-across-the-curriculum programs, for example, there are disagreements between practitioners in various fields and writing specialists from our field. For example, some of our colleagues might favor the styles in works such as *The Double Helix* or Lewis Thomas's *Lives of a Cell* over technical reports and design specifications. They might see "good" scientific writing as philosophical speculation by major scientists, often expressed in genres and on topics fairly far removed from the work that earned them their reputations. We are also familiar with the well-intentioned attempts of our colleagues who try to help students produce "good" social scientific writing, in active voice, with strong verbs and excised prepositional phrases. Such instruction is often criticized when professors in their home departments produce an entirely different style, often what is called "bad" writing in our classes, and wonder why their students' thinking was so subjective and loose. As many members of our profession have noted, discourse communities are not nearly so uniform as our textbooks sometimes suggest. As Joseph Harris has put it, "I think we dangerously abstract and idealize the workings of 'academic' discourse by taking the kinds of rarified talk and writing that go on at conferences and in journals as the norm, and viewing many of the other sorts of talk and writing that occur at the university as deviations from or approximations of that standard" (20).

Nevertheless, there are still some among us who believe that all we really need are uniformity, order, clarity, rules and principles. Allan Bloom argues, for example, that this democracy is really an anarchy, because there are "no recognized rules for citizenship and no legitimate titles to rule" (337). E. D. Hirsch and many others plead for a standard curriculum, standard ways of thinking, shared reading—common ground, in other words. On the other side, there are those who believe that difference is everything, that we should celebrate it in all forms and reject homogenization. Within our own profession, we can name those who represent these political and philosophical poles. In this address, I have argued for diversity because I believe that calls for standardization often mask white, middle-class, male-dominated traditions. Nevertheless, I want to be clear that I do not believe that diversity is an end in itself. As we try to move from "one" right way of thinking and being, let's not get stuck at the stage of "many" right ways of thinking and being, or what we criticize as "hopeless relativism." In some ways, the history of rhetoric is the conflict between those who would spell out rules for rhetorical forms vs. those who would invent new forms to construct new meanings. Surely there are times and places for difference and disagreement and times and places for commonality and community.

Richard Lloyd Jones, in an eloquent vision of our profession, will help me to return to terra firma: "We *can* help students in a democracy understand how language both isolates and builds individuals—all at the same time—and how if we are to live together peaceably we have to learn how we are shaped by discourse as much as we shape discourse" (496). And then he offers some very practical advice: "We need to decide what teaching things we do that are too important to lose, what we can give up with no more than a token fight" (496).

What can we give up with no more than a token fight? I have a long personal list of things I can give up: silly arguments about posture and position, quibbles over the fine points of pedagogical practice, technicalities of writing assessment, narrow conceptions of modes and genres, the need to control my students' writing, and on and on. What things are too important to lose? I put one thing on my list, and after that many other things seem less important: the opportunity to see students grow, not only on the pages of their papers, but also as individuals and as citizens of larger communities. The kind of growth that I'm talking about is the ability to imagine something different, to see things in a new way, to think outside the boundaries of the familiar. That we have to do this is inescapable. Tradition and reform, permanence and change, anarchy and civilization.

These pairings are familiar to us because change is inevitable. But my words have been about the freedom to imagine for ourselves what the changes ought to be. I have chosen to speak on the connections between discourse and transformation in the academy because the pressures to conform and to reproduce are so very powerful. I find myself turning again and again to Freire's *Pedagogy of the Oppressed*, especially to this passage:

> The central problem is this: how can the oppressed, as divided, unauthentic beings, participate in developing the pedagogy of their liberation? . . . . As long as they live in the duality in which *to be* is to *be like*, and to *be like* is to *be like the oppressor*, this contribution is impossible. (33)

If the one way we know to *be* is to *be like*, our visions will continue to run in the old cycles. If we don't understand history, as the saying goes, we are doomed to repeat it. If we can, as Cixous implied, only write our stories to someone else's memory, we will invent courses, syllabi, writing assignments, genres, organizations, institutions, journals, conventions, panel papers, special interest groups, and occasionally even chair's addresses that are entirely familiar. We will not transform. My dream for all of us is that we cherish what is valuable from tradition and that we continue to find new ways of thinking, writing, and acting in the world. This is our common ground in the groves of academe.

Jim Berlin, whom we will remember throughout this convention, helped us to see different pedagogical practices built around our understanding of how language works, either as a transparent vehicle for transmitting reality, as a way of constructing reality, as a way of getting at cultural knowledge, or as a way of exploring individual voice. It was important for our profession to see how our own theoretical positions with regard to language, society, and truth influence the pedagogical practices we choose. I have attempted to place these practices within the dialectic of identity politics and society's aims for education.

Let me conclude now with the rest of Langston Hughes' poem from the book I used the first year I taught:

> Hold fast to dreams
> For when dreams go
> Life is a barren field
> Frozen with snow.

I no longer believe that I can change the world, as I did when I sang along with Joan Baez, but I do believe that I can change my own discourse practices, and in so doing, I may inspire some students in my classrooms. Kenneth Burke taught us a long time ago that rhetoric is the use of language to form attitudes and to influence action. I invite you to use writing to dream about transformations for all of us.

Acknowledgments: Students in my "Feminist Writing Seminar" in the spring of 1994 read my paper and offered many suggestions for additions and notes; they helped me enormously as I tried to turn the spoken words into a written text. Jane Harred was working on the dissertation cited in the notes while I was writing my speech, and traces of our many conversations about authorship appear in my work. That I continue to learn from my students is one of the many reasons why I love our profession. My colleague Lisa Albrecht saw me through this process from the vaguest prewriting to the final draft. Like Cixous, she never fails to push me beyond my comfort level, and I am always glad when I take her advice and take more risks.

Notes

1. The recent textbook co-authored by Andrea Lunsford and John Ruszkiewicz, *The Presence of Others*, was the focus of Limbaugh's comments about the politics of instruction on Limbaugh's show in March of 1994.

2. My essay entitled "Discourse and Diversity," published in *CCC* in 1992, contains a fuller discussion of the connections I try to make between feminist theory and writing.

3. I am indebted to Jane Harred's brilliant work on literary journalism, *Never a Copy: The Conflicting Claims of Narrative Discourse and Its Referent in the Literary Journalism of Truman Capote, Hunter S. Thompson, and Joan Didion.* I recommend her discussion of narrative theory to all who are interested in the question of perspective in nonfiction writing.

Works Cited

Baez, Joan. 1968. *Baptism: A Journey through Our Time.* Vanguard, VSD-79275.

Barber, Benjamin R. 1992. "Jihad vs. McWorld." *Atlantic*, March; 53–62.

Bizzell, Patricia, and Bruce Herzberg. 1990. *The Rhetorical Tradition: Readings from Classical Times to the Present*. Boston: Bedford.

Bloom, Allan. 1987. *The Closing of the American Mind*. New York: Simon.

Bridwell-Bowles, Lillian. 1992. "Discourse and Diversity: Experimental Writing within the Academy," *CCC* 43: 349–68.

Conley, Verena Andermatt. 1991. *Hélène Cixous: Writing the Feminine*. 2nd Ed. Lincoln: University of Nebraska Press.

Didion, Joan. 1993. *Salvador.* New York: Simon.

Foss, Sonja K., Karen A. Foss, and Robert Trapp. 1991. *Contemporary Perspectives on Rhetoric*. 2nd Ed. Prospect Heights, IL: Waveland.

Freire, Paulo. 1970. *Pedagogy of the Oppressed.* Translated Myra Bergman Ramos. New York: Seabury.

Gates, Henry Louis, Jr. 1992. *Loose Canons: Notes on the Culture Wars*. New York: Oxford University Press.

Gere, Anne Ruggles. 1994. "Kitchen Tables and Rented Rooms: The Extracurriculum of Composition." *CCC* 45: 75–92.

Gilyard, Keither. 1991. *Voices of the Self: A Study of Language Competence*. Detroit: Wayne State University Press.

Godzich, Wlad. 1984. "The Culture of Illiteracy." *Enclitic* 8.1–2: 27–35.

Greene, Melissa Fay. 1991. *Praying for Sheetrock*. New York: Fawcett.

Hairston, Maxine. 1985. "Breaking Our Bonds and Reaffirming Our Connections." *CCC* 36: 272–282.

Harred, Jane. 1994. *Never a Copy: The Conflicting Claims of Narrative Discourse and Its Referent in the Literary Journalism of Truman Capote, Hunter S. Thompson, and Joan Didion*. Diss. University of Minnesota.

Harris, Joseph. 1989. "The Idea of Community in the Study of Writing." *CCC* 40: 11–22.

Hughes, Langston. 1966. "Dreams." *Reflections on a Gift of Watermelon Pickle*. Ed. Stephen Dunning, Edward Lueders, and Hugh Smith. Glenview, IL: Scott, 129.

Hurston, Zora Neale. 1978. *Their Eyes Were Watching God*. Urbana: University of Illinois Press.

Kimball, Roger. 1990. *Tenured Radicals: How Politics Has Corrupted Higher Education*. New York: Harper.

Lloyd-Jones, Richard. 1992. "Who We Were, Who We Should Become." *CCC* 43: 486–96.

Lunsford, Andrea A., and John J. Ruszkiewicz. 1994. *The Presence of Others: Readings for Critical Thinking and Writing*. New York: St. Martin's.

Pilger, John. 1983. "Having Fun with Fear." Rev. of *Salvador* by Joan Didion. *New Statesman* 6: 21.

Rich, Adrienne. 1979. *On Lies, Secrets and Silences: Selected Prose 1966–78*. New York, Norton.

Spender, Dale. 1985. *Man Made Language.* 2nd Ed. London: Routledge.
Thomas, Lewis. 1974. *The Lives of a Cell: Notes of a Biology Watcher.*
    New York: Viking.
Watson, James D. 1968. *The Double Helix: A Personal Account of the
    Discovery of the Structure of DNA.* New York: Atheneum.

Chapter 14

A Collage of Time:
Writing and Ritual in Women's Studies

E. M. Broner

I am a collage of my time, of the various movements through which I have read, taught, and marched.

—E. M. Broner

The Times

I taught for a quarter of a century at a large university located in the inner city of Detroit, whose enrollment rose and fell as job opportunities became available or were nonexistent. Around the university, on the stoops of the falling down houses, sat two generations of the unemployed. With unemployment a legacy, the citizens of the city could not prepare themselves for a different life.

The casual using or throwing away of the citizens of a city was impressed upon me. My English classes, when I first began as an instructor, had a substantial number of African Americans. The Pell Grant allowed mothers on welfare to return to class, or to get "off the life" of the streets. I would see, in night classes, my older male students, tired from a day "on the line," the assembly line, often in the boiler room, but touchingly eager to learn.

In those early 60s, the Civil Rights movement was important on campus. In my own English Department, one writing student, Viola Liuzu, went down South to help out in the Selma,

Alabama, march and was murdered, and one instructor, Donald Hope, on a Freedom Ride, was so beaten by truncheons that he died a year later.

Movements Begin in Literature

Writers have their fingers on the pulse. My writing students, before the declared Civil Rights movement, wrote stories of strife, the Caucasians for the first time from the point of view of the African American, while the African American students spoke of what had been silenced before, listing the police violence against them or, later, the careless shooting by the National Guard, from the '67 "riots." They also wrote of a childhood of poverty. One young African American read a poem called "Stomping Roaches at 2 A.M." that became a metaphor for how he and many others had lived.

Another metaphor of that time was "breaking out," and I had nuns as students, still in habit, often writing stories that took place in prison, in confined space, until some of them left the Mother House.

The Vietnam anti-war movement went on for years, and there was a different metaphor, the "trial." There were many trials during that period. The war itself was on trial. I assigned my students to the various sensational trials—or to read the transcripts published in the daily press—and then to write their own trials. We read of the Chicago Seven, and my students wrote Kafkaesque trials of people being charged they knew not what for and judges making injudicious decisions. We were involved in the trial of one man who had been a student at the university. He formed a group called the White Panthers, harassed by the police for having integrated housing, jazz concerts, and poetry readings. Marijuana was planted at this house near campus and large-scale arrests by the vice squad ensued, including the arrest of one of my young colleagues from the English Department who had gone there to visit his student. Ultimately, the White Panthers became a national cause. Those from our class who went to the trial witnessed the organizer of the White Panthers brought in, handcuffed, with the marks of a savage beating still upon him.

Then there was the Vietnam Veterans Against the War, a mock trial set in Detroit, at which the returning veterans threw their medals into waste baskets, each bitterly confessing to an atrocity he had committed.

"I am William Calley," one after another repeated, referring to the soldier who led a troop that participated in killing the innocents of a Vietnam village.

What was in the air was in the classroom. In Playwriting, we were performing dramatic exercises. I asked the students to identify the essence of themselves and to dramatize it. One student, a compulsive talker, filled our ears as he talked his way around the room. He was into Transcendental Meditation, more explanation than meditation. An older student, a Vet with a prematurely grey beard, held his arms stiffly out, like the figure of Justice. His stance was held for a frighteningly long time, and we worried that he was autistic until he gradually relaxed. Could Justice be meted out? Was there justice in the years he had spent in the jungle? During another exercise, we told our dreams. The Vet had a recurring nightmare: a battalion marching, closer, closer, the sound deafening until the army had marched over him. He dreamt of his death, and then he dreamt of our deaths. After the war, the clammy feel of death still pervaded his work.

I told my students, "We are witnesses in our time."

And so we came unto the 70s.

I am convinced that the Women's Movement had its origins in the university. There were the academic pursuits, rigorous, exploratory, adventurous in that new field, but we had other things on our minds in the beginning of the movement.

It was often necessary to send our young women on the "Jane Route," to Chicago, to get abortions. That "Underground Railroad" was, more likely than not, run out of the religious organizations of college campuses. In those early years, our women were fugitives. Then the law was changed, and the women emerged from silence, hearing their own voices, telling the hidden stories. At the Speak Outs on campus, they bravely testified to their experiences with abortion.

There were other Speak Outs. Those women who had graduated from the professional schools returned to tell the undergraduates about sexual harassment of women in the classrooms of the schools of law and medicine, but sternly encouraged the audience to honor their ambitions and assured them that they would eventually win.

What did this have to do with Women's Studies? We were not academicians in the ivory tower. In fact, we often had no tower, no home base at all. In the beginning of the teaching of

Women's Studies, there was a patchwork department at Wayne State—or, even, UCLA—made up of English, history, psychology. Few of the instructors were tenured and they realized, sadly, that this new subject, these experiences and the resultant writings, would not lead to approval at the university tenure committee.

Some of us changed our teaching tactics. I, with writing seminars, had long been informal in manner and dress. I had come down from the podium to join in the circle. Student participation, we learned, educated *us*. Certainly, the diaries that many Women's Studies teachers assigned gave us, their instructors, the texture of the students' lives, their physical safety, even their economics (the Pell student on low stipends worrying about whether to exchange "favors" with the gas station attendant for a full tank).

Class discussions were often so rich that at least two landmark books, both brought out in 1976 (*The Mermaid and the Minotaur* by Dorothy Dinnerstein, a psychoanalytic landmark, and *The Female Imagination* by Patricia Meyer Spacks, feminist literary criticism), gave credit to the students for the collaborative effort.

We in English literature helped the canon to change from the male experience to the acceptance of women whose work would be listed among the modern classics, like Virginia Woolf. In the mid-70s we read of the utopia/dystopia in Marge Piercy's *Women on the Edge of Time*, of mysticism and rebellion in Margaret Atwood's *Surfacing*, of the strange matrilineage in Maxine Hong Kingston's *The Woman Warrior*. My African American students felt their experiences verified in the works of Alice Walker and Toni Morrison and in the short stories collected by Mary Helen Washington in *Black-Eyed Susans*. Women students who were raised Catholic recognized their tales in *Final Payments* by Mary Gordon. We were not strangers in the land any more.

I was starting to get older students, many in their forties, who had married and raised their children, and yet longed for completion of that student part of their lives. I had known some of these women myself in high school, and to see them sitting in the auditorium or seminar room with a multitude of pens, with thick notebooks and attentive faces, was one of my happiest teaching experiences. These women were on the road to change. They did not know then that many of their marriages would fail as the wives changed and the husbands did not. I even received letters from some husbands accusing me of teaching dangerous material. Knowledge is dangerous.

Teaching, then, was action, but writing was my true activism. I wrote *Her Mothers* (Holt, Rinehart and Winston, 1975) about a new kind of search, not the classical hunt of a son searching for his missing father, but mother and daughters searching for themselves in their journeys to one another. Three years later, in 1978, in *A Weave of Women* (Holt, Rinehart and Winston), I wrote of connection rather than separation in a utopian community located in Jerusalem. Jerusalem, the site of the three male religions, also had, deep in the soil, the *teraphim*, the idols of an earlier culture, and there was room, once again, for a women's religion.

The Teaching

At UCLA, in 1979, I demanded a change in classroom style; classes were traditionally taught, with peacock professor, perhaps teaching Poetry of the Romantic Era, striding up and down the stage with an auditorium full of adoring students looking up at him. I demanded a class size where we had the possibility of becoming community and could sit in a circle and hear one another's tales. For some reason, I got what I asked for.

In one of the classes, "Women as Tale Bearer," I asked the students to interview their mothers, aunts, and grandmothers as sources of history, with their papers prepared for presentation to the class.

"Telling the tale," I told them, "is the way we hear who we are, and writing the tale is our way of incorporating it into our history."

Subjects of the published books we read were: "The Immigrant Tale" with Tillie Olsen's *Tell Me a Riddle*; the "Urban Tale" with Grace Paley's *Little Disturbances of Man*; the "Tale of the Black Community" from Mary Helen Washington's *Black-Eyed Susans*; the "Historical Tale," from Susan Cahill's *Women and Fiction*, and the *Gothic Tales* from Isak Dinesen. But it was the reading of the interviews, or learning of the material the students located in trunks in the attic—diaries of great-grandparents who came over the Donner Pass, or of an Italian great-grandmother who worked slavishly as a cook in the lumber camps—that altered my students. They had not conceived of daily heroic actions or of the possibility that their foreign grandmothers could triumph over impossible circumstances. Those readings were the great teachers for all of us.

In a small seminar I also taught "Matriarchy and Myth," with topics like "Woman as Pioneer," with Harriette Arnow's *The Doll-maker*, "The Myths of the Black Mother" with Toni Morrison's *Song of Solomon*, "The Myths of the Chinese Mother" with Maxine Hong Kingston's *The Woman Warrior*, and of "Mother as Connection/ Disconnection" with Adrienne Rich's *Of Woman Born*.

My students, affluent Hollywood babies who wore T-shirts reading: I LOVE BARBRA or I LOVE JANE, found a new kind of history other than celluloid and new topics under which to organize their lives and academic concerns, combining the smeared notebooks of the private self with the presentation of those hidden voices, so their ancestors became acknowledged public selves.

From the Midwest to the West to the Mideast

In 1975, I taught at Haifa University, situated on top of Mount Carmel, overlooking the harbor of the Mediterranean. There was no such thing as Women's Studies in the land, but I turned my English literature classes into that very thing.

In English Composition, I had my students translate the work of their women poets, songwriters, and prose writers into Hebrew. Anthologies of Israeli writing were being published in English with no women in the table of contents. It was an appealing assignment for the students, especially translating the popular culture of songs. This was during the War of Attrition, and many of the songs were written by women longing for peace, such as Nomi Shemer's "We Are Both from the Same Village," which sang of two boy friends of the same age, accent, and height, each going off to war, but, one is "crossing the green field," and the other is "lying behind the fence."

At the end of the semester, in June 1975, we brought out a mimeographed booklet of the class stories and poetry. I wrote the foreword:

> The teaching of English is the writing of English. In Women's Literature we read the writings of contemporary women authors and paralleled them by keeping journals of our fictive selves. If

we read the "father" poems of Diane Wakoski, Sylvia Plath, or Anne Sexton, we wrote our own "Searching for Father." If we read Adrienne Rich's *Diving Into the Wreck*, we explored the sunken vessels of ourselves. We "surfaced" with Margaret Atwood's *Surfacing*. We wrote of our "Sanities and Insanities" with Sylvia Plath's *The Bell Jar*. We explored the "Myth of the Older Woman" with Doris Lessing's *The Summer Before the Dark*. We were charters and cartographers of ourselves.

Teaching the first Women's Studies class—under the guise of Contemporary Literature—was very hard. I could not reach the students. Our cultures were different (as I discovered again when I taught in Israel seven years later).

Some of my assignments were so shocking to the students (i.e., Write of Your Daily Madness) that they reported me to the chair, an American, who stuttered, seemed fearful, but was of stout heart: "T-t-try it. S-s-stick with it!" he encouraged them.

On the day of the assignment on "Sanities and Insanities," the class was silent for the first ten minutes of the period. Then a tall, voluptuous young woman rose.

"I am mad," she announced.

"Sit down!" said a self-conscious faculty wife, "or they'll think you're really *meshugah*."

But the young woman continued.

"I stood outside of my ex-husband's apartment building. He had taken my dog Whiskey. I called Whiskey all the Sabbath, through all the night, until, this morning, when Whiskey jumped out of the window into my arms. I went home to wash before class. So, you can see, I am mad."

There was silence until another student said, at last, "You're not mad. It wasn't the dog you were calling."

A closeness developed, despite our age differences—from twenty (after the army) to seventy, or our lands of origin—from Romania, Poland, Russia, Iraq, the States, to Israel, or from their politics, from left of Labor to right of Likud. Still, in the tradition of Women's Studies classes, they became a community and provided a safe space for one another. I would invite them down the mountain to my apartment in the *Merkaz*, the center of Haifa. Perhaps this is more common of Women's Studies, but our lives were continuous. This group, a mixture of everything in the land, after class would bus down *Har Carmel* and proceed to prepare a meal, energetically cutting the salad into the small pieces of scallion, tomato, cucumber, and pepper with lemon for the Israeli salad. And we would cook chicken together and sit together, our lives an extension of our class. I kept kosher so the religious students could participate in this group activity along with the others.

When our primitive mimeographed publication came out, the class had a party. They honored me for coming and were unhappy that yet another popular teacher was attracted to the romance of the land but then would depart, leaving them to their own devices.

They need not have worried. They had become very resourceful during that course: they had left the comfort of their *mamaloshen*, mother tongue, to write feelingly in a foreign one. They learned in that class not to be so European, stiff, and shy away from intimacy, but, most of all, they discovered that by reading works by women and about women they learned about themselves.

And what did I discover about myself? That I could be an innovator and a leader, not just in the privacy of my studio but in the classroom, at home, and abroad.

It was 1983 before I was to teach again in Israel, this time in Jerusalem, at Hebrew University on top of Mount Scopus, for a summer course combining Israelis and Americans. Hebrew University was the first of the Israeli universities to establish Women's Studies, under Women and Gender. I was to add a new element to Women's Studies, the spiritual component.

I did not realize, however, that, despite having "safe space" on top of a mountain, in a classroom of all women, that the cultural differences between the Israeli and American students almost destroyed the course.

The complaints came largely from the Israelis: the Americans did not show sufficient respect; they were always touching the Israeli women and kissing them on the lips instead of, in the European style, on both cheeks. The Americans were too glib and easily confessional. The Americans were intrusive, asking personal questions. Worst of all, the American women were too safe, unlike the Israelis, who had suffered losses from the actual wars and from living under siege in the wars of attrition. All in all, they said, the American women were spoiled. The American women, in turn, found the Israelis interruptive in the classroom, rude, contradictory, and know-it-alls.

I did not know how to bridge this difference, but one exercise, which threatened to split us even more deeply, turned, instead, into healing us.

The holiday of *Tisha B'Av*, commemorating the loss of the great temples, came in the middle of the summer, during our study course. It is a time of lamentation and of study. The synagogues are open all night; homes become study salons as one reads and learns until dawn. It is customary to read Jeremiah's *Book of Lamentations* during that time. One sings *kinot*, dirges, and remembers, again from Jeremiah, that "There is no balm in Gilead."

How could we turn the classroom into a secular commemoration, a personalizing of loss?

I asked the class, "What of your own lamentations, your expulsions, exodus, alienation?"

They looked at me blankly.

"Mourn for yourselves," I said.

The Israelis could not accept such a personal assignment and could not commit it to paper. Neither their repressed feelings nor lack of ease with the English language would permit this.

However, I called upon one Israeli woman, who happened to be sitting on my right, and I asked if she would begin speaking of loss. The woman had hardly spoken at all during the daily class session. She seldom glanced in my direction. Now she rose and glared at me.

"I would not write it down," she said defiantly.

Then she told her story. She had an adopted family on a kibbutz, like many Israeli city children who were sent to the kibbutzim for the summers. There was the war, the terrible war of 1973, the Yom Kippur war, where her beloved kibbutz brother was killed. She could not bring herself to express her sorrow and sympathy to her family there and so became estranged and stopped speaking to them altogether.

"I hate you," she said to me, in front of the class, "for making me tell this story and for making me weep."

The Israeli women reacted to their compatriot with expression rather than words, but we from the States knew they were thinking, "What do Americans know of such loss?"

I turned to two American students, both mature women, both from California. One was a therapist, and the other was a high school teacher. The therapist, with great difficulty, blowing her nose, speaking wetly, read her lamentation.

To paraphrase: "How I honor my brave son, caught between the extremes of emotions, from manic to depressive, from soaring joy to the depths of despair. With what dignity he has lived these many years in a mental institution."

The class became very quiet. The Israelis, who usually kept up a buzz of conversation, were silenced.

The second student, a slender, energetic woman who taught the children of Hollywood stars at a Beverly Hills high school, read her assignment: "I have learned to love my daughter as a four-year-old, even though she is thirty. I visit her and we play together as we did in her babyhood and I know she will never be more than four. And I never question my love."

After the two women had finished reading their assignments, stumbling over the words, interrupting themselves to gain self-control, the Israeli women turned to embrace them, having learned that there were no Olympic games in suffering.

Shabbat, the Sabbath, was coming. The song of the Sabbath is *L'cha Dodi*, welcoming the bride of the holiday. It is a love song, really. And the other great love song in the land is from the Bible, *Shir Ha'Shirim*, the Song of Songs.

I told the class that we were taking a field trip. We were to meet in the *Hamam*, the bath house, where the women were required to take careful notes. There in the steamy rooms we splashed water upon our perspiring faces, leapt from the cold to the hot tubs, lay on the roof of the *Hamam*, our bellies and breasts domes like the rounded roofs.

"You are to write a *Shir Ha'Shirim l'otzmi*, a Song of Songs to Myself," I assigned.

We were, all of us, shy, I no exception, never having appeared naked before a class.

At the next class meeting at the university I brought a plastic bag that held a cardboard, brush, comb, and scissors.

"I'm going to speak of hair," I said. "I'm going to tell hair-raising stories."

We spoke of the common expressions with "hair," "get in one another's hair," or "letting down our hair," and "hair shirts." We spoke of hair legends, of fairy tales, where the witch called, "Rapunzel, Rapunzel, let down your golden hair."

We spoke of the sadness of Orthodox Jewish women who shaved their heads at their marriages while their bridegrooms' beards and curls would become luxuriant growths. We spoke of "hair fear," in the Samson legend, and of shame, Adam and Eve covering their pubic hair in shame. One member of the group, a Christian minister, spoke of Mary Magdalene wiping the feet of Jesus with her hair.

And then we spoke of the "crowning glory" that is hair, of our mothers combing our hair, of going to the salon where the beauty operators, as my class put it, "make nice to us."

"Now," I told them, "we're going to make nice to another. We will brush the hair of the woman seated on our left."

(The woman on my right who had previously recited about her kibbutz family sat rigidly frightened, until she relaxed under the brush strokes of her seat mate.)

I brushed the long, full head of hair of the young woman on my left. The brush and comb made the rounds of the twenty women as they unpinned each other's hair. We leaned back in pleasure. Soon the room was full of fluffy, purring, curried women.

"Now sing the song of yourselves," I said, "as I assigned."

Lily wrote of her cap of grey curls and her eyes as blue as the skies over Jerusalem. Ellen honored her fingers, the long rounded nails, the strong, capable hands. Another wrote, "I am the meeting places of wet and dry in my body's cavities."

I held up the scissors.

"We're going to make a hair card," I said, "a lock from each of you. It will become a relic for our archives so that it will be known that there was great power in the room."

There was a card with a lock of Ellen's golden hair, Lily's grey curl, and the sleek black hair of the Sephardic students.

For the coming Sabbath, we braided one another's hair while the Christian minister sang, "*Lechi Dodi,* I welcome myself at Sabbath."

Our last action was writing and naming. Barbara was dissatisfied with her name. We discussed alternatives but when she discovered that *Barbara* was from *Barbarian,* connected to other lands, to being on the borders, she kept her name, for that was a brave place to be, on the borders.

Israelis are all trained in the Bible and its corresponding literature. Many were secularists but the Bible was their resource, and they all used it as a point of reference. They spoke of the secret names of God, according to the *Kabbalah.* They spoke of how Adam had named everything in the Garden, not Eve. They spoke of an early sect, the Karaites, that called the Divine Presence *Guf ha Schekhinah*, body of the Female Presence. The Essenes had their naming with an angelology. They said that, according to the Gnostics, every action was sealed by the name of God.

The Israeli women were angry that at public cemeteries, like funerals on the Mount of Olives, the Jewish women's graves were nameless, and they were often buried far from their husbands.

"On Rosh Hashana," said one, "we say, 'May your name be inscribed in the Book of Life.' What is our name, which changes when we marry, which is unrecorded when we die?"

Now in the class were two Leslies. One was in her early twenties and thought of becoming a rabbi. The other Leslie was about forty, from California, and was searching her name.

"Who named you Leslie?" we asked the Californian.

"My mother," she said, "after the movie star, Leslie Howard. She did not care about the sex of her child as long as the name was Leslie for her favorite film actor."

The younger Leslie returned from a women's *yeshivah* where she was studying; only her prayers were different. They feminized the Torah blessing for bringing girls into the world.

Altering language, I told them, is one of the first actions on the way to becoming a feminist.

The Israelis were startled by this act of taking charge of language. In 1983, they saw no reason to take part in a revolution that had barely reached their shores. A lively argument ensued as the Americans predicted that feminism was a wave that would wash up on the beaches of the Mediterranean, of the Kinneret, of the Dead Sea. (And this proved to be true.)

We could not continue our argument about altering language to make it inclusive, for we were altering Leslie. She was selecting a new name. In honor of the seriousness of this occasion, I donned a yarmulke.

"In the names of our foremothers and the energy of the women in this group," I said, "we name you what you name yourself."

Leslie, who had been named capriciously for a 1940s star, looked at the heavens and named herself *Kohava*, star.

The younger Leslie *did* go to the rabbinical school later, giving herself permission to become a different kind of rabbi. And one of the Israeli women fell in love with the German minister and came out of the closet.

When the Americans were to fly back to the States, from Lod, quite some distance from Jerusalem, the Israeli women rose before dawn to accompany them to the airport.

That was a dazzling time, those years ago, when we wrote of what we knew and did not know: of our size, our shape, our dreams, our past, our losses. And each thing we did had not been done before in the land.

Perhaps that is the most a teacher can ask.

Chapter 15

Teaching Elders:
A Journal

Mary Gordon

August 1992

I have been nominated for a Lila Acheson Wallace Reader's Digest Award. One hundred thousand dollars spread over a three-year period. The award has two goals. It wants to free writers from doing things other than their own writing that they must do to earn money, but it also wants to fold writers into the community. So to qualify for the award, each writer must choose an area of community work with which he or she would feel comfortable, which would allow him or her to make a real contribution. A friend of mine says it sounds a little like community service, a sentence in lieu of a jail sentence, given to high-class criminals, like professional athletes caught with drugs.

My feelings are mixed. Why can't people just give me money, no strings attached, no questions asked? But after a little while resenting the soft white hand of philanthropy, I'm very pleased to be doing good works, which I often feel guilty about not doing. Eager to meet kinds of people I don't usually meet: I'm awfully stuck in the white, intellectual/artistic upper-middle class/bohemian world.

When Marci from the Wallace Foundation asks what population I might like to work with, it comes to me in a flash: I'd like to work with older people. This is not entirely disinterested. My mother, who is eighty-four and in a nursing home, is perishing for lack of stimulation. I tried, and failed, to teach a writing course to her and her group. I think that maybe if

213

I work with other older people, I'll learn something that will help her.

Perhaps there is another hope I do not name, that I will find a more hopeful model for aging.

September 1992

The Wallace Foundation puts me in touch with Susan Perlstein, who runs a program called Eldershare the Arts, based in Brooklyn.

Susan went to Barnard, where I went, and where I now teach. She began as a dancer, but was always political. She used to live in a project in the Bronx, lived there for a long time until her young son was put in one too many violent situations. Then she moved to Brooklyn.

She wanted to bring the arts to people in projects. So she and her dance troupe would perform in the lobby of the project buildings. One day, a very old woman came up to her and said, "What about us?" "Nobody," she said, "ever asks the old to sing, or dance, or act, or tell their stories." Susan got the idea, then: she would bring the arts to elders and elders to the arts. She would connect the generations through the arts. On a shoestring, and with a few other committed women, she started Eldershare the Arts. They've gone into some of the toughest neighborhoods in Brooklyn, Queens, and Manhattan. They branch out into nursing homes and V. A. hospitals. They learn techniques to deal with people with limited physical abilities: Alzheimer's patients, people with dementia, the deaf, the blind.

Susan is a hopeful person. She's doing something in the community: it doesn't scare her. She works like a dog and is constantly underfunded. She is exhausted, but not depressed.

She says she'd love to work with me because it would bring a literary element to their work that hasn't been there.

All I can think is that nothing I know or am good at would be of any help to anyone they know. My high standards of language; so that a cliche or a dead word is a physical pain to me. My love of a kind of literature that is difficult and demanding of attention. My fondness for subtlety; my unease with the obvious.

When I taught at a community college I was a failure for these reasons. My students and I didn't share values. I knew that if I'd met them in any other context I would have liked them. They were studying dental hygiene, nursing, police science. If I'd met them as my dental hygienist, the cop on the beat, a nurse changing my IV, I would no doubt have felt a real human bond. But trying to convince them that nuance of language was important, that something written by someone who'd been dead 500 years could matter, I failed. I was uneasy asking them to work hard to understand something—to stay with language that seemed to exclude them. I didn't believe that it would make them better. I didn't even know why I loved it so much— was it partly that it gave me a vision of a world larger, more spacious, than the working class world I grew up in. And was that a good thing for me? That my mother did not understand what I wrote, how I lived as I lived? I didn't think I was larger-minded or larger-hearted than a lot of the kids in my old neighborhood. I just loved this stuff. And I didn't know how to communicate that to people who looked at me, wearily sometimes, cynically others, saying to me: "It's not who we are. It's not our lives."

I asked Susan what I would have to say to these people who had probably lived much more trying and adventurous lives than I did.

"Wait and see," she said. "Believe me, we know what we're doing, and it works."

"But you've never tried to bring literature in before."

"We'll work together," she said.

Susan always makes me feel like we have all the time in the world and in time everything will work itself out.

October 1992–February 1993

I spend time with Susan, and with Joanne Schultz, who coordinates things from the office, and with Peggy Pettit, who's a storyteller, and playwright, and actress. I look at the videotapes they give me and read their material. But I'm still scared; I don't see where I fit in.

Then, one day, I go with Susan to watch Peggy do a storytelling workshop with a group at the Stanley Isaacs project in the South Bronx. Peggy has worked with these people for years; the group has a real cohesion. It's partly the energy of the group itself that makes things work, but it's mostly Peggy. She's magic. She moves in a way that simultaneously suggests endless patience and limitless dynamism. Also, she finds life amusing. She likes to laugh. And she's full of ideas about how the world works; she thinks the world moves on story.

Most of the people in the group are black, as is Peggy. Susan and I are the only whites, except for one man, who's slightly younger than the others. I'm impressed with how sexy and feisty the women are; they're near my mother's age, but they're in there swinging. And trucking. Peggy tells us to pick a partner. We have to take turns pretending to be a gypsy fortune teller. One person has to tell a story and the other has to interpret it. My partner, who must be in her seventies, tells me about a man she's interested in, but she doesn't know if he's interested in her. I tell her about my daughter, who seems hell-bent on not doing what I want if she knows I want it. We listen to each other's stories. Then we have to turn to the group. We have to describe our costume as a fortune teller. Then we have to tell the other person's story, as if it were our own, and then interpret it.

The women really get into it. They are hyperdramatic gypsies. I'm much less able to be free. But after a while, I lose myself in describing my costume. And in giving advice.

I see what formal devices Peggy's been exploring: narrative, point of view, distance, and interpretation.

I wonder how I could modify this with my Barnard students. I wonder how I could get over their initial shyness, the shyness I had, the shyness these women in their seventies and eighties don't have any time for.

February 1993

I agree to participate at the Eldershare Conference. I will read at the end, but I will also take their workshops, in which they try to teach their technique. I choose a session with Susan Perlstein, on taking an oral history. She says that one good exercise is to ask the people to focus on an important historical moment, something where they existed not just as individuals but as part of a group, a nation, perhaps. She says that for us, the important date is JFK's assassination, but for elders it might be the outbreak of the First World War, the Armistice, Pearl Harbor, VE or VJ Day. Again, we choose a partner. She asks me details about what I remember, and I recall that what I felt was annoyance that everyone thinks this is real mourning but that in relation to the loss of my father, this is a minor loss, and for no one can the loss of President Kennedy have been as great as the loss of my father.

Everyone in the room has an individual experience of this day; no one was a cipher, everyone experienced history as themselves.

In the afternoon, I take a workshop with Susan Willerman, who offers two exercises: Write a letter to an ancestor you wish you'd known, asking her the questions about your past, or heritage, that can explain some things you feel are unexplained. I write to my Sicilian great-grandmother. I try to understand what it is like to be trapped in not knowing a language. She never learned English. When she became incontinent, my great-aunt sat her on the toilet all day. My grandmother, her daughter-in-law, rescued her, took her into her home, and cared for her till her death. I wish I liked my grandmother more; always, I must admire her. But her harshness, her stiff back, always intrudes. I am more like her than I was. After we do this, she asks us to remember a piece of clothing in childhood, really to be with it. She takes us through sense-memory exercises: we must feel the cloth against our skin, experience the roughness or smoothness, the freshness or mustiness of the smell. I recall my confirmation dress, which my grandmother made for me. Blue-dotted Swiss. I had to pretend to like it but what I really wanted was the one from Grant's—nylon or rayon or some hideous synthetic fiber—that everyone else in my class had.

Afterwards I talk to Susan Perlstein and Susan Willerman about dealing with Alzheimer's patients. They say a sentence that sears itself in my brain: "Always go for the intact part. That's the thing you have to find."

This is what one must find, first, in all teaching. The intact part. For my students: the shining part, the part of greatest porosity and strength.

Summer 1993

Susan and I meet to try to figure out what kind of setting I would like to teach in, and whom, from Eldershare, I would like to team-teach with.

I have never taught with anyone else. I look forward to doing it because I don't feel I know what I'm doing. If I were in a university setting, where I feel in charge, at home, I'd feel much more anxious about team-teaching. Feel that someone, however, benevolently was looking over my shoulder. Always feel that I hadn't prepared enough, that I could never prepare enough. Now I am the novice, the amateur.

I will work with Fay Ching, who's done a lot of work with Chinese elders. I see the beautiful poems she has written with them. I've also heard Fay read her own work, and I admire it.

The elders' poems are beautiful. It isn't necessary to condescend to them. They're literature.

Ideally, I'd like to teach a group of people whose cultural experience is different from mine. This impulse springs from humility, curiosity, and cannibalism. What can I learn from them that I can use in my work?

Susan and I begin visiting Senior Centers, since we determine that I don't want to work with people who are as far gone, mentally, as my mother. I've had enough of that; it's more than I can bear.

"Knowing what you can bear is an important part of good teaching," Susan says. "And remember, what's not bearable for you is interesting for someone else. Susan Willerman, for example, deals with veterans who often can't talk and have very little cognitive ability. She does drama with them. She does what she likes to do."

Susan Perlstein says it's important to do what you like to do. That's part of what makes it work.

It's not always a luxury one has in college teaching. When I began teaching at the community college, I had to teach what I didn't want to teach to people who didn't want to learn it. How could it not have been a failure?

At Barnard, I get to teach what I want to people who are eager to learn.

I wonder if the elders will be more docile than my Barnard students, more grateful, but less able. I worry about it.

Two of the centers we visit seem too prosperous. People are attended to; they don't need me. They serve populations that are largely Jewish and middle-class. This isn't anything I don't know.

There's a center in Inwood that ought to serve an Irish population, mixed with Dominicans and other Hispanics. It sounds like something I'd like, but when I go there, no one seems interested enough in my project to give it the boost it needs.

I have ideas for how the class could be a success, but without the staff's support, it can't happen.

I leave, feeling guilty. If I wanted to, I could canvas the neighborhood, visit churches, the library, clinics. I could distribute leaflets and speak to people.

The depression of the staff, though, has depressed me, and I lose hope and energy with the project. Susan Perlstein says there are many more places, that I mustn't lose hope.

April and May 1994

I have lost hope, though, and Susan has become busy, so we don't travel to retirement centers until April, and it's not until May that she sends me to Morningside Gardens, which is only ten minutes from where I live.

I'm very impressed with the social workers who run the retirement center. They assure me that I'll have a cross-cultural variety and students who are enthusiastic. One knows because she's already taught a writing course, and the interest is high.

Everything seems right about this, and we immediately shake hands on the deal.

July 1994

Fay develops breast cancer and will be too sick to participate in the project. I will be working with Susan Willerman, who's not a writer, but who has been trained primarily in theater.

This is disappointing to me; I'd been looking forward to working with Fay.

September 1994

Susan and I meet. She says she's nervous to work with me; she's not a writer; she's a little over-awed by me. I never really believe that anyone will be scared of me, but enough people have said it that it must have a grain of truth.

We agree that we'll use the opportunity to exploit our differences. She's done a lot of work in V.A. hospitals with people whose brain damage is severe, and she's learned to work through sensual, rather than intellectual information. Since I believe that most students are sensually deprived, I can't see how this would fail to be a good approach.

We agree that the first class will consist of a couple of exercises to free people up and a bit of talk about who they are and what they want.

I feel that I have no idea what to do, and I look to her for guidance. This is not something I'm used to feeling in relation to teaching.

October 1994

It is a beautiful fall day; there's a tree outside the main building of the center that is transcendentally, extravagantly yellow. I have the usual feeling of dread I have before the first day of any class; the sense that I'm an imposter and will be, any second now, found out. It's exacerbated here because I'm not sure what, if any, will be my students and my common ground.

My first look at them disappoints me. They look so healthy, so prosperous, so middle-class. They're not like the people in Peggy Pettit's class. They're enormously well-spoken. When they describe themselves, they speak of professional success, extraordinary professional success, especially for women. There are ten women and three men. The women have been teachers, social workers, executive secretaries, and hospital administrators. They've traveled around the world.

There is a racial mix, but the social class is uniform: middle.

They're not going to introduce me to the radically unfamiliar world I'd dreamed of. One man, Chinese, in his nineties, is wearing an outlandishly false-looking toupee. All of his sentences go on for at least five minutes, and they're all about his former positions in the world.

I assume they all have novels stashed in their drawers, novels they think are brilliant, novels in the pseudo-genteel style of Belva Plain.

Well, I ask myself, what did you expect?

Something more unfamiliar than this.

Susan's first exercise is one I'm not comfortable with. We have to say our name and name a quality that best describes where we are in life. Then we have to act these words out using movement.

I feel the way I felt when I was at a what were called "hootenanny masses" in the 60s, when everyone was supposed to engage in group hugs. I feel, get me out of here. Can't we diagram sentences or talk about Henry James' idea of significant form?

I don't do this. This isn't me.

When it comes to my turn, I act out: Mary, the overwhelmed.

I give them an assignment to write something about a voice that is calling out their name. I talk to them about voice: the mystery that we all have a different one, the odd thing that we can tell who someone is on the phone even if we don't know them well. We talk about what makes up voice: gender, class, ethnicity, tone, diction.

It's an exercise I do with my college and graduate students, and I'm surprised that these elders respond similarly to their younger counterparts. Except they don't fight me about gender. They all agree that gender counts. Many of the women talk about the things they weren't allowed to say.

I allow that this group may be more surprising than I thought.

They seem very comfortable working as a group, extraordinarily so for people who've just completed their first session. I have to allow that Susan's exercise, although it made me uncomfortable, might have loosened them up.

One woman already annoys me: I think, Bennington 1935. Scarf dances. Thinks she's an artist. Luckily, she's not twenty and I don't have to disabuse her. Some things with this group are easier.

This thought leads me to ponder the nature of teaching that isn't geared toward a student's future. Where you don't feel that what you do is going to have consequences for someone's maturity. Writing in a more or less pure present. Without even a ghost thought about employment. Where money simply isn't in the discourse; where there's no reason for them not to do what they want.

The next week a woman writes about her father's death. Her father died when she was the same age that I was when my father died. What she has written is exactly what I have just finished writing the week before: the anxiety that if your dead father called your name you wouldn't recognize his voice.

And her memory that as a child she heard his voice calling her name from the closet.

An identical memory of mine.

An uncanny sisterhood: the sisterhood of shared imagery, shared loss.

Her language is beautiful; she's a real writer.

She was a secretary and always wanted to write but couldn't because she was the only daughter and had to take care of her mother.

She is simultaneously a character I could have created myself, and a writer writing my text.

The familiar feeling of falling in love with a student, with a new twist: not the student as child/lover, but the student as the mother I have always wanted and not had.

November 1994

The problem of inhibited, too-correct language. The uncomfortableness with the pronoun I. The predilection for the passive voice. The apologetic beginnings when they have to read. Not unlike my students in one way, and yet in some ways very different. "I don't know whether I have the right to write. Literature is so important, such a wonderful thing in this world, what makes me think I can do it. I might not be able to do it right."

My students are not nearly so in awe of literature; it hasn't formed them as it has these elders; they haven't owed it as much. And, for better and for worse, they were educated differently.

I ask the woman who says she's afraid she can't do it right to try to remember who told her there was a right way.

She says, "All those teachers."

I say, "Which one?"

She says, "What do you mean which one. All of them."

I tell them to close their eyes. I tell them to find a face for the voice that tells them there's a right way to write and they can't do it. They must give this face a body and a name. They must call this person to the center of the room. They must give the person a blindfold and a cigarette. Then shoot them.

Everyone enjoys this very much.

I tell them for next week to create a villain.

I tell them there's only one restriction on the assignment. They mustn't try to be either kind or just.

The next week there's a real buzz in the class. All kinds of villains have come to the fore. Teachers. Brutal stepfathers. Sheriffs with dogs on the steps of segregated schools. Boys who call a teenage girl ugly. A boss who fires a young social worker for having lunch with her black colleague. The man who puts

Japanese into concentration camps. A jealous sister. A jealous mother. A brutal, abandoning father. A crippled cousin who uses her handicap to tyrannize. An aunt who hates Roosevelt. Mao tse Tung.

The world has entered the class, a world much wider than the one inhabited by students in their twenties at the university.

For a couple, this is an impossible assignment. They have lived, they say, all the time believing that nobody is all bad. They cannot, they say, write as I suggest.

"Then write a more mixed portrait," I say.

"But that wasn't the assignment."

"Who said that?" asks E. "Put that person in the center of the room, blindfold her, and shoot her."

December 1994

We write about holiday memories. Memories of poverty, of drunkenness. Of heroism. Of loss. Of great wealth. Of exclusion: none of these festivals is mine. Of the joy of being at the right place at the right time. Of failure to create joy that matches joyous memories. Smells: kitchens; a tree cut down in the Black Forest; Christmas in an embassy in Paris, walking off with the ambassador's fountain pen. Thrilling for me: more worlds opening, opening up.

I ponder the distinction between story and anecdote. And I suggest to them: story is able to handle something being itself and its opposite. Anecdote is only one thing at once. I wonder if they're interested in complicating the past, for the sake of what—some standard important to me? I don't yet know—because I'm embarrassed to ask for fear of condescension—what their standards are. How good they want it to be. How hard they want to work.

For now, it seems enough that most of them are writing.

I realize that part of my role with the students I usually teach—extraordinarily gifted young people who are eager to improve, who may even be ambitious for publication and something they would call success—is as a taskmaster. I shove the arrogant out of their complacency, I nudge, gently but firmly, the sensitive, frightened reluctant ones. More, more, I shout or whisper. You can do more. Try this. Read that. I know it's harder for you, but you must. Must.

There is no must with these students, and sometimes, as a teacher, I am unsettled by this.

January 1995

Christmas break. It sometimes shocks me how little I think about my students on breaks. I clear them out of my brain; I want that brain to be a place for my own writing. So it is always with a mixed sense of betrayal and reluctance that I return to my students after break. To pull myself out of the place when my writing is the only writing I have to think about and to turn my attention to the projects and needs of others is a struggle. Every time I tell myself that after a week I'll be back to it again, the new routine will establish itself. But always, the morning for the first class: the old reluctance, the tinge of resentment.

I never want to go back to teaching after time off. I'm always afraid. I always think I don't know how and have no right to do it.

Susan gives them an assignment. Do a self-portrait. Pay particular attention to the place you're in, and what you're wearing. I'm learning a lot from teaching with Susan. I'm learning about teaching for the present, not the future; teaching as process rather than investment. Her assignments spark the students in ways I wouldn't have been able to do; her exercises insist on the presence of the body in both the classroom and the text.

M. has been freed by Susan's assignment to write about her early life. She worked for many years in the Department of Social Security, figuring out people's benefits, preparing their checks. Someone else who couldn't go to college because she had to take care of her mother. Someone else whose father died when she was a child. The place she writes about is her aunt's house, where she is forced to move when her father dies. Another uncanny similarity; her situation was much like mine. The working mother, the mourning child, moved in with relatives. The paradisal home with father, from which you are driven out.

Her mother was a buyer of lace, which she really enjoyed. But her family forced her to get a civil service job in an office so she could have a secure pension. Every day she comes home to the terrible house of her sisters, where she has lost control of the upbringing of her child. She felt she could be happy if she could go back to being a buyer of laces, but she can't.

M. has done it: invented a real room. The heavy furniture, the heavy dishes of hard-won, fearfully clutched respectability. And the weeping mother, a slave to her pension.

When M. herself retires, she offers her services to the United Farm Workers.

Many of the people in this class have been politically active. They believe in politics, political solutions, public identities, and shared, public fates. This makes them extraordinarily youthful and hopeful. They offer me a positive model of aging that my mother's hopelessness has taken away.

Sometimes, though, I have to try to urge them out of language that is too publicly formulaic, too sloganeering, too utopian.

I never have this problem with the twenty-year-olds of the nineties.

It is a problem I love my elders for.

February 1995

We are focusing on memories of clothing. E. writes about a red dress belonging to her governess, which frightened her because it seemed so dangerously sexual.

I am full of praise for this description.

E. says: "But you see, that's the way it always is with me, always has been. I can do something good in a small way, but I never do the big things and I never finish anything."

I don't know what to say to her. "Always" has a meaning for her that it doesn't for my younger students. I have no right to tell her she's wrong, no right to tell her that it might be different from now on.

Only to say, nevertheless what you've done is beautiful.

I know this isn't enough for her.

It is enough for me, though, and we talk about that. The beautiful object, made of prose. Not for anything, but for itself.

March 1995

I have one of those days that comes belatedly sometimes in teaching, when one is humbled and grateful at the same time. Why did it take me so long, but of course, this is what I must do. What I understand for the first time is that within this class

there are two distinct groups. Those who want to work on language, and those who just want to get things done. And that I
have to be a different teacher for each of them.

Susan's more comfortable, we agree, with those who are
just kind of hanging out; she's a more patient person than I,
and a more generous one. We agree that the non-language half
of the class will receive more of her attention, and I'll focus on
the ones who want—what? More craft, more challenge. I'm trying not to call them the more serious ones, trying not to judge
them, but it's not really possible. I am who I am; I am as a
teacher the person I am in the world.

I bring in a passage of Proust: the beginning of *Remembrance of Things Past*, when he talks about the state of being in
between wakefulness and sleep. A couple of them have read it.
A few feel they have no right to be reading Proust. Just listen, I
say. I talk to them about how important it is to realize that a
state, psychic or physical, is not monochrome or monolithic: it's
a surface that must be broken up to be properly described. We
talk about breaking up experience in order to write about it.
Turning it over, looking at it from different perspectives, different angles.

E., who wrote about her dead father's voice, writes a beautiful description of being in her crib and waiting for her father to
come and get her in the morning. She says she doesn't know
how she remembers this, but it is the truth. She studies with a
woman who works on meditation techniques; for her, writing is
a spiritual journey. The truth is of, and with, God.

I take her aside afterward. "You have it," I say to her. "You're
the real thing. Do you want me to work with you privately?"

She says she has to think about it, because she's spent so
many years avoiding writing that it might be too much for her
now. She'll be eighty in September; it might be too late.

I tell her I know it's not.

"Give me some time to think about it," she says. "I'm
scared."

April 1995

The winter, although mild, keeps lingering, and people are
suffering from colds and flu. Two of the students are in their
nineties, some are in their late eighties, and every time I don't

see one of them, I worry that they're dying. And I wonder if I've done well enough by them; that if mine was their last brush with writing, was it a good enough, an enriching-enough brush? This, of course, is something I don't have to worry about with twenty-year-olds. I know that after me, there will be more. I might not know what the more will be, but I know I'm not the last chapter.

We do another exercise with their names, one that I've done successfully with my younger students. They must write a meditation on their names and say whether or not they think they've been given the right name, if their name expresses their true nature, what associations their name brings up for them, and what the context of their name—familial or historical—might be.

This seems to be a very fruitful assignment. N., who's the oldest in the class and has been nearly silent all of these months, writes a beautiful meditation on the biblical Naomi, her namesake, and the wandering of this woman with her daughter-in-law. She talks about herself as a wanderer. I'd written her off as an ex-school teacher, hobbled by respectability. She sees herself as a sojourner, a journeyer, never having settled down.

I think if God has a body or a face, it would be the face and body of D. She's a beautiful. African American with liquid movements and a magically rich voice. She's been an actress, an activist, a teacher. Now she's writing children's books. She talks about her childhood in Florida and the grief of having had to change her name every time her mother remarried. Not knowing what her real name was—her father's, her mother's. The trauma of having to take a new name at her marriage. Then the memory of having been called "fatty" and eating the chocolate bars in her grandmother's store for consolation.

A., also in his nineties, writes about the mixed exhilaration and grief of having to change his Chinese name for a Western one. It is the first time he's focused, hasn't lost himself and us in a wooly fabric of tall tales. Whatever he's saying now is the truth.

A reporter from the *Times* comes to observe and write about the class. His description of the students is condescending: they are dear old things, sitting on park benches, feeding the pigeons, tottering into the room for the shred of illumination in their drab, little lives. They're furious. They write a group letter mentioning all of their activities: theater groups, voter registration, tutoring children in Harlem, pro-choice work, teaching dance. The letter is a marvelous piece of focused outrage. It does not get printed in the *New York Times*.

May 1995

We plan a joint reading of the elders and my Barnard students. It's difficult to find dates that will be good for everyone, but finally we do, and both classes are thrilled.

I order pizza so the two groups can get to know one another, but so many of my students come late (it's finals week, and they're frazzled), and the elders feel shy in a college setting (not their turf) that very little conversation is made. And I'm frantic, as I always am, when I'm responsible for feeding more than two people at once.

I pair each elder with a young student, hoping that the readings will be an implied conversation. It works. The frames of reference are different, the elders place themselves in a more public world, and, of course, the time perspectives are radically disparate. But for all of these students, the process of writing is the same, and the enterprise is the same: How do I use language to understand being alive? The reading goes on for two hours, and no one wants to leave.

Something has happened in the world that is hopeful.

The student newspaper reports the event and quotes D. as saying, "Mary is very good at packing a lot of information into a little bit of time, which is good, because time is one thing we don't have much of, at our age."

For my younger students, the clock strikes at the end of the semester. For the elders, the clock is ticking away the last days of their lives.

June 1995

Our farewell party falls on the day when I'm moving my father's remains from one grave to another. It's something I've wanted to do for almost thirty-five years, and I've done it. I've talked to E. and to M. about it because although some of my younger friends think I'm being mad, ghoulish, or obsessive, they understand. They understand the importance of a name carved in stone, of a place to visit. They understand the tremendous importance of memory.

I tell the students I don't know if I'll be able to make it to the party, and of course they understand. But after this enormously emotional day, when I've touched a coffin with whatever is left of my beloved father—ashes, a few chips of bone—when I've prayed and thrown flowers and stones and prepared a feast for the friends who accompany me, I long to be with my elders to tell them about it.

They're thrilled for me, without ambivalence. We eat grapes and brie and drink wine. Susan and I hold each other and cry.

It's not a question of what has been accomplished. It's a question of what happened. Something entirely hopeful, entirely loving. A spot of light. An enclosed garden. Presence, and the present. A nest of language for the past. Or just, for a few hours, less than forty, perhaps a way of being in the world.

Chapter 16

Engaged Pedagogy (from *Teaching to Transgress: Education As the Practice of Freedom*)

bell hooks

To educate as the practice of freedom is a way of teaching that anyone can learn. That learning process comes easiest to those of us who teach who also believe that there is an aspect of our vocation that is sacred; who believe that our work is not merely to share information but to share in the intellectual and spiritual growth of our students. To teach in a manner that respects and cares for the souls of our students is essential if we are to provide the necessary conditions where learning can most deeply and intimately begin.

Throughout my years as student and professor, I have been most inspired by those teachers who have had the courage to transgress those boundaries that would confine each pupil to a rote, assembly-line approach to learning. Such teachers approach students with the will and desire to respond to our unique beings, even if the situation does not allow the full emergence of a relationship based on mutual recognition. Yet the possibility of such recognition is always present.

Paulo Freire and the Vietnamese Buddhist monk Thich Nhat Hanh are two of the "teachers" who have touched me deeply with their work. When I first began college, Freire's thought gave me the support I needed to challenge the "banking system" of education, that approach to learning that is rooted in

Reprinted from *Teaching to Transgress: Education as the Practice of Freedom* by bell hooks (1994), by permission of the publisher, Routledge: New York and London, and by permission of the author.

the notion that all students need to do is consume information fed to them by a professor and be able to memorize and store it. Early on, it was Freire's insistence that education could be the practice of freedom that encouraged me to create strategies for what he called "conscientization" in the classroom. Translating that term to critical awareness and engagement, I entered the classroom with the conviction that it was crucial for me and every other student to be an active participant, not a passive consumer. Education as the practice of freedom was continually undermined by professors who were actively hostile to the notion of student participation. Freire's work affirmed that education can only be liberatory when everyone claims knowledge as a field in which we all labor. That notion of mutual labor was affirmed by Thich Nhat Hanh's philosophy of engaged Buddhism, the focus on practice in conjunction with contemplation. His philosophy was similar to Freire's emphasis on "praxis"—action and reflection upon the world in order to change it.

In his work, Thich Nhat Hanh always speaks of the teacher as a healer. Like Freire, his approach to knowledge called on students to be active participants, to link awareness with practice. Whereas Freire was primarily concerned with the mind, Thich Nhat Hanh offered a way of thinking about pedagogy which emphasized wholeness, a union of mind, body, and spirit. His focus on a holistic approach to learning and spiritual practice enabled me to overcome years of socialization that had taught me to believe a classroom was diminished if students and professors regarded one another as "whole" human beings, striving not just for knowledge in books, but knowledge about how to live in the world.

During my twenty years of teaching, I have witnessed a grave sense of dis-ease among professors (irrespective of their politics) when students want us to see them as whole human beings with complex lives and experiences rather than simply as seekers after compartmentalized bits of knowledge. When I was an undergraduate, Women's Studies was just finding a place in the academy. Those classrooms were the one space where teachers were willing to acknowledge a connection between ideas learned in university settings and those learned in life practices. And, despite those times when students abused that freedom in the classroom by only wanting to dwell on personal experience, feminist classrooms were, on the whole, one location where I witnessed professors striving to create participatory spaces for the sharing of knowledge. Nowadays, most women's studies professors are not as committed to exploring new pedagogical strategies. Despite this shift, many students still seek to enter feminist classrooms because they continue to believe that there, more than in any other place in the academy, they will have an opportunity to experience education as the practice of freedom.

Progressive, holistic education, "engaged pedagogy" is more demanding than conventional critical or feminist pedagogy. For, unlike these two teaching practices, it emphasizes well-being. That means that teachers must be actively committed to a process of self-actualization that promotes their own well-being if they are to teach in a manner that empowers students. Thich Nhat Hanh emphasized that "the practice of a healer, therapist, teacher or any helping professional should be directed toward his or herself first, because if the helper is unhappy, he or she cannot help many people." In the United States it is rare that anyone talks about teachers in university settings as healers. And it is even more rare to hear anyone suggest that teachers have any responsibility to be self-actualized individuals.

Learning about the work of intellectuals and academics primarily from nineteenth-century fiction and nonfiction during my pre-college years, I was certain that the task for those of us who chose this vocation was to be holistically questing for self-actualization. It was the actual experience of college that disrupted this image. It was there that I was made to feel as though I was terribly naive about "the profession." I learned that far from being self-actualized, the university was seen more as a haven for those who are smart in book knowledge but who might be otherwise unfit for social interaction. Luckily, during my undergraduate years I began to make a distinction between the practice of being an intellectual/teacher and one's role as a member of the academic profession.

It was difficult to maintain fidelity to the idea of the intellectual as someone who sought to be whole—well-grounded in a context where there was little emphasis on spiritual well-being, on care of the soul. Indeed, the objectification of the teacher within bourgeois educational structures seemed to denigrate notions of wholeness and uphold the idea of a mind/body split, one that promotes and supports compartmentalization.

This support reinforces the dualistic separation of public and private, encouraging teachers and students to see no connection between life practices, habits of being, and the roles of professors. The idea of the intellectual questing for a union of mind, body, and spirit had been replaced with notions that being smart meant that one was inherently emotionally unstable and that the best in oneself emerged in one's academic work. This meant that whether academics were drug addicts, alcoholics, batterers, or sexual abusers, the only important aspect of our identity was whether or not our minds functioned, whether we were able to do our jobs in the classroom. The self was presumably emptied out the moment the threshold was crossed, leaving in place only an objective mind—free of experiences and biases. There was fear that the conditions of that self would interfere with the teaching process. Part of the luxury and privilege of the role of teacher/professor today is the absence of any requirement that we be self-actualized. Not surprisingly, professors who are not concerned with inner well-being are the most threatened by the demand on the part of students for liberatory education, for pedagogical processes that will aid them in their own struggle for self-actualization.

Certainly it was naive for me to imagine during high school that I would find spiritual and intellectual guidance in university settings from writers, thinkers, scholars. To have found this would have been to stumble across a rare treasure. I learned, along with other students, to consider myself fortunate if I found an interesting professor who talked in a compelling way. Most of my professors were not the slightest bit interested in enlightenment. More than anything they seemed enthralled by the exercise of power and authority within their mini-kingdom, the classroom.

This is not to say that there were not compelling, benevolent dictators, but it is true to my memory that it was rare—absolutely, astonishingly rare—to encounter professors who were deeply committed to progressive pedagogical practices. I was dismayed by this; most of my professors were not individuals whose teaching styles I wanted to emulate.

My commitment to learning kept me attending classes. Yet, even so, because I did not conform—would not be an unquestioning, passive student—some professors treated me with contempt. I was slowly becoming estranged from education. Finding Freire in the midst of that estrangement was crucial to my survival as a student. His work offered both a way for me to understand the limitations of the type of education I was receiving and to discover alternative strategies for learning and teaching. It was particularly disappointing to encounter white male professors who claimed to follow Freire's model even as their pedagogical practices were mired in structures of domination, mirroring the styles of conservative professors even as they approached subjects from a more progressive standpoint.

When I first encountered Paulo Freire, I was eager to see if his style of teaching would embody the pedagogical practices he described so eloquently in his work. During the short time I studied with him, I was deeply moved by his presence, by the way in which his manner of teaching exemplified his pedagogical theory. (Not all students interested in Freire have had a similar experience.) My experience with him restored my faith in liberatory education. I had never wanted to surrender the conviction that one could teach without reinforcing existing systems of domination. I needed to know that professors did not have to be dictators in the classroom.

While I wanted teaching to be my career, I believed that personal success was intimately linked with self-actualization. My passion for this quest led me to interrogate constantly the mind/body split that was so often taken to be a given. Most professors were often deeply antagonistic toward, even scornful of, any approach to learning emerging from a philosophical standpoint emphasizing the union of mind, body, and spirit, rather than the separation of these elements. Like many of the students I now teach, I was often told by powerful academics that I was misguided to seek such a perspective in the academy. Throughout my student years I felt deep inner anguish. Memory of that pain returns as I listen to students express the concern that they will not succeed in academic professions if they want to be well, if they eschew dysfunctional behavior or participation in coercive hierarchies. These students are often fearful, as I was, that there are no spaces in the academy where the will to be self-actualized can be affirmed.

This fear is present because many professors have intensely hostile responses to the vision of liberatory education that connects the will to know with the will to become. Within professorial circles, individuals often complain bitterly that students want classes to be "encounter groups." While it is utterly unreasonable for students to expect classrooms to be therapy sessions, it is appropriate for them to hope that the knowledge received in these settings will enrich and enhance them.

Currently, the students I encounter seem far more uncertain about the project of self-actualization than my peers and I were

twenty years ago. They feel that there are no clear ethical guide-
lines shaping actions. Yet, while they despair, they are also
adamant that education should be liberatory. They want and demand more from professors than my generation did. There are
times when I walk into classrooms overflowing with students
who feel terribly wounded in their psyches (many of them see
therapists), yet I do not think that they want therapy from me.
They do want an education that is healing to the uninformed,
unknowing spirit. They do want knowledge that is meaningful.
They rightfully expect that my colleagues and I will not offer
them information without addressing the connection between
what they are learning and their overall life experiences.

This demand on the students' part does not mean that they
will always accept our guidance. This is one of the joys of education as the practice of freedom, for it allows students to
assume responsibility for their choices. Writing about our
teacher/student relationship in a piece for the *Village Voice*,
"How to Run the Yard: Off-Line and into the Margins at Yale,"
one of my students, Gary Dauphin, shares the joys of working
with me as well as the tensions that surfaced between us as he
began to devote his time to pledging a fraternity rather than cul-
tivating his writing:

> People think academics like Gloria [my given name] are all about
> difference: but what I learned from her was mostly about same-
> ness, about what I had in common as a black man to people of
> color; to women and gays and lesbians and the poor and anyone
> else who wanted in. I did some of this learning by reading but
> most of it came from hanging out on the fringes of her life. I lived
> like that for a while, shuttling between high points in my classes
> and low points outside. Gloria was a safe haven . . . Pledging a
> fraternity is about as far away as you can get from her class-
> room, from the yellow kitchen where she used to share her
> lunch with students in need of various forms of sustenance.

This is Gary writing about the joy. The tension arose as we discussed his reason for wanting to join a fraternity and my disdain for that decision. Gary comments, "They represented a
vision of black manhood that she abhorred, one where violence
and abuse were primary ciphers of bonding and identity." Describing his assertion of autonomy from my influence he writes,
"But she must have also known the limits of even her influence
on my life, the limits of books and teachers."

Ultimately, Gary felt that the decision he had made to join a fraternity was not constructive, that I "had taught him openness" where the fraternity had encouraged one-dimensional allegiance. Our interchange both during and after this experience was an example of engaged pedagogy.

Through critical thinking—a process he learned by reading theory and actively analyzing texts—Gary experienced education as the practice of freedom. His final comments about me: "Gloria had only mentioned the entire episode once after it was over, and this to tell me simply that there are many kinds of choices, many kinds of logic. I could make those events mean whatever I wanted as long as I was honest." I have quoted his writing at length because it is testimony affirming engaged pedagogy. It means that my voice is not the only account of what happens in the classroom.

Engaged pedagogy necessarily values student expression. In her essay, "Interrupting the Calls for Student Voice in Liberatory Education: A Feminist Poststructuralist Perspective," Mimi Orner employs a Foucauldian framework to suggest that

> Regulatory and punitive means and uses of the confession bring to mind curricular and pedagogical practices which call for students to publicly reveal, even confess, information about their lives and cultures in the presence of authority figures such as teachers.

When education is the practice of freedom, students are not the only ones who are asked to share, to confess. Engaged pedagogy does not seek simply to empower students. Any classroom that employs a holistic model of learning will also be a place where teachers grow, and are empowered by the process. That empowerment cannot happen if we refuse to be vulnerable while encouraging students to take risks. Professors who expect students to share confessional narratives but who are themselves unwilling to share are exercising power in a manner that could be coercive. In my classrooms, I do not expect students to take any risks that I would not take, to share in any way that I would not share. When professors bring narratives of their experiences into classroom discussions it eliminates the possibility that we can function as all-knowing, silent interrogators. It is often productive if professors take the first risk, linking confessional narratives to academic discussions so as to show how experience can illuminate and enhance our understanding of academic material. But most professors must practice being vulnerable in the classroom, being wholly present in mind, body, and spirit.

Progressive professors working to transform the curriculum so that it does not reflect biases or reinforce systems of domination are most often the individuals willing to take the risks that engaged pedagogy requires and to make their teaching practices a site of resistance. In her essay, "On Race and Voice: Challenges for Liberation Education in the 1990s," Chandra Mohanty writes that

> resistance lies in self-conscious engagement with dominant, normative discourses and representations and in the active creation of oppositional analytic and cultural spaces. Resistance that is random and isolated is clearly not as effective as that which is mobilized through systemic politicized practices of teaching and learning. Uncovering and reclaiming subjugated knowledge is one way to lay claims to alternative histories. But these knowledges need to be understood and defined pedagogically, as questions of strategy and practice as well as of scholarship, in order to transform educational institutions radically.

Professors who embrace the challenge of self-actualization will be better able to create pedagogical practices that engage students, providing them with ways of knowing that enhance their capacity to live fully and deeply.

Chapter 17

Composing a
Pleasurable Life

Sondra Perl

What is deeply pleasurable in life? For me, the answers come quickly: teaching, writing, being married, raising my children, walking my dogs, spending time in the cool of an old art museum, hiking, eating, loving, being a friend—not necessarily in that order.

How do I know this? Out of all the chaos of existence, how is it that these experiences come to me? What do the words signify? What do they say to you?

This much I do know: I never intended to be a teacher. For many years, after an early, aborted marriage, I never intended to get married again. Once remarried, I resisted the idea of having children. And now, when I think back on the statements I made about what I did or did not desire, I know that seeking pleasure has had little to do with my choices. Rather, pleasure has come to me uncalled for, unbidden, from giving myself to what I care for.

Schooling/Teaching/Living

I was not one of those girls who, in her spare time, corralled her friends into "playing school." In the requisite twelve years of schooling, I never had a teacher I actually liked. As a child and then a teenager, I couldn't imagine anything more tedious than getting up every day and teaching a bunch of kids.

But then, growing up as I did in the fifties, I rarely thought about getting up and going to work at all. It was understood

239

that I would attend college as did most daughters of upwardly mobile, successful Jewish parents from northern New Jersey. But it was also understood that my goal was to bring back the title of "Mrs." as well as a bachelor's degree—the former a far more important pedigree than the latter.

I chose a women's college. I remember thinking that I wanted to be able to study without worrying about how I looked—ignoring while I could the burdensome concerns of a young woman whose ultimate goal was marriage.

And study I did. Worlds opened to me. Art history. Literature. Language. Eric Lustig taught me to stand before a painting and wait. To let the painting speak to me and then to record what I was seeing and hearing in an art journal. Charles L'Homme chainsmoked while reciting poetry and brought Yeats into my life. I spent three months living in Madrid with a Castillian family and discovered the chameleon who lived inside of me.

A dutiful daughter, first-born, I did not disappoint my parents. I completed college with a BA in art history, dropped the idea of entering the Peace Corps, and married a doctor during my senior year. We rented an apartment in New Jersey, near my parents' home, and I lived the life I thought I was destined to live. I didn't look for a job; I didn't need to, having moved from my father's care to my husband's. To occupy my time, I volunteered at the Women's Auxiliary of the hospital and took a Chinese cooking course with my mother. I played tennis and shopped. Had my nails done weekly. And began to wonder why I was so miserable.

The marriage lasted a year and a half, by which time I realized it was my father who delighted in the man I had married, not I. And my father's delight was no longer sufficient. Shocking as it was to disrupt familial life, to divorce before most of my friends had even married, I was yearning for something I had not yet experienced and some submerged part of me rose up, remembered art history and literature and Spain—and left.

* * *

It's the day after Labor Day, 1970. I take the bus from New Jersey to the Port Authority in New York. I am alone. I have never taken the subway. When I ask the token collector how to get to Greenwich Village, he gruffly responds, eliding his words, "Take the "ate" train, lady." I think he's saying, "Eight—take the eight train." To be sure, I ask hesitantly, my voice rising, "Eight?"

He looks at me as if I'm a moron and in a tone drenched with disgust, he responds, once again, "No, lady, A, A, not eight—A, get it?" After a few more rounds, I figure out it's letters not numbers he's talking about, and overcome by my own ignorance, clutching my bag, I race downstairs to catch the train that will take me away, out of his sight, to disappear at lightening speed through the dark tunnels of Manhattan.

I find an apartment to share on the corner of Fifth Avenue and 10th Street. The only thing I know I'm fairly good at is school. To do graduate work in art history, I need to learn German, but having inherited from my mother a deep suspicion of anything remotely related to the German Reich, I decide to switch my focus to English literature. Columbia's English department says it's too late to apply. NYU says it's okay. I become a student again.

I find my classes boring. It's the 70s, the war is on, and I'm studying Celtic myths, being lectured at by men in ties. I walk the streets of the Village and imagine families inside the brownstones, their wooden shutters closed to the cold outside, warm in front of their working fireplaces. I wonder if loneliness in a New Jersey suburb with a husband who repeatedly asks me to return is preferable to loneliness on 10th Street. I feel the power of the city churning beneath me and can envision no future for myself here. My father will not visit. He cannot bear to see the occasional roach that scurries across the sink or on my mattress on the floor.

I assume a degree in English will prepare me to be an editor or a teacher. I'm not sure either one appeals to me, but a fellow student suggests I walk over to the School of Education to find out if I can do some student teaching. "They're pretty flexible over there," he says, "and it's a sure way to find out about life in a classroom."

At NYU's School of Education, I meet Gordon Pradl and John Mayher. Their hair is long, 70s style. They sit, often on top of their desks, in one large room on the third floor of the Press Building. Funny, ironic, each man is, in his own way, accessible. John sends me to Seward Park High School on the lower East Side as a student teacher. I have never been to the lower East Side, but by now I have at least learned how to read a subway map. It takes less than three minutes in front of a class for me to know I am home.

What was it? What is it still? What occurs each time I face a group of students? It's happened so many times in so many different ways with so many different groups, it's hard to say precisely. There they are. Sitting. Waiting. Here I am. Looking. Standing. I know that if I welcome them and see them, reach across this invisible divide and invite them out, they will speak. I experience the challenge of meeting them. It's right there. I can begin with my notes and classroom business or I can pause and wait. Look. See who is in the room. Read the space. It's not that I stand there in a trance without speaking. It's that my speaking is initiated in response to their presence and so I begin—with what I hope the course will be about, by what I sense is possible for all of us this term. Usually after I say a few words, I invite everyone to write: what comes to mind when each of us considers the content of the course? Often I write too. Then I ask each person to introduce himself or herself by reading a bit of what she or he has written. A brave soul begins. Then someone else joins in. Soon one voice echoes another. Common threads begin to appear. Questions. Laughter. Concerns. Their voices fill the room. I take in what I hear and ask myself, how can I best meet these people?

I have learned to listen carefully. It is not unlike what Eric taught me about paintings. To look closely at what is in front of me and to listen to what is being spoken. As I meet the challenge to take in what my students say and ask, I am simultaneously called out of myself. My preoccupation of the day does not intrude in this space. The speeding ticket on the way to work, the article in the *Times* about the impending cuts to higher education, tonight's dinner—all miraculously disappear if I'm truly in my classroom, doing what gives me deep pleasure: asking, listening, responding, pointing out commonalities, dealing with confusions, adding my own point of view or formulating, often freshly, an idea that has emerged from all my students have said.

Finding Work/Discovering Love

Eugenio María de Hostos Community College of the City University of New York. It's the last college on the CUNY list. It's in the South Bronx. I've never even been to the Bronx, let alone its infamous southern section. But I desperately want to teach, and although all of the other English departments have filled their adjunct positions by the time I make my calls in

September 1971, I tell myself to be thorough, to call every college on the list.

The woman who answers the phone says they might have a section of Freshman composition from five to six, Monday, Wednesday, Friday. Can I come up and wait to see how many students show up? If there are more than thirty-four, they will make two sections. Can I? I've already taken out my subway map.

I sit at the back of the room and count: twenty students, twenty-five, twenty-eight, thirty-two, (Oh please God, a few more) thirty-five and counting. The class has forty students and I have my first teaching job: one section of Freshman composition.

Hostos is brand new, one of the community colleges created by the advent of the Open Admissions policy CUNY instituted in 1968, to provide higher education to anyone in New York with a high school diploma. By the time I become the first adjunct in the English department, the college has been open two years, has already worn out several administrations, and is now under the direction of Candido de Leon, whose mission is to build a bilingual institution in the Bronx. After my first year as an adjunct, I am hired full-time. I am an instructor with an MA degree and very happy.

* * *

Open Admissions brought both excitement and turmoil to CUNY. English faculties from different campuses were eager to meet. Mina Shaughnessy was gathering people together to discuss the teaching of composition. I felt honored to represent Hostos. And in those CUNY-wide meetings, I met, for the first time, colleagues, far more experienced than I, who cared about the teaching of writing: John Brereton, Ken Bruffee, Marsha Cummins, Judith Fishman, Betsey Kaufman, Richard Larson, Bob Lyons, Don McQuade, Marie Ponsot, Sandra Schor, Lucille Shandloff, Richard Sterling, Lynn Troyka, Harvey Weiner, and many others.

By this time, I realized that I had not exactly chosen a career. I had made my way hesitantly into a classroom and only once I was inside, teaching, did I realize I belonged there. Now, I knew, I had some decisions to make: stop teaching, attend graduate school full-time and get a Ph.D. as quickly as possible, or remain at Hostos teaching full-time and work on the degree more slowly. While there were career ramifications either way, to me there was only one real choice. I was at my best when I was teaching. And what I was learning in my classroom fueled my desire to study, to discover what others in the field of language and literature were writing. Somehow, too, I seemed to trust that tenure and promotion, the tangible signs of success, would come if I continued to follow what truly interested me and what brought me the deepest pleasure.

In addition to teaching experience, Hostos also brought me lifelong colleagues. Lois Lambdin and Dexter Fisher were the first women with whom I shared work interests. It was natural enough for me to assume we would discuss the details of our personal lives with one another, but I had never before known the binding force of shared work commitments, the pleasure of time spent thinking creatively and abstractly, wrestling with the impact of curricular decisions, or imagining a new sequence to address a problem we faced. Later on, Diana Diaz, Linda Hirsh, and Alfredo Villanueva joined the group of faculty I counted as my friends.

I spent seven years at Hostos. During that time, I experimented with many different approaches to teaching. I taught in an interdisciplinary program, eventually becoming its director. I took a seminar sponsored by CUNY on cognitive styles. I read about writing apprehension, tagmemics, sentence-combining, and other issues. And I realized that no one really knew much about the ways underprepared college students composed. I found, in essence, the heart of a matter that to this day still fascinates me, a question to study, to live with, to mull over, and a focus, as well, for a doctoral dissertation. I decided to observe basic writers as they composed, and in doing so, to begin an inquiry into the nature of the composing process.[1]

* * *

It's September 1977. A friend in clinical psychology is getting divorced. He calls. Wonders if I am free. We go out. We discover we have a lot to say to one another. The pull, the attraction, is as intellectual as it is physical. I find that I can talk to him about my dissertation. He listens. He's passionate about ideas. I inform him, in no uncertain terms, that I have no desire to get married or to have children. He doesn't go away.

A year later, he raises some questions. "What are your goals? What vision do you have for your future?" I look at him skeptically. "I don't have a vision," I say. "I don't think like that. Things just happen to me. I don't plan them." I can tell he's not satisfied. He doesn't think my answers are sufficient.

A few months later. The Bronx Botanical Gardens. We sit on a hill overlooking the woods. Again he asks, "So what goals do you have for yourself? Where would you like to be professionally in, say, five or ten years?" Again I tell him, "I don't have a five-year plan. That's what countries have." It sounds oddly economic to me. "I don't know how to think like that."

But I begin to wonder. Is this what certain boys are taught? Are there men, at least from middle- or upper-class families, who grow up knowing they will play a role in the affairs of the world, knowing in their bones that they will find a place for themselves?

He pushes me gently. "So, can you begin to envision something?" I start to cry. This is hard. I've never tried to think in such big terms. I am afraid to say "I want this." To claim something as mine. It's not polite.

But, slowly, I begin to sense both the injustice and the weakness inherent in my position. No, I've not been taught to think like this. But why can't I? Why can't I ask what kind of professional life I want to lead and listen to what comes back? Why can't I envision a career path? Why not set goals? At first, my answers are shaky, uncertain. But I feel as if this man named Arthur has given me a gift. It turns out to be one of many.

The Writing Project

In the spring of 1978, I completed my doctoral dissertation on the composing processes of unskilled college writers, with support from Gordon Pradl, who served as chair, and many more talks with Arthur, who began to hold an increasingly important place in my life. In 1979, the dissertation brought me an NCTE Promising Researcher Award and national recognition. Finding the question that guided the study, collecting the data, and devising methods of analysis taught me how to engage in fine-grained research. Working seriously, for several years, on a sustained piece of inquiry showed me that I could tackle a large question and move from concrete details to larger, more theoretical constructs. Through this research, I learned about the ways that unskilled writers composed. And I began to think about ways to teach these writers that would help them through the tangles in their composing processes, rather than create more knots.

My own thinking about the teaching of writing, however, only took convincing shape in 1978, after Richard Sterling,

John Brereton, and I received funding to start a branch of the National Writing Project at Lehman College, CUNY, and had begun to work in earnest on the development of the New York City Writing Project.

*   *   *

It's May 1978. Jim Gray, the founder and director (until 1995) of the National Writing Project, flies to New York to tell us what he expects to see in the summer institute he is funding. "Teachers must write every day," Jim says, his blue eyes flashing. Okay, we nod. I take notes. "And," he continues, "we expect them to write in different points of view." Okay again. I jot down 'Jim Moffett's influence is obvious here, sounds interesting.' "And, of course, every afternoon, you will have writing response groups," he remarks. What? Richard, John, and I roll our eyes and grimace at one another. Response groups? This sounds a bit too much like therapy for us. Maybe teachers in California sit around and willingly expose their written work to people they barely know, but teachers in New York? Never.

I smile now when I recall our doubts of almost twenty years ago. The basic model Jim described is what I still follow today in almost every class I teach—in writing, literature, or women's studies. Whether I am teaching undergraduates in Freshman composition or Ph.D. candidates in a doctoral seminar, writing underlies everything we do. I ask students to write in class on issues that are raised through discussion; I ask them to keep response logs as they are reading; I ask for pieces of writing in different forms or from different points of view; for dialogues written between texts or authors; for reflective pieces in which students consider their progress with the course material or with their writing. Similarly, it is a rare class when students do not spend some time working collaboratively, reading work to each other in pairs or reading and writing in small groups.

I do not devise these approaches on my own. Those who have joined me in creating the work of the project over the years, Elaine Avidon, Linette Moorman, Ed Osterman, Marcie Wolfe, and many others, bring their own interests in students, their own creative takes on how to fashion a learner-centered classroom, their own interpretations of texts. Together we design and experiment with structures: Saturday meetings, inservice courses, summer institutes. Sometimes we argue. Frequently we write. But together we struggle to build a project sensitive to the needs of its constituencies—both teachers and students.

I serve as a director of the New York City Writing Project for ten years. During this time, I work with some of the most dedicated teachers I have ever met. Some invite me into their classrooms, behind the scenes, to witness their successes and struggles. Many of these teachers work in difficult schools where broken windows, leaky ceilings, and concealed weapons are commonplace, but they refuse to give up on the urban poor who inhabit them.

These teachers challenge me to consider how the theories I espouse about writing and learning fit with the daily life of teaching as they know it. How, for example, can students work in groups when the desks and chairs they sit in are bolted to the floor? When the seats themselves, dating back to the turn of the century, were designed for immigrants who were physically smaller than those who now occupy them? What do writing process and point-of-view have to do with passing Regents exams and competency tests? How can teachers allow for student-centeredness and spontaneity when they are mandated to follow lesson plans preapproved by their assistant principals? Thorny issues. Hard questions. Teaching dilemmas not readily resolved.

In 1979, the project takes me to Shoreham-Wading River on Long Island, when Richard Sterling and I are invited by Mark Goldberg, an exuberant and thoughtful administrator, to teach first one summer institute and then another to the teachers in his district. I return to Shoreham one year later, having received federal funding to conduct an ethnographic study on the teaching of writing occurring in the district. For two years, two research assistants and I visit classrooms from grades one through twelve, meet weekly with teachers in a study group, and work together on our understanding of the ways teachers take the lessons learned in summer institutes and turn them into effective classroom practices.

I spend most of my time in the home and classrooms of Diane and Ross Burkhardt, where I learn about the rhythms of daily life in the eighth grade. I discover how exciting teaching in a public school can be when teachers have resources and support and are not afraid to care for their students, and I learn how wonderful it is to have children in my life.

Lehman College/Writing/Babies

When I returned from Shoreham to New York City, I brought back in my car more than boxes of data crammed with student writing, teachers' journals, and fieldnotes. I brought back the physical sensation of first graders crawling onto my lap as they read me their stories. I brought back the memory of the sun warming my shoulders as I rooted for Matt and Brian after school at their baseball game. I brought back a knowledge about schooling and children and teachers that would take years to digest and would have an impact on the direction my life would take.

Nor did I bring these memories back alone. James Carter, who served as one of the research assistants on this project, returned to his high school teaching job. But Nancy Wilson, my other assistant, brought back her data and her memories too: of high school events and of the teachers and students she had come to know best. Together we talked out, talked over, wrote, and rewrote our stories of that project. Together at Lehman College we stayed late into the night, figuring out how to turn thousands of pages of data into a book about the daily lives of teachers committed to teaching writing. Over Chinese food on 95th Street or Indian food on Columbus Avenue, we read our drafts to one another, laughed, cried, commiserated, and cheered one another on until we each found what we wanted to say.

I was by now an assistant professor at Lehman College, having moved there in 1978 when the Writing Project received its first funding. Soon I would come up for tenure and promotion. It would have been in my professional interest, many argued, to be the sole author of the book Nancy and I were working on. Nancy would understand. She had been hired as an assistant, not a co-author. But the self-interested approach seemed empty to me. To assert my authority at the end of the project when all along we had worked as a team and I had consistently spoken for the value of collaboration seemed, at best, disingenuous. A high-handed move in my mind at least. So, I invited Nancy to be my co-author on the book that resulted from our research, a decision I have never regretted.[2]

In 1980, just before the beginning of the Shoreham project, I agreed, much to my surprise after all my earlier protestations, to marry Arthur Egendorf. The first year of our married life was spent with Arthur kissing me good-bye on Sunday nights when

I left for the district and welcoming me home on Thursday or Friday evening when I returned. He understood the authorship issue. Having watched this project evolve, having seen the way my collaboration with Nancy had grown, he knew, as I did, that this was a shared work.

At the same time, Nancy and Arthur watched me move from a woman who stated categorically that she did not want children to one who openly embraced the idea. It occurred to me that by living in Manhattan and teaching adults, it had been easy for me to avoid contact with children. But after living in Shoreham, after spending close to two years inside schools, after working in classrooms and watching kids and their writing grow and change, I knew that I wanted to have children in my life. Not as a teacher of someone else's youngsters but as a mother of my own.

* * *

In 1984, my daughter, Sara, is born. Three years later, wishing for just one more child, I give birth to identical twin sons. Sara is an easy child, graceful and articulate from an early age; the boys are her opposite. Fitful and restless, Josh and Sam sleep only intermittently. They spend a good deal of their days and most nights crying. And for the first time in many years, the life I have so carefully constructed comes crashing down.

Sleep deprivation for several years is a terrible thing. Arthur and I walk around like zombies. The slightest provocation can set us reeling. I feel as if my skin has been scratched by razors. The first sane thing I do is resign as director of the Writing Project. Then I request as simple a teaching schedule as possible. Then I stop presenting at national conferences. Then I stop attending local meetings. I have already stopped writing.

As my professional world recedes, I am distraught. Losing the sense of myself as someone who has work in the world has been my greatest fear. Certainly I have been warned by women writers that children (more than one, Alice Walker cautions) will thwart creativity. Now, here I am, teaching, still, but only as a break from what I have strenuously avoided all my life and which now dominates my entire existence: two crying babies, one toddler, dirty diapers, piles of laundry, ear infections, antibiotics, Sesame Street, and hours of Dumbo.

Men/Feminism/Writing

How does it change? When does it get better? Slowly, gradually. The boys stop crying. They look around. They reach out and discover one another. Who else is there? I'm there. Their mother. Their father is there too. And their sister. We have to learn how to become a family of five. I have to learn how to embrace two at once.

It is hard work, this learning to be a mother of sons. It does not come easily to me. Most of my close friends are women. My mother and grandmother have passed on a clannishness about female concerns that makes it easy for me to be a sister and to mother a daughter. But boys? I find it hard to match their rhythms, to follow their lead, to rejoice in their strutting and screeching.

But wait, I say. They are my sons. They will grow up to be men in the world. What sort of men will I, consciously or not, help to shape? If I cannot reach out and accept them, as they are, in the way I look to reach out and accept whoever enters my classroom, how can I ever think I will teach them anything? If I think it is my job to nurture the voices in my classroom, isn't it equally my task to nurture the voices of my children? To be present and appreciative as they try out the many voices inside them, and as they go on, one hopes, to construct new ones?

And wait another minute. If I look back on this tale I have just told, what do I notice? From the time I was in college, male professors taught me, guided me, and helped me find my way. My story is full of male teachers, male administrators, even male collaborators, on projects. It is also true that female administrators and professors were few in number, but in any event, males did not ignore me or try to prevent my success. On the contrary, men—at least those I chose to work with—listened to me, took me seriously, encouraged me, and respected me.

And then I notice this: the friendships I value most are based on shared commitments, not gender. The exchange takes place over ideas we are committed to, over projects we envision. We may, my friends and I, enact our visions differently, but what we share is a commitment to the same sort of world, a similar sense of values, an interest in one another's stories, and often the desire to discover through conversation, in cafes, over coffee, in museums, at concerts, even in playgrounds, where our visions might lead.

One of my most enduring visions concerns the classroom. The one I envision is a lively, exciting, challenging, demanding, nurturing, intellectual space. It may be labeled "feminist" in that it is often filled primarily with women, we often discuss issues related to women, and we often read texts written by women. In some courses, I focus explicitly on the roles women have played or been forced to play (in literature, in cultures) throughout the world and the options currently open to them. In all courses, I look to create a caring environment. I work hard to encourage all students in the class to speak, especially those who find themselves disagreeing with what I say. I look to create a classroom that, in current academic parlance, is dialogic rather than monologic. I look to make it rich and nuanced in experience, filled with many different voices, and I especially cultivate the moments that are humorous. I know the class is working well when students speak up, when they read something they have written with conviction or with real gusto in their voices, and most often when I notice we are all laughing. And, lest it be mistaken, let me make myself clear: in my way of thinking, it is the speaking up, the sharing of writing, and the discovery of one's voice (in many different tones, levels, and registers) that marks the first step toward agency.

But I wonder, is such an approach especially feminist? Have women cornered the market on the desire to create nurturing classrooms? Are we the only ones concerned with the development of voice(s)? Certainly we are not the only ones interested in the enfranchisement of our students. Are the men who share our visions to be labeled "feminist" as well? What about the women who work in more standard, academic fashion? Are they less feminist because they teach in a less learner-centered style? Is there room in the academy for so many different feminisms? If so, of what use is the term? But if not, what have we created? For while I am not unaware of the many ways in which patriarchies have, for centuries, excluded, silenced, and marginalized women, I fear we are creating our own exclusive club when we label as feminist practices that are essentially human.

If I have learned anything by teaching writing for twenty-five years, it is that the struggle to write is a struggle for entitlement, for the right to have one's words matter. It is as much a struggle for men as it is for women, for professors as for their students, for those who come from privileged backgrounds as for those who do not. We may struggle differently, with different levels of concern, but for most of us (if not all), writing entails commerce with a self we do not entirely know and an unceasing search to discover how best to represent who we are and what we think in print.

Most adults I meet do not willingly choose to write. Their memories of writing classrooms are charged with defeat, of somehow "doing it wrong." Those of us who continue to write, to explore our lives and our thoughts in print, must have some other experience, must know deep within, often without admitting it, that this search brings rewards, insight, even at times pleasure. It is a struggle we contend with, seek and give ourselves to, because, we think, something is at stake. What we have to say matters. Or will matter, we hope, to those who read our words.

The only way I know to enable students to become better writers, then, is to listen to them in such a way that they come to know that their words matter. It is to take what they write, however meager, and listen to it so that they, too, can begin to hear what is there. Then, if they truly accept that their words matter to their classmates and to me, an interesting phenomenon occurs: they write more; the writing begins to improve; their voices begin to shake as they read aloud a piece they have come to care about. As I see it, they have begun to make connections between language and life, between their use of words and their dawning sense of self. They have begun to imagine themselves as writers, men and women alike.

Pleasure

Examining my own teaching practice, I know that I consciously look to make my classroom pleasurable for everyone who is there, myself included. But then the question comes, why pleasure? What is that? And I realize that for me, pleasure is not merely the result of having fun. It is what I derive from being connected to others and what I experience when I am called on to respond. Of course, there are moments when not responding is equally pleasurable, when, for instance, I spend time at the beach and relax into the sand. Or when my children visit friends overnight, Arthur and I are alone together, and the house becomes perfectly quiet. But every summer, when vacation ends, I feel a quickening within myself, an eagerness to return to the scenes that most call me, scenes filled with colleagues and friends, students and texts, a life of challenge and work.

* * *

When I fled New Jersey and walked alone on the streets of New York, I did not know what might lie ahead of me. I did not know that a life committed to work could be so satisfying. I did not know that pleasure could be derived from working hard, from immersing myself in the details of a project until that project felt like a second skin. I did not know that this immersion is both a surrender and a way of inhabiting another world, or that it would carry within itself the "absorbedness" Donald Hall speaks of in *Life Work* (Hall 1993, 62) as the fleeting but true value of a life's vocation. I did not even suspect that such experiences existed and certainly not that women might be entitled to them. It took living it to learn that doing the work I value, in as committed a way as I can muster, at times falling short, always expecting more, within a community of like-minded colleagues, could and would become a source of unending pleasure.

Notes

1. Perl, Sondra. 1978. *Five Writers Writing: Case Studies of the Composing Processes of Unskilled College Writers*. Diss. New York University.

2. Perl, Sondra, and Nancy Wilson. 1986. *Through Teachers' Eyes: Portraits of Writing Teachers at Work*. Portsmouth, NH: Heinemann Educational Books.

Works Cited

Hall, Donald. 1993. *Life Work*. Boston: Beacon.

Chapter 18

As if your life depended on it
(from *WHAT IS FOUND THERE:*
Notebooks on Poetry and Politics)

Adrienne Rich

You must write, and read, as if your life depended on it. That is not generally taught in school. At most, *as if your livelihood depended on it:* the next step, the next job, grant, scholarship, professional advancement, fame; no questions asked as to further meanings. And, let's face it, the lesson of the schools for a vast number of children—hence, of readers—is *This is not for you.*

To read as if your life depended on it would mean to let into your reading your beliefs, the swirl of your dreamlife, the physical sensations of your ordinary carnal life; and, simultaneously, to allow what you're reading to pierce the routines, safe and impermeable, in which ordinary carnal life is tracked, charted, channeled. Then, what of the right answers, the so-called multiple-choice examination sheet with the number 2 pencil to mark one choice and one choice only?

To write as if your life depended on it: to write across the chalkboard, putting up there in public words you have dredged, sieved up from dreams, from behind screen memories, out of silence—words you have dreaded and needed in order to know you exist. No, it's too much; you could be laughed out of school, set upon in the schoolyard, they would wait for you after school, they could expel you. The politics of the schoolyard, the power of the gang.

Or, they could ignore you.

To read as if your life depended on it—but what writing can be believed? Isn't all language just manipulation? Maybe the poet has a hidden program—to recruit you to a cause, send you into the streets, to destabilize, through the sensual powers of language, your tested and tried priorities? Rather than succumb, you can learn to inspect the poem at arm's length, through a long and protective viewing tube, as an interesting object, an example of this style or that period. You can take refuge in the idea of "irony." Or you can demand that artists demonstrate loyalty to that or this moral or political or religious or sexual norm, on pain of having books burned, banned, on pain of censorship or prison, on pain of lost public funding.

Or, you can say: "I don't understand poetry."

Chapter 19

We Was Girls Together:
Race and Class and Southern Women

Hephzibah Roskelly

When I was eight or nine, I had a friend whose name was Marie. Pronounced with a drawn-out short *a* and a long long *e*, it sounded beautiful, the name of a French queen. When I visited my grandmother's house in New Orleans, she would come to play. She was the daughter of my aunt's cook, and she was black.

I don't know that I thought much about that. I didn't think about the fact that Emma, her mother, cooked every day for my aunt and for us when my family came "home" on yearly vacations. Emma made gumbo and fried chicken and one night a magical baked Alaska, and yet neither she nor Marie ever sat down to dinner with us. At eight or nine, if you're white, perhaps it's hard to see that the small, safe world that encloses also excludes. Emma worked in the kitchen; Marie and I played. We jumped off the porch into the cushiony St. Augustine grass, chased each other around the fig tree, and played dolls in the cool, sandy dirt under the house.

One day, we were upstairs in the small room my grandmother had made into a den. We were giggling, maybe tickling one another or pulling hair. I remember someone coming in, my grandmother's friend, and taking my arm, setting me upright. We stopped laughing abruptly, and the friend said something stern to me about behaving "like a lady." Nothing much happened after that I think; no scenes, no racial discussions. But Marie's visits dwindled and then stopped. It has taken me over thirty-five years to understand that I was being taught a lesson that day. It has taken me this long to articulate a new lesson that helps me confront the old one and confront as well my sense of loss.

How much of race and class and gender converge in the admonition to me to sit up straight and "act like a lady!" I didn't hear its undertones then, even though I felt them. But Marie and her mother, having suffered the tidy, genteel oppression that constituted black and white relationships between Southern females in the Fifties no doubt got the message. White and black girls are not friends or compatriots. One must be a lady; the other never can be.

Marie and I were separated in ways defined by our geography, sex, and place—as well as by our color. Race and class and gender weave together in this story so tightly that it is not possible to pick at one strand without pulling out the other threads. That interpenetration of conditions, of color and sex and social standing, is mutually reinforcing and constraining in our culture and certainly in the classroom. But the complexities of how race, class, and gender work together often stymie teachers and scholars as they attempt to discuss them with students and with their colleagues.

The feminist movement has given much help to teachers who would find ways to make their classrooms more equitable places. But even feminist theory, so determined to examine the politics of culture and of difference, often has failed in its attempt to talk about the other factors that impinge upon gender considerations, those of race and class. Recent conflicts in the feminist movement between women of color and their white colleagues hinge on that failure. bell hooks argues that the women's movement in the Sixties refused to see distinctions: "Since so many of the early feminist books really reflected a certain type of white bourgeois sensibility, this work did not touch many black women deeply; not because we did not recognize the common experiences women shared, but because those commonalities were mediated by profound differences in our realities created by the politics of race and class" (hooks 1995, 47). Katherine Mayberry's recent report of a women's studies conference, where African American women walked out of a panel on Toni Morrison because it was being presented by white women, demonstrates that hooks' contentions about early feminists hold firmly today.[1]

Feminists, especially Southern women, struggle to talk honestly about the racial and class dimensions of gender; race remains too painful and class too embedded to explore clearly and sensitively. Yet, as the conflicts in the women's movement illustrate and as our own teaching should suggest, it's both useful and necessary to do so. Uncovering the stories of race and class and gender in our own pasts becomes a potentially powerful method for confronting the issues in our teaching and in our research.

Both white privilege and white poverty have informed my Southern culture, the construction of my gender, and my attitudes about race. My mother's family represented the white educated class that kept black servants, paid them well for the times, remained kind, and firmly prevented any kind of equal communication. My father's family were Southerners too, of another class. Poor white tenant farmers in northern Florida, they hired no servants and had no servants' daughters around to play with. African American families lived near them, families who had been there for years and who sharecropped alongside my father and his brothers and sisters. As an adult, I discovered how they had shared resources as well as the land during the hard times of the Depression, cooperating to survive. Equals in many ways, especially in their marginal status in the larger culture, these two groups remained separated by race when social situations—sitting on the porch together, for example—highlighted and reinforced painful differences.

Both these class cultures, inscribed by race, have caused me to speculate about the way that class and race intersect with gender and about what responsibility I should have as a teacher in a Southern university where many of my students could tell stories like mine, of understanding and loss, of class and race and gender, but never do. I believe that feminist theory needs to listen to those stories, as well as to the stories of the many third-world feminists who are speaking out, who are insisting on the importance of context as feminists make theories. Andre Lorde's impassioned "Open Letter to Mary Daly" is an early example of that insistence: "The oppression of women knows no ethnic or racial boundaries, true, but that does not mean it is identical within those boundaries. To deal with one without even alluding to the other is to distort our commonality as well as our difference" (Lorde 1983, 96).

bell hooks grew up in a rural, racially segregated Southern town in the Fifties and remembers few relationships at all between black and white women. "I knew of no intimacy, no deep closeness, no friendship between black and white women. Though never discussed, it was evident in daily life that definite barriers separated the two groups, making close friendship impossible" (hooks 1995, 94). Just like Marie and me, bell hooks was taught the hard lesson of segregation. Yet, in the South, white and black women historically have been together in the most personal of settings, defined alike by their roles in kitchen and bedroom, and if never friends they have often been intimates. Divided by enormous gaps in class and by the abyss of racial difference, both were caught in a tight patriarchal grip that exerts some pressure even today.

Mary Boykin Chestnut, the wife of a planter in the antebellum South, seems to understand that connection as she writes in her diary: "All married women, all children and girls who live in their father's houses are slaves" (Chestnut 1990, 15). Few white wives and daughters consciously understood that link. Their own powerlessness, in fact, often made them strike out at their even more powerless "rivals," punishing slave women severely, often by selling slaves' light-skinned children away from them.[2] The reality and horror of slavery, the legacy of slavery in Jim Crow laws, and the continuing patriarchy in the South, with its regressive legislation on women's issues from marital rape to child support, have placed burdens on white and black women living in the South and continue paradoxically both to divide and connect us.

So the question for the Southern white feminist, especially a teacher, becomes how to talk across these borders and through such historic bitterness. How do we confront the class differences between rural and urban, poor and wealthy, and the racial difference that continues to haunt us? How do we provoke talk about issues that have historically been "unladylike" to discuss?

The first step seems to me to involve a real recognition of the difference race and class makes in any discussion of gender. Southern white women who are feminists and who believe in racial justice want so badly to connect—to make up—that we try to merge or erase difference. But because we are part of the larger white culture, our merging almost always means diminishing, or even coopting, the African American cultural experience we try to identify with. The appropriation the black women academics decried at the Women's Studies Conference is a cry of frustration at white women's refusal to understand context.

I recently became uncomfortably aware of how easy it is to give in to the temptation to ignore difference. In an Institute on race and gender sponsored by my university, consultants who had been brought to our group to take faculty through a series of exercises designed to promote racial awareness asked us to think about emotions we had been encouraged and discouraged from having. My African American colleague Sally Anne mentioned that in her experience growing up in a segregated rural town in the South she was discouraged from melancholy or sadness. "Get going," her mother would say, giving her chores, keeping her busy. I chimed in, telling about my Florida grandmother who, like Sally Anne's mother, insisted on no idle hands and had me sweeping, cleaning, and peeling endlessly. I was brought up short by the insistence of the facilitator that I look at the differences between us, the gap between a melancholy borne of oppression that might never be overcome if given in to and a bored sadness that at most was transitory.

Some feminists, reacting to the problem of cooptation, simply refuse to deal with minority cultural experience in their work. Quoting Phyllis Chesler, Patricia Meyer Spacks writes in *The Female Imagination* that she, like Chesler, is "reluctant and unable to construct theories about experiences I haven't had" (Spacks, ix), and she uses that argument to explain why her study of imagination and literature concentrates on works like *Jane Eyre* and *Middlemarch*, books that she claims "touch on familiar experience, familiar cultural settings." Alice Walker goes to the heart of the difficult problem for white feminists who would confront the race/class/gender web of connections in their writing and teaching as she responds to Spacks' comment with a pointed observation of her own in an essay in the collection *But Some of Us Are Brave*. "Perhaps this is the white female imagination, one that is reluctant and *unable* to construct theories about 'experiences I haven't had.' Yet Spacks never lived in 19th century Yorkshire, so why theorize about the Brontes?" (Walker 1982, 43).

Walker lets me know that it's a mistake to ignore race and class if I intend to talk about gender, just as much of a mistake as pretending that my experience is the same as that of my African American colleague. Fear prevents us from speaking about our cultural experience and how it might connect to others', but fear limits the imagination and the possibility for transformation. Walker suggests that white feminists are unwilling to construct theories where race and presumably class is a factor, because they have been unwilling to see themselves as constructed by those realities. Obviously, however, white people are constructed just as African Americans are, by their own ethnicities and social conditions. And, they are capable of talking about racism from their own experience. As Christine Sleeter says, "White people know a great deal about how racism works because we have observed white people intimately all our lives" (Sleeter 1994, 7). Once white teachers and students begin the process of examining our own racially and socially constructed backgrounds, we finally begin to unpack what Peggy McIntosh calls "this invisible knapsack of white privilege" (McIntosh 1988, 10).

White privilege, like male privilege, like middle-class privilege, is a kind of unconscious understanding, so much a part of the fabric of daily life that most people, especially if they are white or male or middle class, regard it as neutral, universal, normal, rather than constructed. It's what allows my students to say—and believe it—that race isn't a problem anymore. "It's all what the individual decides to do with his life, nothing else anymore," one student tells his group in a class discussion about affirmative action. As McIntosh (1988) says in her famous essay "White Privilege and Male Privilege," "Many, perhaps most, of our white students in the U.S. think that racism doesn't affect them because they're not people of color." In other words, white students don't see whiteness as a racial identity, and middle-class white students don't see their class as a constructed identity. But unearned privilege of color, class or gender distorts reality, and not only the humanity of disenfranchised groups but the humanity of those holding the privilege.

To become conscious of how we're constructed, *that* we're constructed, would seem to be a first step toward understanding. Black women critics who write of white Southern writers teach me how to use my experience to connect—not distort—the experience of others different in race and class from me. When Alice Walker writes about Flannery O'Connor in *In Search of Our Mothers' Gardens*, she says, "I remind myself of her courage and of how much—in her art—she has helped me to see. She destroyed the last vestiges of sentimentality in Southern writing; she caused white women to look ridiculous on pedestals, and she approached her black characters—as a mature artist—with unusual humility and restraint" (Walker 1983, 59). Walker's comments come from her place as reader and writer, and she uses context, rather than suppresses it, as she discusses that place. Other writers and critics, like Toni Morrison and Audre Lorde and bell hooks and Patricia Williams, help me understand how to make context become the beginning point for dealing with matters of race in my writing and teaching.

I can write about the work of these writers by asserting my own place within that work, by acknowledging the context of experience I bring to my reading, and I can teach the work of these writers by showing students how to make their own socially constructed identities a part of their own interpretations of what they read and what they write.

Feminist theory already contains within it the means to deal with context, with the difference class and race make, if feminists will remember to make *method* as well as *content* their pedagogical agenda. Some of those methods change patterns of responsibility and authority in ways that promote consciousness of power relationships cross-gender, cross-race, cross-class. Group work, long advocated by feminist theory for its encouragement of collaborative talk, undermines in positive ways the "class privilege" of the teacher, allowing student agendas to guide the work. Collaboration, in writing and talk, insists that writers and speakers learn from—and use—the insights and experiences of partners, who bring a variety of cultural, ethnic, and social contexts. Journal writing, dialogues, informal responses, and a host of other writing tasks can foster negotiation, challenging received ideas of all kinds, including privilege.

One of the most productive writing assignments I've used recently asks students to tell of their earliest memory in encountering someone of another race. The stories students write are revealing in their vagueness about how budding relationships ended. They are often poignant, often about loss. "I don't remember why I never went back to her house," said one young man telling about dinner at a white playmate's house. "Maybe she moved." The kind of negotiation that goes on as we read and hear about these stories allows students to come to new understandings about matters they might have ignored. "Multiculturalism" becomes much more than an education buzz word; it's a description of the people in the classroom and their relationships.

Hearing these stories may be the most powerful way for students to understand race, class and gender since it connects and distances experience at the same time. I've learned that reading stories, their own and others', brings students an understanding and consciousness of their own and others' contexts that allows them to grapple with the frustrating and painful issues they have grown up with and have hidden. Toni Morrison's novel *Sula* is a story of survival of a small African American community called "The Bottom" (white people live down the hill—ironically "on top" of the blacks they discriminate against). It's also a story of female friendship that survives class distinctions. I've taught this novel, and I use it to help my students frame discussions of race and culture and power. I use it now, too, to help me frame the story of my own race and class and context. The friends are reunited only after one is dead, but the realization of their connection is for the surviving friend, "like getting the use of an eye back, having a cataract removed" (Morrison 1987, 95).

My New Orleans' friend Marie and I weren't friends; we never got a chance to be. But telling our story, and reading Morrison's, feels like getting the use of an eye back. This is how the novel ends:

> And the loss pressed down on her chest and came up in her throat. "We was girls together," she said as though explaining something. "O Lord, Sula," she cried, "girl, girl, girlgirlgirl."
> It was a fine cry—loud and long—but it had no bottom and no top, just circles and circles of sorrow. (Morrison 1987, 230)

I respect the difference between the two pairs of girls, one bound by community and connection, the other separated by community and difference. I know that Sula and her friend Nell are not Marie and Hephzibah. And yet I know "we was girls together." Black and white women—and men—in the South can find a way to be whole when we tell and hear all our stories, the stories of employed and employer, farmer and merchant, poor white and poor black, finally to face the circles and circles of sorrow that surround and connect us.

Notes

1. Katherine Mayberry's essay, "White Feminists Who Study Black Writers," appeared in the *Chronicle of Higher Education*, November 1994

(p. 39). In it, she not only recounted the events at the Women's Studies Conference where African American women walked out of a session on Toni Morrison where only white women were presenting, but also described the false position of the white scholar, who "carries a false sense of our own power and of the docility of the texts we claim to master." Her position led to other discussions about the viability of white feminists writing about black authors.

2. Deborah Gray-White's *Arn't I A Woman* (NY: Knopf, 1987) examines the relationship of black and white women in the antebellum South, locating evidence of plantation mistresses selling children of slave women who "looked suspiciously white," obviously suspecting their husbands of having fathered the children.

Works Cited

Chestnut, Mary Boykin. 1990. *Diary from Dixie*. Boston: Harvard University Press.

hooks, bell. 1995. *Teaching to Transgress*. NY: Routledge.

Lorde, Audre. 1983. "An Open Letter to Mary Daly." *This Bridge Called My Back: Writings by Radical Women of Color*. Edited by Cherri Moraga and Gloria Anzaldúa. NY: Kitchen Table Press.

McIntosh, Peggy. 1988. "White Privilege and Male Privilege: A Personal Account of Coming to See Correspondences Through Work in Women's Studies." Wellesley, MA: Wellesley College Center for Research on Women.

Morrison, Toni. 1987. *Sula*. NY: Plume/Dutton.

Sleeter, Christine. 1994. "White Racism." *Multicultural Education*. Spring: 5–9.

Spacks, Patricia Meyer. Quoted in Walker, Alice "One Child of One's Own: A Meaningful Digression Within the Work(s)."

Walker, Alice. 1982. "One Child of One's Own: A Meaningful Digression Within the Work(s)." *All the Women are White, All the Blacks are Men, But Some of Us Are Brave: Black Women's Studies*. Edited by Gloria T. Hull, Patricia Bell Scott, and Barbara Smith. Old Westbury, NY: The Feminist Press, 37–44.

———. 1983. *In Search of Our Mothers' Gardens*. NY: Harcourt Brace.

Chapter 20

Time Alone, Place Apart: The Role of Spiracy in Using the Power of Solitude

Jacqueline Jones Royster

Growing up as an only child, I found myself alone frequently, and in the early years, I struggled mightily to distinguish between being alone and being lonely, being apart and being isolated, living differently and being different. Ultimately, I came to understand distinctions among solitude, loneliness, isolation, and alienation, and across the matrix of these experiences, I learned to appreciate the power of solitude. I consider myself fortunate that I had parents who helped me to like and to value myself without external affirmation. I grew to enjoy my own company. With their guidance, times alone became opportunities to enter the worlds of books, to reflect, to explore possibilities, to process observations and experiences, to act out in my own head untold possibilities, to imagine. My parents listened to my ravings and my cravings, and they encouraged me to study, to grow, and to develop.

Further, during the times alone, I learned to focus my energy toward action and productivity. I was able to crystallize my imaginings in words, in pictures, in colors. Perhaps my greatest asset, beyond loving and supportive parents, was that there was no shortage of books, paper, pencils, crayons, or other tools that might facilitate such explorations. I harbored theories and concepts, neither of which I would have labeled such high-sounding words. I identified solutions to little problems in my own life and big problems out in the world. In other words, in the safe space of my own solitude, having time alone and place apart, I let myself loose in the world.

As a young child, then, I had the luxury of time. I had the security of places that were my own. I had spiritual and physical nourishment from my parents, and I had a peace of mind that comes with respecting one's own talents and abilities. I was able to feel the joy and power of solitude, and I experienced its blessings as evidenced particularly by the validation of academic success. I was able to see firsthand what the solitary activities of thinking and writing alone with one's self can do. I learned early to rejoice in the potential of being alone.

Life, however, has a way of continuing and changing. As an adult who has adult responsibilities, I have been plagued by this image of solitude, by the challenge of finding time alone and place apart. These are luxuries that get harder and harder to come by. When we have jobs that are time-consuming; when we value relationships with others (partners, children, parents, friends, other significant others) that require maintenance and demand time, thoughtfulness, and energy, how do we maintain a balance that allows time and space for self in solitude? What happens if this luxurious image of solitude cannot hold? If we do not have ready access to this potential, how, then, do we remain productive? How do we reach and sustain a state of being that allows us to make good use of our talents and abilities as thinkers and writers?

I am an active teacher, writer, scholar; a mother of two; a wife of an active professional; a daughter of a woman from whom I still draw strength and who deserves to know my love and appreciation; a friend to a relatively small group of people who are invaluable in my life; a person within a closely knit family who lives in a city filled with family; a member of a socially conscious community organization that dedicates itself to public service and political action. I have multiple loyalties beyond myself, and there is never enough time to do all that ideally either I would want to do or should do. Or, on the occasions when I do have time alone, there are still multiple obligations across which to divide my thinking and my energy, and few spaces, large or small, that I can claim as exclusively my own. When I feel most distracted by the fullness of my life, I allow myself the luxury of imagining a future state when my felt needs are ideally met. In the meantime, however, I resist the desire to let myself drown in a sea of obligations that are at the same time also my pleasures and my passions. Instead, I look for inspiration and for alternatives.

Again and again, I have turned to the world of African American women writers. They have articulated my thoughts and desires, helped me to name my struggle, and demonstrated with their lives that productivity is possible even when conditions are not at their best. Across the generations, these women have been, for me, beacons of light in what can often feel like pervasive darkness. From their lives and words, I breathe into myself hope, courage, and grit, and I can see myself beginning to fashion what I need: new pathways to solitude, new ways of looking at time and at time alone, new ways of conceiving a notion of place, and other ways, if not new ones, to create places apart.

I feel kinship, for example, with Gertrude E. H. Bustill Mossell, who in 1908 wrote *The Work of the Afro-American Woman* under the name Mrs. N(athan) F(rancis) Mossell. Mossell was a journalist who wrote for the periodical press, both white and African American. In one of the essays in this collection, "A Lofty Study," Mossell describes a visit to the home of a member of the Society of Friends during which she has a moment of insight. The woman took Mossell to a room in the attic, the woman's study. Mossell describes its suitability for work (i.e., for writing): "It was so quiet, so peaceful, the air was so fresh and pure, it seemed like living in a new atmosphere" (p. 127). The sight of this room, so pleasingly decorated, so specifically appropriate for study showed her what was missing from her own environment. She was amazed that she had not thought of such a thing, a place of her own, if not a room in the attic, then "at least a corner" (p. 128). She says: "What a satisfaction to put everything in order, turn the key, and feel that all is safe—no busy hands, no stray breeze can carry away or disarrange some choice idea kept for the future delectation of the public! Besides this, one who writes much generally finds that she can write best at some certain spot. Ideas come more rapidly, sentences take more lucid forms. Very often the least change from that position will break up the train of thought" (p. 129).

A reader of this short essay can easily receive the impression that between these lines Mossell alludes to the encumbrances on her own work, or in the very least, to her understanding of adjustments that women often must make in anticipation of the hands of children or the needs and preferences of professional husbands who are "educated to work alone" (p. 128). The reader can also infer that Mossell recognizes that the woman's own work, her own intellectual enterprises rather than her household/family duties, may not have central priority in the home. We can infer that she understands that women may not be "educated to work alone" or "educated" to feel entitled to the privilege of time and place alone. We may also infer that at some level Mossell seems to understand that the first barrier to a place of one's own is, perhaps, in the woman's own mind. She writes: "I just sat down and wondered why I had never thought of this very room for a study" (p. 127).

With the sight of this room, Mossell awakens to a need for solitude, for a place apart. Twenty-one years later, Virginia Woolf makes this same case quite powerfully in *A Room of One's Own* (1929). Eight decades later in our own day, often women like myself who think and write still must awaken or be awakened to the necessity of recognizing, naming, and claiming a need for solitude. We must also awaken to the necessity of feeling entitled to a place apart.

I feel similar kinship with Anna Julia Cooper whose thoughts extend the sense of need beyond solitude as a place apart. Cooper was a former slave who went on to become a teacher, a writer, a scholar, a social activist, a woman who was among the first African American women to earn a Ph.D., and the first from this group to be named president of a college. Sixteen years earlier than Mossell, in 1892, Cooper wrote in *A Voice from the South*:

> One mind in a family or in a town may show a penchant for art, for literature, for the learned professions, or more bookish lore. You will know it when it is there. No need to probe for it. It is a light that cannot be hid under a bushel—and I would try to enable that mind to go the full length of its desires. Let it follow its bent and develop its talent as far as possible: and the whole community might well be glad to contribute its labor and money for the sustenance and cultivation of this brain. Just as earth gives its raw material, its carbons, hydrogen, and oxygen, for the tree which is to elaborate them into foliage, flower and fruit, so the base elements, bread and money furnished the true brain worker come back to us with compound interest in the rich thought, the invention, the poem, the painting, the statue. (pp. 262–63)

In this passage, Cooper brings to life images that are elemental, basic, foundational. She conjures visions of growth and development from the realm of the ordinary, and through the implied contrasts with the ways in which we do and do not support the development of human beings, she places American society before a tribunal of reason and justice as she appeals for a place in which academic pursuits and learned enterprises are valued and specifically nourished, given the context of the book, even for women. Cooper appeals for "bread" to sustain both body and soul and entreats her audience to understand that "base" elements (bread, money) are the foundation from which excellence grows and through which the society reaps reward. In her own case, with a mind so ingenious and vibrant, she received precious little of either, such that she says, "I constantly felt (as I suppose many an ambitious girl has felt) a thumping from within unanswered by any beckoning from without" (p. 76). We hear an undernourished spirit. We know her pain and her frustration. But if we look at her life and contributions, we also see her resiliency and her determination to be productive and to make a difference.

Like Cooper, I sometimes long for easier access to conditions—the time, space, resources, circumstances, the peace of mind—that would allow me to devote sustained energy to thinking, reading, writing as I feel inclined to engage in them and not at the will and/or demand of others; to exchanging ideas with others in the interest of spiritual and intellectual stimulation and not just toward the completion of assigned tasks, to searching for truth/sense/understanding and not just for ways to get things done in the face of encumbrances and constraints amid balances of power, policy, or privilege that are not tilted in my direction. I would like the time and space that money can buy but also spiritual nourishment so that I can sustain and insulate myself as well as conserve and maximize my energy as I work. Like Cooper, sometimes, I feel "a thumping from within." Unlike her, occasionally I hear resonant chords in the distance, but still I long for them to be closer, clearer, more full-bodied, and more consistently available. I look at Cooper, however, and all that she was able to do with less than I, and I am renewed.

A third African American woman writer from whom I gather strength and inspiration is Maria W. Stewart, a free-born woman who wrote in the 1930s and who is generally acknowledged by scholars as the first African American woman political writer. She was a pioneer in a day when precious few women, and certainly not African American women, either spoke or wrote in public arenas. In her very first publication, a tract addressed to the people of color in Boston, Massachusetts, Stewart reflects on her actions in a way that helps me to implant, not just the need for solitude, but more the need to make use of the power of solitude within a more meaningful framework. She wrote that

> what I have done, has been done with an eye single to the glory of God, and to promote the good of souls. I have neither kindred nor friends. *I stand alone in your midst* [emphasis mine], exposed to the fiery darts of the devil, and to the assaults of wicked men. But though all the powers of earth and hell were to combine against me, though all nature should sink into decay, still I would trust in the Lord, and joy in the God of my salvation. For I am full persuaded that he will bring me off conqueror, yea, more than conqueror, through him who hath loved me and given himself for me. (p. 41)

As an academic, I have found that time alone and place apart are vitalized by what I have come to call, for lack perhaps of a better term, a sense of spiracy. I have come to understand this term as a recognition of the ways in which I am situated or situate myself within the worlds in which I live and breathe. It is not just a sense of self. It is a more a sense of self in particular space as such territory may be defined in variable but meaning-filled ways. I find that with a sense of spiracy, there is the capacity to be propelled toward solitude as a state of consciousness.

Maria Stewart wrote, "I stand alone in your midst," and like her, at some point along my way, I sensed in myself the need to find a breathing space, even in the midst of others, from which I could do more than just breathe and experience the world, but also from which I could envision it. The process of trying to meet this need has felt like a cleansing, clarifying process, one that I have had to manage in the midst of "the fiery darts of the devil, and the assaults of wicked men." Moreover, as I have gained a better notion of good breathing and greater visibility, I have discovered that often these spaces are very personal, solitary ones, places that are hand-fashioned to meet individual needs, but in being so, they tend to be, as I have come to recognize and understand them, well-fortified, richly generative, and wondrously self-sustaining, even in the face of ongoing darts, devils, and wickedness.

In my life as an academic, this sense of spiracy seems to emerge from points of convergence in literacy studies, Women's Studies, and African disapora studies. This is the space from which I envision the world. In each discipline, separately, I can feel connection, but I feel most energized, most capable of productivity at a point of convergence. In Black Women's Studies, a point at which women's studies meet African diaspora studies, I have found many moments of intellectual and spiritual synergy, which, in my experience, seems essential to our abilities to maximize our uses of the power of solitude. I feel most synergetic, however, when all three disciplines converge at points that allow for a multidimensionality of connection and vision. Through this multidimensional experience, I live and breathe, sense my own potential, and feel capable of productivity. I feel in focus, attuned to my thoughts.

As I have reflected on this process, I have become aware that the synergy, the sense of connectedness, the sense of spiracy comes, in part at least, from a coalescing of values, beliefs, priorities, interests, experiences, and training. However, I recognize the three disciplines—sites of training, research, and learning—as lenses through which I can make sense of this spectrum, see the world, think, write, and search for truths. On a spiritual level, therefore, I feel well-seated and generously endowed with possibility.

As in Stewart's case, this process seems to have brought me to a sense of mission, and in keeping with the tradition of Black feminist thought (see Royster 1990), intellect, ethics, and action seem to have become one. Stewart considered herself to be chosen as an instrument of God and dedicated herself to "the Glory of God" as she sought to "promote the good of souls." One might say that she was a politically conscious evangelist, seeing evils in the world that could be addressed through the good will, hard work, and good sense of men and women.

In similar manner, I consider myself to be an academic activist, a person who has chosen (even if I have not been chosen) to be a politically conscious watchdog, a sentry for the need for positive change in the world of education. My mission is twofold: (1) to document to the extent that I can the lives, conditions, and achievements of women of African descent, both historically and currently; and (2) to use the understanding that I acquire of life, literacy, and learning in the interest of academic excellence, intellectual growth, and the individual development of my students. At this point in my understanding, then, I am beginning to see solitude less as a physical state of being, which I cannot always maintain, than as a state of consciousness, which I can maintain more easily. I find that, even though I still look toward some future state of solitude within which I am ideally nurtured, I am more at peace than I might have been about finding ways to use the power of time alone and place apart, despite the limitations in access that are imposed by my circumstances.

First of all, I find that I am much better at creating illusions than I used to be. As Mossell has urged, I create the illusion of space at the corner of a table, at a chair in an otherwise crowded room, in piles of file folders with descriptive labels, or boxes of diskettes, all of which help to provide for me a sense of order and organization to a sometimes chaotic existence. I maintain a sense of continuity, order, and privacy, and I name these small organizers of my life and my work the exclusive room of my own. I find my own place within the covers of multicolored folders and within the tiny spaces of little boxes.

In addition, I take time where I find it. With a heightened consciousness of good, meaningful work, I find solitude even amid a crowd—on an airplane, among children at play, during any of an endless number of meetings, lectures, or other public events; or I find it in atypical places, like my favorite place this year—the shower. I listen, not to the chaos around me, but to myself. My thoughts claim authority regardless of my physical surroundings, and I listen. I find it wise, therefore, never to be far from my journal, the encoded key by which I can go about the business of my days and still have a mechanism that can record any movements toward focus and unlock both potential and productivity.

This conglomeration of things is the way that I have found to make use of the power of solitude when I do not have the luxury of sustained times alone or exclusive places apart. Through such mechanisms, I try to maintain balance, sometimes with more success than others. I make time for family, for job, for friends, occasionally for community service, and I feel that all is relatively well. However, when illusions become too inadequate, I stop pretending and also make time for myself in more traditional ways. I claim at that point, as I feel that I am entitled to claim, more substantial chunks of time and a literal room of my own, temporary though they will have to be. I understand clearly that my solutions are not magic ones, but they are workable ones. For me, they have become the truth until some other truth arrives.

At the base of it all, I distinguish the vital role that my parents played in the formation of fundamental notions of potential and productivity, and I feel privileged. At base, also, is a sense of spiracy that has brought me focus, and with sincere gratitude, I honor the lives and legacies of African American women writers for being so instructive and so inspirational. With their help, I feel even greater privilege. I count this twofold heritage as my intellectual ancestry (see David 1987), and from this place, I find solace and solitude, and feel empowered to make whatever use I can of whatever potential is available in my efforts to preserve, to carry forth, and to add to the legacies of black women's writing.

Works Cited

Cooper, A. J. 1988. *A Voice from the South.* New York: Oxford University Press (Schomburg Library of Nineteenth-Century Black Women Writers).

David, D. 1987. *Intellectual Women and Victorian Patriarchy: Harriet Martineau, Elizabeth Barrett Browning, George Eliot.* New York: Cornell University Press.

Mossell, Mrs. N. F. 1988. *The Work of the Afro-American Woman.* New York: Oxford University Press (Schomburg Library of Nineteenth-Century Black Women Writers).

Richardson, M., ed. 1987. *Maria W. Stewart, America's First Black Woman Political Writer.* Bloomington, Ind.: Indiana University Press.

Royster, J. J. 1990. Perspectives on the Intellectual Tradition of Black Women Writers. *The Right to Literacy.* Edited by A. Lunsford, H. Moglen and J. Slevin. New York: Modern Language Association, 103–12.

Woolf, V. 1989. *A Room of One's Own.* San Diego, Calif.: Harcourt Brace Jovanovich.

A Selected Bibliography

Autobiography Studies

This bibliography contains selected autobiographies, autobiographical essays, and secondary sources.

Adams, Timothy Dow. 1990. *Telling Lies in Modern American Autobiography.* Chapel Hill: University of North Carolina Press.

Allen, Paula Gunn. 1986. *The Sacred Hoop: Recovering the Feminine in American Indian Traditions.* Boston: Beacon.

Allende, Isabel. 1994. *Paula.* New York: Harper Collins.

Allison, Dorothy. 1995. *Two or Three Things I Know For Sure.* New York: Dutton.

Angelou, Maya. 1969. *I Know Why the Caged Bird Sings.* New York: Random.

Anzaldúa, Gloria. 1987. *Borderlands/La Frontera: The New Mestiza.* San Francisco: Aunt Lute.

Ascher, Carol, Louise De Salvo, and Sara Ruddick, eds. 1984. *Between Women: Biographers, Novelists, Critics, Teachers, and Artists Write About Their Work on Women.* Boston: Beacon.

Ashton-Warner, Sylvia. 1967. *Myself.* New York: Simon.

———. 1963. *Teacher.* New York: Simon.

Baker, Houston A., Jr. 1975. "The Problem of Being: Some Reflections on Black Autobiography." *Obsidian* 1: 18–30.

Bateson, Mary Catherine. 1990. *Composing a Life.* New York: Plume.

Belenky, Mary Field, Blythe McVicker Clinchy, Nancy Rule Goldberger, and Jill Mattuck Tarule. 1986. *Women's Ways of Knowing: The Development of Self, Voice and Mind.* New York: Basic.

Benstock, Shari, ed. 1988. *The Private Self: Theory and Practice of Women's Autobiographical Writing.* Chapel Hill: University of North Carolina Press.

Bizzell, Patricia. 1992. Introduction. *Academic Discourse and Critical Consciousness.* Pittsburgh: University of Pittsburgh Press: 3–30.

Bloom, Lynn Z. 1991. "Teaching College English as a Woman." *College English* 54: 818–825.

Boland, Eavan. 1995. *Object Lessons: The Life of the Woman and the Poet in Our Time.* New York: Norton.

Braham, Jeanne. 1995. *Crucial Conversations: Interpreting American Literary Autobiographies by Women.* New York: Teachers College.

Braxton, Joanne M. 1989. *Black Women Writing Autobiography.* Philadelphia: Temple University Press.

Bridwell-Bowles, Lillian. 1995. "Freedom, Form, Function: Varieties of Academic Discourse." *CCC* 46: 46–61.

Brodkey, Linda. 1994. "Writing on the Bias." *College English* 56: 527–547.

Brodzki, Bella, and Celeste Schenck, eds. 1988. *Life/Lines: Theorizing Women's Autobiography.* Ithaca: Cornell University Press.

Bruner, Jerome. 1986. *Actual Minds, Possible Worlds.* Cambridge, MA: Harvard University Press.

———. 1983. *In Search of Mind: Essays in Autobiography.* New York: Harper.

Bruss, Elizabeth. 1976. *Autobiographical Acts: The Changing Situation of a Literary Genre.* Baltimore: Johns Hopkins University Press.

Bunkers, Suzanne. 1993. "What do Women Really Mean? Thoughts on Women's Diaries and Lives." *The Intimate Critique: Autobiographical Literary Criticism.* Edited by Diane P. Freedman, Olivia Frey, and Frances Murphy Zauhar. Durham: Duke University Press, 207–221.

Butterfield, Stephen. 1974. *Black Autobiography in America.* Amherst: University of Massachusetts Press.

Cary, Lorene. 1991. *Black Ice.* New York: Vintage.

Chernin, Kim. 1983. *In My Mother's House: A Daughter's Story.* New York: Harper.

Cliff, Michelle. 1985. *The Land Of Look Behind.* Ithaca, NY: Firebrand.

Cofer, Judith Ortiz. 1990. *Silent Dancing: A Partial Remembrance of a Puerto Rican Childhood.* Houston: Arte Publico.

Cooper, Joanne E. 1991. "Telling Our Own Stories: The Reading and Writing of Journals and Diaries." Witherell and Noddings 96–112.

Couser, Thomas G. 1989. *Altered Egos: Authority in American Autobiography.* New York: Oxford.

———. 1979. *American Autobiography: The Prophetic Mode.* Amherst: University of Massachusetts Press.

Culley, Margo. 1985. *A Day at a Time: The Diary Literature of American Women from 1764 to the Present.* New York: Feminist.

———. 1992. *American Women's Autobiography: Fea(s)ts of Memory.* Madison: University of Wisconsin Press.

Cutuly, Joan. 1993. *Home of the Wildcats: Perils of an English Teacher.* Urbana: NCTE.

Dahl, Karin L, ed. 1992. *Teacher as Writer: Entering the Professional Conversation.* Urbana: NCTE.

Didion, Joan. 1961. "On Keeping a Notebook." *Slouching Toward Bethlehem* (1979). New York: Simon, 131–141.

Dillard, Annie. 1987. *An American Childhood.* New York: Harper.

Eakin, Paul John. 1985. *Fictions in Autobiography: Studies in the Art of Self-Invention.* Princeton: Princeton University Press.

Earle, William. 1972. *Autobiographical Consciousness.* Chicago: Quadrangle.

Erikson, Erik. 1968. *Identity Youth and Crisis.* New York: Norton.

Field, Joanna. 1981. *A Life of One's Own.* Los Angeles: J. P. Tarcher.

Florio-Ruane, Susan. 1994. "The Future Teachers' Autobiography Club: Preparing Educators to Support Literacy Learning in Culturally Diverse Classrooms." *English Education* 26.1: 52–66.

Fowler, Lois J., and David H. Fowler. 1990. *American Women in Autobiography.* Albany: State University of New York Press.

Freedman, Diane P., Olivia Frey, and Frances Murphy Zauhar, eds. 1993. *The Intimate Critique: Autobiographical Literary Criticism.* Durham: Duke University Press.

Gilyard, Keith. 1991. *Voices of the Self: A Study of Language Competence.* Detroit: Wayne State University Press.

Gornick, Vivian. 1987. *Fierce Attachments.* New York: Simon.

Hampl, Patricia. 1981. *A Romantic Education.* Boston: Houghton.

Heilbrun, Carolyn G. 1988. *Writing A Woman's Life.* New York: Ballantine.

Helle, Anita Plath. 1991. "Reading Women's Autobiographies: A Map of Reconstructed Knowing." Witherell and Noddings 48–66.

Hellman, Lillian. 1973. *Pentimento: A Book of Portraits.* Boston: Little.

———. 1976. *Scoundrel Time.* Boston: Little.

———. 1969. *An Unfinished Woman.* Boston: Little.

hooks, bell. 1989. *Talking Back. thinking feminist: thinking black.* Boston: South End.

———. 1994. *Teaching to Transgress: Education as the Practice of Freedom.* New York: Routledge.

Howarth, William L. 1974. "Some Principles of Autobiography." *New Literary History* 5: 363–381.

Jelinek, Estelle C. 1976. "Teaching Women's Autobiography." *College English* 38: 32–45.

———. 1986. *The Tradition of Women's Autobiography: From Antiquity to the Present.* Boston: Twayne.

———, ed. 1980. *Women's Autobiography: Essays in Criticism.* Bloomington: Indiana University Press.

Juhasz, Suzanne. 1978. "Some Deep Old Desk or Capacious Hold All: Form and Women's Autobiography." *College English* 39: 663–70.

Kingston, Maxine Hong. 1976. *The Woman Warrior: Memoirs of a Girlhood Among Ghosts.* New York: Knopf.

Lifshin, Lyn, ed. 1982. *Ariadne's Thread: A Collection of Contemporary Women's Journals.* New York: Harper.

Lionnet, Francoise. 1989. *Autobiographical Voices: Race, Gender, Self-Portraiture.* Ithaca: Cornell University Press.

Lorde, Audre. 1980. *The Cancer Journals.* San Francisco: Spinster/Aunt Lute.

———. 1984. *Sister Outsider: Essays and Speeches by Audre Lorde.* Freedom, CA: Crossing.

———. 1982. *Zami. A New Spelling of My Name: A Biomythography.* Freedom, CA: Crossing.

Lu, Min-zhan. 1987. "From Silence to Words: Writing as Struggle." *College English* 49: 437–448.

Mairs, Nancy. 1994. *Voice Lessons: On Becoming a (Woman) Writer.* Boston: Beacon.

McCarthy, Mary. 1957. *Memories of a Catholic Girlhood.* New York: Harcourt.

McQuade, Donald. 1992. "Living In-And On-the Margins." *CCC* 43: 11–22.

Miller, Nancy K. 1991. *Getting Personal: Feminist Occasions and Other Autobiographical Acts.* New York: Routledge.

Moraga, Cherrie. 1983. *Loving in the War Years.* Boston: South End.

Moraga, Cherrie, and Gloria Anzaldúa, eds. 1981. *This Bridge Called My Back: Writings by Radical Women of Color.* Watertown, MA: Persephone.

Morrison, Toni. 1987. "The Site of Memory." Zinsser 101–124.

Murray, Donald M. 1991. "All Writing Is Autobiography." *CCC* 42: 69–74.

Neuman, Shirley, ed. 1991. *Autobiography and Questions of Gender.* London: Frank Cass.

Olney, James, ed. 1980. *Autobiography: Essays Theoretical and Critical.* Princeton: Princeton University Press.

———. 1972. *Metaphors of Self: The Meaning of Autobiography.* Princeton: Princeton University Press.

Olsen, Tillie. 1978. *Silences.* New York: Delacorte.

O'Reilley, Mary Rose. 1993. *The Peaceable Classroom.* Portsmouth, NH: Boynton Cook/ Heinemann.

Ostriker, Alicia. 1983. *Writing Like a Woman.* Ann Arbor: University of Michigan Press.

Pascal, Roy. 1960. *Design and Truth in Autobiography.* Cambridge: Harvard University Press.

Peterson, Linda H. 1991. "Gender and the Autobiographical Essay: Research Perspectives, Pedagogical Practices." *CCC* 42: 170–83.

Porter, Roger. 1977. "Word, Mirror, and Self: Autobiography in the Classroom." *The English Record* 18: 2–5.

Rich, Adrienne. 1986. *Blood, Bread and Poetry: Selected Prose 1979–1985.* New York: Norton.

———. 1979. *On Lies, Secrets and Silence: Selected Prose 1966–1978.* New York: Norton.

————. 1993. *What Is Found There: Notebooks on Poetry and Politics.* New York: Norton.

Rose, Mike. 1989. *Lives on the Boundary.* New York: Free.

Ruddick, Sara, and Pamela Daniels, eds. 1977. *Working It Out: Twenty-Three Women Writers, Artists, Scientists, and Scholars Talk About Their Lives and Work.* New York: Pantheon.

Salvidar, Ramon. 1985."Ideologies of the Self: Chicano Autobiography." *Diacritics* 15. 3: 25–33.

Sarton, May. 1973. *Journal of a Solitude.* New York: Norton.

Schwartz, Mimi, ed. 1991. *Writer's Craft: Teacher's Art.* Portsmouth, NH: Boynton Cook/Heinemann.

Shea, Daniel B. Jr. 1969. *Spiritual Autobiographical in Early America.* Princeton: Princeton University Press.

Shumaker, Wayne. 1954. *English Autobiography: Its Emergency, Materials and Form.* Berkeley: University of California Press.

Smith, Sidonie. 1987. *A Poetics of Women's Autobiography: Marginality and the Fictions of Self-Representation.* Bloomington: Indiana University Press.

————.1993. *Subjectivity, Identity and Women's Autobiographical Practices in the Twentieth Century.* Bloomington: Indiana University Press.

————. 1974. *Where I'm Bound: Patterns of Slavery and Freedom in Black American Autobiography.* Westport, CT: Greenwood.

Smith, Sidonie, and Julia Watson, eds. 1992. *De/Colonizing the Subject: The Politics of Gender in Women's Autobiography.* Minneapolis: University of Minnesota Press.

Sommers, Nancy. 1992. "Between the Drafts." *CCC* 43: 23–31.

————. "I Stand Here Writing." 1993. *College English* 55: 420–428.

Spacks, Patricia M. 1973. "Reflecting Women." *Yale Review* 63: 26–42.

Spacks, Patricia Meyer. 1977. "Women's Stories, Women's Selves." *Hudson Review* 30: 29–46.

Spengemann, William C. 1980. *The Forms of Autobiography: Episodes in the History of a Literary Genre.* New Haven: Yale University Press.

Staunton, Donna C. 1987. *The Female Autograph: Theory and Practice of Autobiography from the Tenth to the Twentieth Century.* Chicago: University of Chicago Press.

Steinem, Gloria. 1983. *Outrageous Acts and Everyday Rebellions.* New York: Holt.

Stepto, Robert. 1979. *From Behind the Veil: A Study of Afro-American Narrative.* Urbana: University of Illinois Press.

Sternburg, Janet, ed. 1980. *The Writer on her Work.* Vol. 1. New York: Norton.

————, ed. 1991. *The Writer on Her Work.* Vol. II. New York: Norton.

Stone, Albert. 1982. *Autobiographical Occasions and Original Acts.* Philadelphia: University of Pennsylvania Press.

Swann, Brian, and Arnold Krupat, eds. 1987. *I Tell You Now: Autobio-graphical Essays by Native American Writers.* Lincoln: University of Nebraska Press.

Tokarcyzk, Michelle M., and Elizabeth A. Fay, eds. 1993. *Working-Class Women in the Academy: Laborers in the Knowledge Factory.* Amherst: University of Massachusetts Press.

Tompkins, Jane. 1987. "Me and My Shadow." *New Literary History* 19: 169–178.

———. 1996. *A Life in School: What the Teacher Learned.* Reading, Massachusetts: Addison-Wesley.

Villanueva, Victor, Jr. 1993. *Bootstraps: From An American Academic of Color.* Urbana: NCTE.

Walker, Alice. 1983. *In Search of Our Mothers' Gardens.* New York: Har-court.

Warner, Sylvia Ashton. 1967. *Myself.* New York: Simon.

———. 1963. *Teacher.* New York: Simon.

Wear, Delese, ed. 1993. *The Center of the Web: Women and Solitude.* Al-bany: State University of New York Press.

Weintraub, Karl J. 1978. *The Value of the Individual: Self and Circum-stance in Autobiography.* Chicago: University of Chicago Press.

Welty, Eudora. 1984. *One Writer's Beginnings.* Cambridge: Harvard University Press.

Williams, Patricia J. 1991. *The Alchemy of Race and Rights: Diary of a Law Professor.* Cambridge: Harvard University Press.

Wolf, Christa. 1970. *The Quest for Christa T.* Translated by Christopher Middleton. New York: Farrar.

Woolf, Virginia. 1976. *Moments of Being.* San Diego: Harcourt.

———. 1929. *A Room of One's Own.* New York: Harcourt. (Reprinted in 1957.)

———. 1953. *A Writer's Diary.* New York: Harcourt.

Zinsser, William, ed. 1987. *Inventing the Truth: The Art and Craft of Memoir.* Boston: Houghton.

Feminist Theory and Pedagogy and Composition Studies

Abel, Elizabeth, ed. 1982. *Writing and Sexual Difference.* Chicago: Uni-versity of Chicago Press.

Abel, Elizabeth, Marianne Hirsch, and Elizabeth Langland, eds. 1983. *The Voyage In: Fictions of Female Development.* Hanover, NH: Uni-versity Press of New England.

Aisenberg, Nadya, and Mona Harrington. 1988. *Women of Academe: Outsiders in the Sacred Grove.* Amherst: University of Massachu-setts Press.

Alcoff, Linda. 1988. "Cultural Feminism versus Poststructuralism: The Identity Crisis in Feminist Theory." *Reconstructing the Academy:*

Women's Education and Women's Studies. Edited by Elizabeth Minnich, Jean O'Barr, and Rachel Rosenfeld. Chicago: University of Chicago Press, 257–288.

Annas, Pamela. 1985. "Style as Politics: A Feminist Approach to the Teaching of Writing." *College English* 47: 360–372.

———. 1987. "Silences, Feminist Language Research, and the Teaching of Writing." Caywood and Overing 3–18.

Anzaldúa, Gloria, ed. 1990. *Making Face, Making Soul: Haciendo Caras. Creative and Critical Perspectives by Feminists of Color.* San Francisco: Aunt Lute.

Ashton-Jones, Evelyn, ed. 1990. "Gender, Culture, and Ideology." Special Issue of *Journal of Advanced Composition* 10.

Ashton-Jones, Evelyn, and Dene Kay Thomas. "Composition, Collaboration, and Women's Ways of Knowing." Ashton-Jones 275–292.

Bauer, Dale M. 1990. "The Other 'F' Word: The Feminist in the Classroom." *College English* 52: 385–396.

Berg, Temma F., ed. 1989. *Engendering the Word.* Chicago: University of Illinois Press.

Bishop, Wendy. 1990. "Learning Our Own Ways to Situate Composition." Ashton-Jones 339–356.

Bizzell, Patricia. "Rhetorical Authority as a Woman." Phelps and Emig 27–42.

Bleich, David. 1990. "Sexism in Academic Styles of Learning." Ashton-Jones 231–248.

Bloom, Lynn Z. 1990. "Why Don't We Write What We Teach? And Publish It?" Ashton-Jones 87–100.

Bridwell-Bowles, Lillian. 1995. "Discourse and Diversity: Experimental Writing Within the Academy." Phelps and Emig 43–66.

Brown, Lyn Mikel, and Nancy Hoffman, eds. 1991. "Women, Girls and the Culture of Education." *Women's Studies Quarterly* 1 & 2.

Bunch, Charlotte and Sandra Pollack, eds. 1983. *Learning Our Way: Essays in Feminist Education.* Trumansburg, NY: Crossing.

Butler, Judith. 1990. *Gender Trouble: Feminism and the Subversion of Identity.* New York: Routledge.

Caywood, Cynthia L., and Gillian R. Overing, eds. 1987. *Teaching Writing: Pedagogy, Gender, Equity.* Albany: State University of New York Press.

Chodorow, Nancy. 1978. *The Reproduction of Mothering: Psychoanalysis and the Sociology of Gender.* Berkeley: University of California Press.

Christian, Barbara. 1985. *Black Feminist Criticism: Perspectives on Black Women Writers.* New York: Pergamon.

———. 1980. *Black Women's Novelists: The Development of a Tradition.* Westport, CT: Greenwood.

Cixous, Hélène. 1980. "The Laugh of the Medusa." Translated by Keith Cohen and Paula Cohen. *New Feminisms: An Anthology.* Edited by Elaine Marks and Isabelle de Courtivron. Amherst: University of Massachusetts Press, 245–264.

Clark, Beverly Lyon, and Sonja Wiedenhaupt. 1992. "On Blocking and Unblocking Sonja: A Case Study in Two Voices." *CCC* 43: 55–74.

Culley, Margo, and Catherine Portuges, eds. 1985. *Gendered Subjects: The Dynamics of Feminist Teaching.* Boston: Routledge.

Daumer, Elisabeth, and Sandra Runzo. 1987. Caywood and Overing 45–64.

Dingwaney, Anuradha, and Laurence Needham. 1992. "Feminist Theory and Practice in the Writing Classroom: A Critique and a Prospectus." *Constructing Rhetorical Education: From the Classroom to the Community.* Edited by Marie Secor and Davida Charney. Carbondale: Southern Illinois University Press, 6–25.

Dinnerstein, Dorothy. 1976. *The Mermaid and the Minotaur: Sexual Arrangement and Human Malaise.* New York: Colophon.

DuBois, Ellen Carol, et al. 1985. *Feminist Scholarship: Kindling in the Groves of Academe.* Urbana: University of Illinois Press.

Ebert, Teresa L. 1991. "The 'Difference' of Postmodern Feminism." *College English* 53: 886–904.

Eichhorn, Jill, et al. 1992. "A Symposium on Feminist Experience in the Composition Class." *CCC* 43: 297–337.

Enos, Theresa. 1990. "Gender and Journals: Conservers or Innovators." *PRE/TEXT* 9: 209–214.

Ferguson, Mary Anne, ed. 1986. *Images of Women in Literature.* 4th ed. Boston: Houghton.

Fetterley, Judith. 1978. *The Resisting Reader: A Feminist Approach to American Fiction.* Bloomington: Indiana University Press.

Flynn, Elizabeth. 1988. "Composing as a Woman." *CCC* 39: 423–435.

———. 1990. "Composing 'Composing as a Woman': A Perspective on Research." *CCC* 41: 83–89.

———. 1991. "Composition Studies from a Feminist Perspective." *The Politics of Writing Instruction: Postsecondary.* Edited by Richard Bullock and John Trimbur. Portsmouth, NH: Boynton Cook/ Heinemann, 55–84.

Flynn, Elizabeth, and Patrocino Schweickart, eds. 1986. *Gender and Reading: Essays on Readers, Texts, and Contexts.* Baltimore: Johns Hopkins University Press.

Fontaine, Sheryl I., and Susan Hunter, eds. 1993. *Writing Ourselves into the Story: Unheard Voices from Composition Studies.* Carbondale: Southern Illinois University Press.

Freire, Paulo. 1981. *Pedagogy of the Oppressed.* Translated by Myra Bergman Ramos (1968). New York: Continuum.

Frey, Olivia. 1990. "Beyond Literary Darwinism: Women's Voices and Critical Discourse." *College English* 52: 507–526.

———. 1987. "Equity and Peace in the New Writing Class." Caywood and Overing 93–106.

Fuss, Diana. 1987. *Essentially Speaking: Feminism, Nature, and Difference.* New York: Routledge.

Gabriel, Susan L., and Isaiah Smithson, eds. 1990. *Gender in the Class-room: Power and Pedagogy.* Urbana: University of Illinois Press.

Gannett, Cinthia. 1995. "The Stories of Our Lives Become Our Lives: Journals, Diaries and Academic Discourse." Phelps and Emig 109–136.

Gates, Henry Louis, Jr, ed. 1990. *Reading Black, Reading Feminist: A Critical Anthology.* New York: Meridian.

Gearhart, Sally Miller. 1979. "The Womanization of Rhetoric." *Women's Studies International Quarterly* 2: 195–201.

Gilbert, Sandra, and Susan Gubar. 1979. *The Madwoman in the Attic: The Woman Writer and the Nineteenth Century Imagination.* New Haven: Yale University Press.

———. 1987, 1989. *The War of the Words: No Man's Land: The Place of the Woman Writer in the Twentieth Century.* Vol. 1 and 2. New Haven: Yale University Press.

Gilligan, Carol. 1982. *In A Different Voice: Psychological Theory and Women's Development.* Cambridge: Harvard University Press.

Goetsch, Lori. 1991. "Feminist Pedagogy: A Selective Annotated Bibliography." *National Woman's Studies Association Journal* 3: 422–429.

Goulston, Wendy. 1987. "Women Writing." Caywood and Overing 19–29.

Green, Gayle, and Coppelia Kahn. 1986. *Making a Difference: Feminist Literary Criticism.* London: Methuen.

Greene, Maxine. 1988. *The Dialectic of Freedom.* New York: Teachers College.

Grumet, Madeleine R. 1988. *Bitter Milk: Women and Teaching.* Amherst: University of Massachusetts Press.

———. 1991. "The Politics of Personal Knowledge." Witherell and Noddings 67–77.

Hays, Janice. 1995. "Intellectual Parenting and a Developmental Feminist Pedagogy of Writing." Phelps and Emig 153–190.

Heilbrun, Carolyn G. 1990. "The Politics of Mind: Women, Tradition, and the University. " Gabriel and Smithson 28–40.

Holbrook, Sue Ellen. 1991. "Women's Work: The Feminizing of Composition." *Rhetoric Review* 9: 201–229.

Howe, Florence. 1971. "Identity and Expression: A Writing Course for Women." *College English* 32: 863–871.

Hull, Gloria, et al., eds. 1982. *All the Women are White, All the Blacks Are Men, But Some of Us Are Brave.* New York: Feminist.

Hunter, Susan. 1991. "A Woman's Place Is in the Composition Class." *Rhetoric Review* 9: 230–245.

Jacobus, Mary. 1987. *Reading Women: Essays in Feminist Criticism.* New York: Columbia University Press.

Jarrett, Susan. 1991. "Feminism and Composition: The Case for Conflict." *Contending with Words: Composition and Rhetoric in a Post-modern Age.* Edited by Patricia Harkin and John Schilb. New York: MLA, 105–123.

Juncker, Clara. 1988. "Writing with Cixous." *College English* 50: 424–436.

Kamuf, Peggy. 1980. "Writing Like a Woman." *Women and Language in Literature and Society.* Edited by Sally McConnell Ginet, Ruth Borker, and Nelly Furman. New York: Praeger Special Studies, 284–299.

Kaplan, Alice. 1993. *French Lessons.* Chicago: University of Chicago Press.

Kaufman, Linda, ed. 1989. *Gender and Theory: Dialogues in Feminist Criticism.* Oxford, England: Basil Blackwell.

Kirsch, Gesa E. 1993. *Women Writing the Academy: Audience, Authority, and Transformation.* Carbondale: Southern Illinois University Press, NCTE.

Kramarae Cheris, and Paula A. Treichler. 1990. "Power Relationships in the Classroom." Gabriel and Smithson 41–59.

Lamb, Catherine. 1991. "Beyond Argument in Feminist Composition." *CCC* 42: 11–24.

Lauter, Paul. 1983. *Reconstructing American Literature Courses: Syllabi, Issues.* New York: Feminist.

Lewis, Magda Gere. 1993. *Without a Word: Teaching Beyond Women's Silence.* New York: Routledge.

Maher, Frances, and Mary Kay Tetreault. 1994. *The Feminist Classroom.* New York: Basic.

Marks, Elaine, and Isabelle de Courtivron, eds. 1980. *New French Feminisms.* Amherst: University of Massachusetts Press.

McConnell-Ginet, Sally, Ruth Borker, and Nelly Furman. 1980. *Women and Language in Literature and Society.* New York: Praeger.

McCracken, Nancy Mellin, and Bruce C. Appleby. 1992. *Gender Issues in the Teaching of Writing.* Portsmouth, NH: Boynton Cook/Heinemann.

Middleton, Sue. 1993. *Educating Feminists. Life Histories and Pedagogy.* New York: Teachers College.

Miller, Janet. 1982. "Feminist Pedagogy: The Sound of Silence Breaking." *Journal of Curriculum Theorizing* 4.1: 5–11.

Miller, Nancy. 1986. *The Poetics of Gender.* New York: Columbia University Press.

Miller, Susan. 1991. "The Feminization of Composition." *The Politics of Writing Instruction: Postsecondary.* Edited by Richard Bullock and John Trimbur. Portsmouth, NH: Boynton Cook/Heinemann, 39–53.

Minnich, Elizabeth. 1990. *Transforming Knowledge.* Philadelphia: Temple University Press.

Minnich, Elizabeth, Jean O'Barr, and Rachel Rosenfeld, eds. 1988. *Reconstructing the Academy: Women's Education and Women's Studies.* Chicago: University of Chicago Press.

Moi, Toril. 1985. *Sexual/Textual Politics: Feminist Literary Theory.* London: Methuen.

Nicholson, Linda J., ed. 1990. *Feminism/Postmodernism*. New York: Routledge.

Noddings, Nel. 1984. *Caring: A Feminine Approach to Ethics and Moral Education*. Berkeley: University of California Press.

———. 1991. "Stories in Dialogue: Caring and Interpersonal Reasoning." Witherell and Noddings 157–170.

Osborn, Susan. 1991. " 'Revision/Re-Vision': A Feminist Writing Class." *Rhetoric Review* 9: 258–273.

Payne, Michelle. 1994. "Rend[er]ing Women's Authority in the Writing Classroom." *Taking Stock: The Writing Process Movement in the 90s*. Edited by Lad Tobin and Thomas Newkirk. Portsmouth, NH: Boynton Cook/Heinemann.

Peterson, Jane E. 1991. "Valuing Teaching: Assumptions, Problems, and Possibilities." *CCC* 42: 25–35.

Phelps, Louise Wetherbee. 1995. "Becoming a Warrior: Lessons of the Feminist Workplace." Phelps and Emig 289–339.

Phelps, Louise Wetherebee, and Janet Emig, eds. 1995. *Feminine Principles and Women's Experience in American Composition and Rhetoric*. Pittsburgh: University of Pittsburgh Press.

Poovey, Mary. 1988. "Feminism and Deconstruction." *Feminist Studies* 14: 51–65.

Pratt, Mary Louise. 1991. "Arts of the Contact Zone." *Profession* 91: 33–40.

Ritchie, Joy S. 1990. "Confronting the 'Essential' Problem: Reconnecting Feminist Theory and Pedagogy." Ashton-Jones 249–273.

Ruddick, Sara. 1989. *Maternal Thinking*. Boston: Beacon.

Russ, Joanna. 1983. *How To Suppress Women's Writing*. Austin: University of Texas Press.

Sadker, Myra, and David Sadker. 1990. "Confronting Sexism in the College Classroom." Gabriel and Smithson 176–187.

Schweickart, Patrocino P. 1990. "Reading, Teaching and the Ethic of Care." Gabriel and Smithson 78–95.

Shor, Ira. 1981. *Culture Wars*. Boston: Routledge.

Showalter, Elaine. 1985. *The New Feminist Criticism. Essays on Women, Literature and Theory*. New York: Pantheon.

Spender, Dale. 1980. *Man Made Language*, 2d ed. New York: Routledge.

Steinitz, Victoria, and Sandra Kantor. 1991. "Becoming Outspoken: Beyond Connected Education." *Women's Studies Quarterly* 19: 138–153.

Tedesco, Janis. 1991. "Women's Ways of Knowing/Women's Ways of Composing." *Rhetoric Review* 9: 246–257.

Tompkins, Jane. 1990. "Pedagogy of the Distressed." *College English* 52: 653–660.

Tornsey, Cheryl. 1989. "The Critical Quilt: Alternative Authority in Feminist Criticism." *Contemporary Literary Theory*. Edited by C. Douglas

Atkins and Laura Morrow. Amherst: University of Massachusetts Press, 180–199.

Treichler, Paula A., Cheris Kramarae, and Beth Stafford, eds. 1985. *For Alma Mater: Theory and Practice in Feminist Scholarship.* Urbana: University of Illinois Press.

Washington, Mary Helen, ed. 1975. *Black-Eyed Susans: Classic Stories By and About Black Women.* Garden City, NY: Anchor.

Washington, Mary Helen. 1987. *Invented Lives: Narratives of Black Women 1860–1960.* Garden City, NY: Doubleday.

Weedon, Chris. 1987. *Feminist Practice and Poststructuralist Theory.* Cambridge, MA: Blackwell.

Weiler, Kathleen. 1988. *Women Teaching for Change: Gender, Class, and Power.* New York: Bergin.

Witherell, Carol, and Nel Noddings, eds. 1991. *Stories Lives Tell: Narrative and Dialogue in Education.* New York: Teachers College.

Zawacki, Terry Myers. 1992. "Recomposing as a Woman—An Essay in Different Voices." *CCC* 43: 32–38.

Contributors

Lynn Z. Bloom is Professor of English and Aetna Chair of Writing at the University of Connecticut, Storrs. She is the author of *Doctor Spock: Biography of a Conservative Radical* and the co-author of *American Autobiography 1945–1980: A Bibliography* (with Briscoe, Tobias). She has edited two diaries of civilian women's internment in Japanese camps in the Philippines throughout World War II, Natalie Crouter's *Forbidden Diary* and Margaret Sams's *Forbidden Family*. *Coming to Life: Reading, Writing, Teaching Autobiography* is forthcoming from Prentice Hall.

Lillian Bridwell-Bowles is Professor of English, Director of the Center for Interdisciplinary Studies of Writing, Co-director of the Minnesota Writing Project, and Faculty Affiliate in Women's Studies at the University of Minnesota. She has published extensively (articles, chapters, books) in the areas of rhetorical theory, linguistics, and gender studies.

Linda Brodkey, Associate Professor of Literature at the University of California-San Diego, directs the Warren College Writing Program and teaches undergraduate and graduate courses on literacy and writing. Her publications include *Academic Writing As Social Practice* and many essays on writing theory and practice.

E. M. Broner lives in New York City and is Professor Emerita of Wayne State University. She has taught as professor or visiting writer at U.C.L.A., Sarah Lawrence College, Tulane/Emily Newcomb, Oberlin College, Haifa University-Israel, and elsewhere. Broner is an international lecturer and the author of nine books, including *A Weave of Women*, *The Telling*, *Mornings and Mourning*, and *Ghost Stories*. She is also the co-author of *The Women's*

Haggadah, with Nomi Nimrod, a retelling of the Exodus. Dr. Broner has won two National Endowment for the Arts for her fiction and a Wonder Woman Award for her revised ceremonies.

Karen Ann Chaffee is an adjunct instructor in the English Department at The State University of New York, New Paltz, where she teaches Preparatory Writing and Freshman Composition. Her interests in the teaching of writing, women's writing, and the uses of autobiography in academic writing have led her to The State University of New York at Albany, where she is a doctoral candidate focusing on composition and rhetoric. Karen lives in Saugerties, New York, with her husband and two daughters where she writes poetry in her free time.

Pamela Chergotis is the editor of a weekly newspaper and literary periodical in upstate New York and is a former editor of scholarly books. She is an M.A. candidate in the English Department of the State University of New York, New Paltz, where she taught freshman composition as a teaching assistant.

Judith Ortiz Cofer is Professor of English at the University of Georgia, where she teaches literature and creative writing. She is the author of several volumes of poetry, including *Terms of Survival* and *Reaching for the Mainland*; a novel, *The Line of The Sun*; a collection of poetry and prose, *The Latin Deli*; and an autobiographical memoir, *Silent Dancing: A Partial Remembrance of a Puerto Rican Childhood*, which received the 1991 PEN/ Martha Albrand Special Citation for Nonfiction.

Lynne Crockett received her Master's degree in English from the State University of New York, New Paltz, where she taught freshman composition for three years while employed as a teaching assistant. She is pursuing a Ph.D. in Literature at New York University where she is teaching in the Expository Writing Program.

Ann Victoria Dean is Assistant Professor of Educational Foundations at the State University of New York, New Paltz. She completed her Ph.D. at Dalhousie University, Halifax, Nova Scotia, in 1992. Her research interests include narrative inquiry and autobiography in education, anti-racist-sexist-classist education, and critical pedagogy.

Diane Glancy is Associate Professor of English at Macalester College, where she teaches Native American literature, creative writing, and script writing. She has published a novel, *Pushing The Bear*; several short story collections, including *Trigger Dance*, which received the Charles Nilon Fiction Award; and several poetry volumes (e.g., *Iron Woman*, and *Boom Town*). Her latest work is an essay collection, *The West Pole*, to be published by University of Minnesota Press.

Mary Gordon holds the McIntosh Chair as Professor of English at Barnard College. Her published works include four novels *Final Payments*, *The Company of Women*, *Men and Angels*, and *The Other Side*; an essay collection, *Dead Girls and Bad Boys and Other Essays*; a collection of short stories, *Temporary Shelter*; and a book of novellas, *The Rest of Life*. She has received the Lila Acheson Wallace Reader's Digest Writer's Award and a Guggenheim Fellowship. Her most recent work, *The Shadow Man*, an autobiographical memoir about her father, was published in 1996.

bell hooks is Distinguished Professor of English at City College in New York. She has authored many books, including *Ain't I a Woman: Black Women and Feminism*; *Talking Back: Thinking feminist, Thinking black*; *Outlaw Culture: Resisting Representations*; and *Teaching to Transgress*. She writes and speaks extensively about issues of race, gender, and class.

Min-zhan Lu is Assistant Professor of English at Drake University, where she teaches composition, literary and cultural criticism, and autobiography. Her latest work focuses on multicultural issues and the use of cultural dissonance in teaching.

Elaine P. Maimon is Provost and Professor of English at Arizona State University West. Formerly, she was Dean of Experimental Programs at Queens College/CUNY and Associate Dean of the College at Brown University. At Beaver College, in 1974, she created and then administered one of the nation's first programs in writing across the curriculum. In her honor, Beaver College has created the Elaine P. Maimon Award for Excellence in Writing. Her B.A., M.A., and Ph.D. in English are from the University of Pennsylvania. Her publications include *Writing in the Arts and Sciences*, *Readings in the Arts and Sciences*, and *Thinking, Reasoning, and Writing*.

Gillian B. Maimon holds a B.A., with a concentration in Literature and Society, from Brown University and holds an M.S. in Education from the University of Pennsylvania. Her play, "Old Aunt Bea," was produced by the National Improvisational Theatre in 1992. She currently teaches in the Philadelphia School District.

Sondra Perl is Professor of English at Lehman College and the Graduate School and University Center of the City University of New York. She is editor of *Landmark Essays on Writing Process* (Erlbaum) in which she describes the development of composing studies, critiques their impact, and calls for research in which investigators are both fully engaged and take full account of their presence. Her most recent account of her teaching appears as "Composing Texts/Composing Lives" in the Winter 1994 issue of the *Harvard Educational Review*. She is currently working with Ira Shor to develop the Ph.D. specialization in composition theory and rhetoric at the CUNY Graduate School.

Adrienne Rich is the author of more than fifteen volumes of poetry, including *Snapshots of a Daughter-in-law, Diving into the Wreck, The Atlas of the Difficult World: Poems 1988–1991* and several essay collections (e.g., *On Lies, Secrets, and Silence: Selected Prose, 1966–1978*; *Blood, Bread and Poetry: Selected Prose, 1979–1986*; and *What Is Found There: Notebooks on Poetry and Politics*). Among her many awards and accomplishments are the National Book Award, the Ruth Lilly Poetry Prize, and the Fellowship of the Academy of American Poets.

Hephzibah Roskelly is Associate Professor of English and Director of Composition at the University of North Carolina, Greensboro, where she teaches courses in rhetoric and composition, pedagogy, and American literature. She is completing a book on teaching with Kate Ronald—*Reason to Believe: Romanticism, Pragmatism and the Teaching of Writing*.

Jacqueline Jones Royster, Associate Professor of English at Ohio State University and 1995 Chair of the Conference on College Composition and Communication, defines her primary area of research as the history and uses of literacy among African American women. Her publications include a co-edited anthology, *Double-Stitch: Black Women Write about Mothers and Daughters*; a language arts textbook series, *Writer's Choice, Grades 6–8*; an edited volume, *Southern Horrors and Other Writings: The Anti-Lynching Campaign of Ida B. Wells-Barnett, 1892–1900*; and various articles in women's studies and literacy studies.

Jan Zlotnik Schmidt is Professor of English and Coordinator of the Composition Program at the State University of New York, New Paltz, where she teaches composition, creative writing and autobiography courses. The co-author with the late Dr. Carley Bogarad of a literature for composition textbook—*Legacies: Fiction, Poetry, Drama, Nonfiction* (Harcourt Brace), she also has published articles on writing theory and instruction and autobiography in such journals as *Journal of Advanced Composition* and *CEA Critic*. A poet, her work has been published in many journals, and her poetry volume, *We Speak in Tongues*, appeared in 1991.

Nancy Sommers is Director of the Expository Writing Program at Harvard University. The co-author of several college writing textbooks, she has published widely, and her articles on writing theory and practice have appeared in such journals as *CCC* and *College English*. Sommers received the National Council of Teachers of English Promising Research Award for her work on revision and the Richard Bradcock Award in 1983 and 1993.